Alternative Salvations

Also available from Bloomsbury

The Study of Religion, 2nd edition, George D. Chryssides and Ron Geaves
Christianity and the University Experience, Mathew Guest,
Kristin Aune, Sonya Sharma and Rob Warner
Sacred and Secular Musics, Virinder S. Kalra

ALTERNATIVE SALVATIONS

Engaging the Sacred and the Secular

Edited by
Hannah Bacon, Wendy Dossett and Steve Knowles

Bloomsbury Academic
An imprint of Bloomsbury Publishing Plc

B L O O M S B U R Y

LONDON · OXFORD · NEW YORK · NEW DELHI · SYDNEY

Bloomsbury Academic

An imprint of Bloomsbury Publishing Plc

50 Bedford Square	1385 Broadway
London	New York
WC1B 3DP	NY 10018
UK	USA

www.bloomsbury.com

BLOOMSBURY and the Diana logo are trademarks of Bloomsbury Publishing Plc

First published 2015

British Library Cataloguing-in-Publication Data
A catalogue record for this book is available from the British Library.

ISBN: HB: 978-1-4725-7994-2
ePDF: 978-1-4725-7995-9
ePub: 978-1-4725-7996-6

Library of Congress Cataloging-in-Publication Data
Alternative salvations: engaging the sacred and the secular/edited by Hannah Bacon, Wendy Dossett, and Steve Knowles.
pages cm
Includes bibliographical references and index.
ISBN 978-1-4725-7994-2 (hb) – ISBN 978-1-4725-7996-6 (epub) –
ISBN 978-1-4725-7995-9 (epdf) 1. Salvation.
2. Salvation–Comparative studies. I. Bacon, Hannah, 1978- editor.
BL476.A48 2015
234–dc23
2015031569

Typeset by Deanta Global Publishing Services, Chennai, India
Printed and bound in Great Britain

Contents

Part II
RE-READING TRADITIONS

Robert B. Arrowood is a graduate student working under Dr Ralph W. Hood, Jr. in the Psychology of Religion Lab at The University of Tennessee at Chattanooga. He received his Bachelor of Arts in psychology from Tusculum College and is currently working on his Masters of Science in research psychology. His primary interests include Terror Management Theory, in which he seeks to examine the interaction between death awareness and religious orientation to affect worldview defence. Additionally, he seeks to examine death awareness's influence on broader issues such as optimism, sexual interest and cognitive resources. He also has a general interest in social psychology and successful teaching practices.

Irene Ayallo is lecturer in Social Practice at Unitec Institute of Technology, New Zealand. Her research interests include gender studies, politics (political theories, political participation, social justice and human rights), HIV-AIDS care and prevention, political theology and marginalized groups.

Hannah Bacon is senior lecturer in Feminist and Contextual Theology at the University of Chester, UK. Her current research focuses on the theological dimensions of secular, commercial weight loss programmes and engages with ethnographic work she has conducted inside an organized weight loss group in the UK. She is the author of *What's Right with the Trinity? Conversations in Feminist Theology* (Ashgate, 2009) and co-editor with Wayne Morris and Steve Knowles of *Transforming Exclusion: Engaging Faith Perspectives* (Continuum, 2011).

Madeleine Castro is senior lecturer in Interdisciplinary Psychology at Leeds Beckett University, UK. Her research interests include the sociology and psychology of paranormal or extraordinary experiences, contemporary spiritualties and methodology in the social sciences. Her most recent work focuses on the concept of transcendent experiences (outside of a religious context) as catalysts for personal transformation in contemporary society. She also co-directs a network for researchers interested in subjects such as the paranormal called *Exploring the Extraordinary*.

Thomas J. Coleman III is the director of the Ralph W. Hood Jr. Psychology of Religion Laboratory and a graduate student in the Research Psychology Master programme at the University of Tennessee at Chattanooga. He is an assistant editor for the journal *Secularism & Nonreligion*, and The Religious Studies Project. His current interests span research in cultural psychology, the cognitive sciences and the philosophy of science, focusing on theory of mind and folk psychology.

Jenny Daggers is associate professor in Christian theology at Liverpool Hope University, UK, where she teaches in the Department of Theology, Philosophy and Religious Studies. Her research and teaching interests are in twentieth- and twenty-first- century theology, particularly as it relates to issues of gender in postcolonial and postmodern perspectives. Recent publications include *Postcolonial Theology of Religions: Particularity and Pluralism in World Christianity* (Routledge, 2013). She has also co-edited with Grace Ji-Sun Kim *Christian Doctrines for Global Gender Justice* (forthcoming Palgrave, 2015) and *Reimagining with Christian Doctrines: Responding to Global Gender Injustices* (Palgrave, Pivot, 2014). She is editor of *Gendering Christian Ethics* (CSP, 2012) and author of a number of articles on feminist theology, and women and Christianity in the nineteenth and twentieth centuries.

Douglas Davies is director of the Centre of Death and Life Studies at Durham University, UK and author *of The Mormon Culture of Salvation* (Ashgate, 2000); *A Brief History of Death* (Blackwell, 2004), *Emotion, Identity, and Religion: Hope, Reciprocity, and Otherness* (OUP, 2011) and jointly with Hannah Rumble *Natural Burial: Traditional-secular Spiritualties and Funeral Innovation* (Continuum, 2012). He has authored numerous other publications in theology and social anthropology, death studies and Mormonism. His research interests include contemporary death and funerary practices. He was president of the British Association for the Study of Religions 2009–12.

Wendy Dossett is senior lecturer in Religious Studies at the University of Chester, UK. She was for a decade an associate director of the Alister Hardy Religious Experience Research Centre and is now principal investigator of the Higher Power Project which explores spirituality among people in recovery through the Twelve Steps. She is co-editor with Chris Cook of Religion and Addiction: a special issue of *Religions*. She has worked in a Residential Drug and Alcohol Addiction Rehabilitation Centre. She is also author of numerous A-level textbooks in Buddhism and religious studies.

Kris Hiuser recently completed his PhD from the University of Chester, UK. His thesis considered the question of why God became human – particularly addressing this question in the light of the topic of non-human animals – and what ethical implications this has for humans. He has published journal articles on God's covenantal relationship with non-human animals, the capacity of non-human animals to sin, and how they feature in the theology of Maximus the Confessor.

Jon Hoover is associate professor of Islamic studies at the University of Nottingham, UK. His research focuses on the major medieval Muslim theologians Ibn Taymiyya and Ibn Qayyim al-Jawziyya and their subsequent reception. His publications include the book *Ibn Taymiyya's Theodicy of Perpetual Optimism*; several articles on Ibn Taymiyya's and Ibn Qayyim al-Jawziyya's views on creation, theodicy, universal salvation and Christians; and a number of essays on contemporary Christian – Muslim relations.

Steve Knowles is senior lecturer in Religion and Popular Culture at the University of Chester, UK. His research interests include contemporary apocalyptic ideologies and Christian fundamentalism; sociology of risk; and religion and digital media. He is the author of *Beyond Evangelicalism* (Ashgate, 2010) and co-editor with H. Bacon and W. Morris of *Transforming Exclusion: Engaging Faith Perspectives* (Continuum, 2011).

Paul Middleton is senior lecturer in New Testament and Early Christianity at the University of Chester. His research interests include violence and martyrdom in the ancient and modern world, constructions of early Christian identities and the Book of Revelation. He is the author of *Radical Martyrdom and Cosmic Conflict in Early Christianity* (T & T Clark, 2006) and *Martyrdom: A Guide for the Perplexed* (T & T Clark, 2011).

Wayne Morris is senior lecturer in contextual and practical theology and head of Theology and Religious Studies at the University of Chester, UK. He is author of *Theology without Words: Theology in the Deaf Community* (Ashgate, 2008) and *Salvation as Praxis: A Practical Theology of Salvation for a Multi-Faith World* (Bloomsbury, 2014). His research interests include practical theologies of disability, religions and spiritualities and the rights of linguistic minority groups.

Emily Pennington recently gained a PhD in feminist theology from the University of Chester. She is now Theological Partnerships Leader and Co-ordinator at the University of Winchester, UK. Her research explores the interface between Christian eschatology and the creative and sensual experiences and expressions of women's bodies. She is author of *Feminist Eschatology: Embodied Futures* (Ashgate, forthcoming).

Kornelia Sammet is interim professor for qualitative methods in social research at Bielefeld University in Germany. She researches across the fields of sociology of religion, gender studies, social inequality and qualitative methodology. She is author of *Frauen im Pfarramt: Berufliche Praxis und Geschlechterkonstruktion* (Ergon, 2005) and with Gert Pickel, *Einführung in die Methoden der sozialwissenschaftlichen Religionsforschung* (Springer VS, 2014). She is also co-editor of *Transformations of Religiosity. Religion and Religiosity in Eastern Europe 1989–2010* (VS-Verlag, 2012).

William Stephenson is a reader in English at the University of Chester, UK. His latest academic book is *Gonzo Republic: Hunter S. Thompson's America* (Continuum, 2011). He has published two books on John Fowles and numerous articles on contemporary novelists including J. G. Ballard, Iain Banks, Bret Easton Ellis, Alex Garland, Hunter S. Thompson and Irvine Welsh. His first poetry collection *Rain*

Dancers in the Data Cloud (Templar, 2012) won an Iota Shots Award; his second collection *Source Code* (Ravenglass, 2013) won the Ravenglass Poetry Prize.

Katja Stuerzenhofecker is lecturer in Gender Studies in Religion at the University of Manchester, UK and is currently enrolled on the Doctorate of Professional Studies in Practical Theology at the University of Chester. Her doctoral research investigates the purpose and form of teaching practical theology to students of all faiths and none in a secular setting of higher education. Her further research interests include gender studies and feminist method and theory in theology and education. She has published on the topic of sustainability in the theology curriculum.

Acknowledgements

Like many edited collections, this one arose from a sociable, after-work conversation between colleagues in which it emerged that some of our research preoccupations constellated around a single yet fluid theme: *salvation*. The deepening of that conversation, along with the realization that this theme functioned in our work in such contrasting and even contradictory ways, eventually developed into a clear direction, and the idea of a conference was mooted on the theme. The realization that the trope of salvation was significant to us all was not immediately obvious. Some of us working outside of Christian settings would at the very least not have naturally used the term. Others were actively challenging received Christian tradition, and viewed common configurations of salvation as deeply suspect. The historical periods explored in our work spanned millennia, so it was not even the case that we all shared an interest in the contemporary language of salvation. It took the development of a multilevelled yet shared vision to grasp that 'salvation' might be a common theme. Our first acknowledgement is to each other, not only within our editorial team, but to the wider group within the Department of Theology and Religious Studies at the University of Chester among whom that initial conversation emerged. Some (but not all) of the conversation partners have their own work represented here, but their contribution went far beyond this, into the formation of the vision for the volume.

Three departmental colleagues in particular, in addition to those in the list of contributors, played a significant part in those early conversations and the evolving structure of the conference; namely Dr Ben Fulford, Dr Dawn Llewellyn and Professor Chris Baker. Even then, it was not until the tremendous response to the call for papers for the Alternative Salvations conference held in Chester September 2012 that our sense of the theme as genuinely analytically productive began to take hold.

Our second set of acknowledgements, then, is to the contributors to the conference, who brought their disciplines, approaches and research data into conversation with us around our theme. We were particularly delighted that the project attracted contributors from Germany, New Zealand and the United States, as well as from many parts of England, Scotland and Wales.

Sincere thanks are due to our editors at Bloomsbury, Lalle Pursglove and Anna MacDiarmid, who applied precisely the right combination of pressure and encouragement to enable this volume to see the light of day. We are thankful that they understood and appreciated our project. Similarly, we are grateful to the anonymous peer-reviewers both for their encouragement (which we needed) and for their careful consideration and critique. This led to some substantial restructuring of the proposal to better reflect our purposes. The volume is improved as a consequence.

The artwork on the front cover is a painting by St Ives-based artist Angela Diggle, a friend of one of the editors. The water-colour collage is appropriately entitled 'The Fall, falling, fallen ...' (www.stives-artist.com/). We thank 'Diggle' for the permission to use the painting. We thank Berni Hunt for undertaking the massive task of indexing. Our gratitude is also extended to the staff at Gladstone's library (www.gladstoneslibrary.org/) which served as a welcome bolthole on several occasions for the editorial team. Surrounded by W. E. Gladstone's own library (and beautiful food) we found we worked far more effectively than back at Hollybank, home of the Department of Theology and Religious Studies on the Chester campus. While one reason for that is the fact that our students also live in Hollybank, we do want to thank them too. We consider ourselves privileged to be working in a Department of Theology and Religious Studies in which there is expertise across a wide range of subject areas from contextual and systematic theology, to biblical studies and ancient history; from the sociology of religion, to the study of indigenous religions and global traditions. Part of that privilege comes from working with students who are as interested as the staff in contributing to the conversation which the department is having with itself and with others.

***

The Twelve Steps are reprinted with the permission of Alcoholics Anonymous World Services, Inc. (AAWS). Permission to reprint the Twelve Steps does not mean that AAWS has reviewed or approved the contents of this publication, or that AAWS necessarily agrees with the views expressed herein. AA is a programme of recovery from alcoholism only – use of the Twelve Steps in connection with programmes and activities which are patterned after AA, but which address other problems, or in any other non-AA context, does not imply otherwise.

Introduction

Hannah Bacon, Wendy Dossett and Steve Knowles

The phrase 'alternative salvations' is contentious, immediately provoking the question, 'alternative to what?' Such questions about the norms and established conventions of how salvation is understood constitute the heart of this volume, as contributors disturb the very notion of a dominant centre. In adopting the Christian theological term 'salvation', our aim is not to position Christianity as normative for understanding other faiths or to assume that such theological language can be imposed on other faith or secular settings. Instead, the chapters here interrogate a wide range of possible interpretations of the term in order to trouble a hard and fast binary between the sacred and profane, problematizing essentialized distinctions between 'religious' and 'secular'. They explore in some cases the complexities of what 'salvation' means both within and beyond traditional religion, and in others take the notion of salvation, experimentally, as a hermeneutical lens.

The genesis of this volume is located in conversations which took place between colleagues in the Department of Theology and Religious Studies at the University of Chester in 2012 about overlapping research interests and fields of inquiry. Identifying 'alternative salvations' as a possible way to name and express some of the synergies we saw prompted a decision to hold a day-long conference focused on exploring this tentative category. The conference sought to explore a number of themes, including how 'unorthodox' readings of sacred texts might inform salvation experience; how life transformations outside of religious contexts might be considered spiritual; how ideas of this-worldly salvation might be politicized; how ideas of salvation might be simultaneously secularized and infused with new power; what alternative salvations might be discovered within dominant religious discourse and how they might be practised. Most of the contributions in this volume began as papers presented at that conference.

Why Salvation?

While the trope of salvation appeared to link many of the diverse research projects being undertaken in the Department of Theology and Religious Studies at the time, and seemed useful thematically, we were mindful of the problems inherent in applying a term with heavily Christian connotations to other contexts. The study of religion has been dogged by the tendency to organize knowledge according to a Christian template, and all of the projects represented here would reject this tendency. Religious studies as it emerged in the British context was shaped by the liberal Christian project of 'understanding our neighbours'. Even now a comparative approach which maps aspects of religions onto a liberal Christian worldview dominates not only education, but public discourse about religions in general (Owen 2011). Thus 'religions' are expected to have founders and texts, beliefs and practices, doctrines and behavioural codes, institutions and ritual specialists, and structured cosmologies which account for suffering and promote spiritual goals. The precise 'ingredients' may be different in each case, but structural similarity prevails. In such a model, it would be common to encounter the assumption that Hindus, for example, 'believe in' salvation, but call it *mokṣa* which translates as liberation. The problems inherent in such an approach are obvious. It structures knowledge based on an assumed Christian norm. It abstracts, decontextualizes and essentializes a concept selected according to Christian values, and it organizes information on the basis of similarity. This volume, by collecting narrative case-studies embedded in a diverse range of contexts, seeks to explore structural difference and dissonance, as well as similarity. Readers hoping for an account of 'how different religious traditions see salvation' are liable to be disappointed. While contextual diversity was a crucial consideration in the selection of the chapters, and traditions other than Christianity are referenced, a 'world religions' approach was not the organizational strategy.

That said, positioned as we are in a culture shaped by Christian images and motifs in which the term salvation continues to have currency, acknowledging its Christian roots is important. The term is derived from the Latin *salvare* and is connected to the Latin *salus* meaning 'health' (Higton 2008: 260). In Christian belief and practice, the term retains associations with health and healing but also reflects secular meanings given to the term; those depicting rescue, protection and prevention from danger (Astley 2010: 108). The Greek *sozo* ('I save') and *soteria* ('salvation') are used in the New Testament, for example, to express healing and wellness. It is this notion of salvation that Morris argues is present in the Gospels; in Luke (8.48) where Jesus tells the woman with a haemorrhage that 'your faith has made you well' (Morris 2014: 55). Salvation is aligned with healings from physical and mental illness; with the 'making well' of the sick. Jesus 'makes well' Jairus' daughter (Mk 5), but he also identifies his mission with the 'making well' of sinners and thus with spiritual redemption as well as physical and psychological wholeness (Astley 2010: 108). In Mark's Gospel, when the scribes and Pharisees see Jesus eating with the sinners and tax collectors, Jesus responds to their reproach with the words, 'Those who are well have no need of a physician, but those who are sick; I have come to call not the righteous but sinners' (Mk 2.17). Salvation as rescue from danger, however, is also an important soteriological image. It appears in the New Testament, for example, when, confronted with stormy waters and fearing for their lives, the disciples beseech a sleeping Jesus, 'Lord, save us! We are perishing' (Mt. 8.25).

When considering Christian soteriology then, it is important to appreciate that salvation is imaged in a diversity of ways. Trevor Hart talks about a 'kaleidoscope of metaphors' in the Bible, including metaphors of 'release', 'transformation' and those which have to do with a new, restored relationship between God and sinners (1997: 194–5), which attempt to describe the nature of the threat and the means of rescue (1997: 189). Within Christian theology more broadly, salvation has been imaged as reconciliation, liberation, healing, sanctification, justification, deification, revelation, satisfaction, victory, ransom, expiation, to name but a few common tropes (Higton 2008: 262; Hart 1997: 196–204). At the centre of most is an understanding that God's intended good for the world has been corrupted and that the world is thus now distorted and disordered. 'Sin' has commonly named the problem as personal rebellion against God but the influence of liberation theologies has recovered social and political dimensions to Christian theologies of sin, naming as sin the social evils embodied in the political systems of capitalism, colonialism, heterosexism, racism, patriarchy and so forth. In all instances, however, salvation is typically constructed as a movement towards the making whole of that which is broken, whether that be the restoration of relationship with self, God and other or freedom from the systemic and political 'powers and principalities' that conspire against spiritual, physical and mental wholeness.

This volume addresses many aspects of such theological traditions. However, rather than assuming Christianity to be normative the term salvation is utilized because it gives voice to the valence the term continues to have today and is expressive of the way the Western cultural imaginary has been historically shaped by Christian thought. The chapters in this volume show that the term continues to be invested with meaning and power, drawing on its heritage while having currency beyond this. As such, the term is adopted as a device which authors invest with meanings emerging from their various research contexts.

'Alternative' to What?

Given this, authors name various narratives as 'alternative'. Each author queries in different ways and to different degrees the stability of established orthodox accounts of salvation, whether these emerge within religious traditions or within cultural settings. In Part 1, salvation is configured 'alternative' on the grounds that narratives develop outside religious contexts – in atheistic conceptions of salvation in the 'here' and 'now' (Chapter 1), in Twelve-Step recovery programmes (Chapter 2), in public policy surrounding HIV-AIDS in Kenya (Chapter 3), in secular commercial weight loss settings (Chapter 4), in transcendent experiences outside of institutional religious contexts (Chapter 5), in the attempt at salvation through the use of 'psychedelic technologies' (Chapter 6), in non-church responses to the question, 'What comes after death?' (Chapter 7), in the use of plausibility theory as a tool for finding meaning in secular notions of salvation in the NHS and woodland burial (Chapter 8). Although operative outside traditional religious settings, salvation here is not free from religious symbolism.

Part 2 focuses upon cases of salvation which disrupt dominant interpretations or practices of salvation within religious traditions. Contributors set about recovering marginalized theological and religious perspectives on salvation and sometimes engage with unconventional dialogue partners in order to challenge dominant traditions. In so doing, these chapters open up new spaces for alternative readings of religious traditions. Established orthodoxies are confronted by a critical questioning of cultural and religious assumptions about 'normalcy' (Chapter 11), gender binaries (Chapter 12) and the status of animals (Chapter 13). Dominant religious interpretations of salvation are challenged by subversive accounts of martyrdom in Christianity (Chapter 10), fundamentalist eschatology (Chapter 16) and universal salvation in Islamic thought (Chapter 15). Entrenched theological views are reframed by engaging the concept of 'flourishing' and by drawing on experiences of teaching and learning within the higher education classroom (Chapter 14). The 'generic habit' of assuming Christian supremacy and normalcy, demonstrated by the way other faith traditions are labelled 'alternative', is also critiqued. Aptly, the very notion of 'alternative salvations' is challenged and the Christian, Eurocentric and colonial nature of this category probed (Chapter 9).

Despite the variety of topics considered here, however, two themes characterize our debate (this is reflective of the debate within contemporary academic scholarship outlined further below): first, the problematizing of the binary between the so-called 'sacred' and 'profane', and second, the use of ordinary lived experience to trouble totalizing metanarratives about salvation.

Problematizing the Sacred and the Secular

Émile Durkheim's *The Elementary Forms of Religious Life: A Study in Religious Sociology*, published in 1912 was instrumental in positing a distinction between the sacred and profane. This distinction, which inevitably generates over-simplistic analyses, has been the subject of much scrutiny in the literature of the sociology and anthropology of religion, and in cultural studies since (Paden 1991, 2011; Anttonen 2000; Knott 2005; Fitzgerald 2000; Lynch 2012; Day, Vincett and Cotter 2013). By selecting a notion ('salvation') whose natural classification would be 'sacred', and subjecting it to sustained analysis within a range of theoretical frameworks and case-study settings, this volume offers a further contribution to debates in this field. Gordon Lynch explains that Durkheim's own schema did not itself rest on a simplistic or theoretical religious/secular divide.

> Durkheim was not using the sacred simply as a synonym for things that we conventionally define as 'religious'. ... Rather, he saw sacred objects as being defined by the distinctive ways in which people experienced them and related to them. (2012: 23)

Many of the chapters in this volume affirm this reading of Durkheim, and make cases for the legitimacy of 'porting' the language of salvation to settings that are not conventionally religious. Kim Knott has argued that the 'sacred' should be understood not as a specifically religious category, nor as a concept that stands against the secular. Furthermore, the secular should not be thought of as being unable to 'host the sacred' (2013: 160). Rather, the idea of the 'sacred' can be ascribed to either (secular or religious) perspective. Clearly some of the contributors to this volume would resonate with such a view. However, other chapters explore settings which go beyond even this theoretical framework. It is one thing (and uncontroversial) to say people outside of institutionally religious contexts report 'spiritual' experiences; it is quite another to say, as Bacon does, that the experience of embodiment is predicated on a powerful, potentially distorted, yet hidden, Christian soteriology. The chapters indicate that salvation, or analogues of salvation, are sought, found, or unconsciously implied in the everyday, in the vernacular. The suggestion that religious forms may be 'read into' or 'read from' ordinary life is not new, and has been explored via the use of frameworks such as 'implicit religion', (Bailey 1999), 'invisible religion' (Luckmann 1967), 'surrogate religion' (Robertson 1970) and quasi-religion (Griel and Robbins 1994). While many of these categories might illuminate the cases explored in these pages, we have found none of them useful for every case, and all of them prone to a re-inscribing of the very essentialisms they sought to correct.

Taken together, the chapters in this volume profoundly challenge not only the notion of a sacred/secular binary, but even the idea of a 'spiritual but not religious' space 'between' them. All these categories may be helpful to some extent, but only if they remain provisional. In Russell McCutcheon's words,

> As scholars of social classification, we can see no reason to assume, as do many of the people that we happen to read, that the categories of 'religion' and 'politics', or 'sacred' and 'secular', refer to actual qualities in the real world.... Instead they are nothing more than codependent, portable discursive markers. (in Arnal and McCutcheon 2013: 132)

Listening to Ordinary lived Experience

In emphasizing salvation narratives as they emerge within everyday contexts, many contributions echo shifts within the disciplines of religious studies and Christian theology. The last decade has seen a self-conscious turn to 'lived', 'everyday' or 'vernacular' religion in religious studies, for example (Primiano 1995; Ammerman 2007; McGuire 2008a; Harvey 2009, 2013; Bowman and Valk 2012). This has involved the eschewing of grand narratives and scholarly categories in favour of detailed attention to the stuff of everyday life: materiality, embodiment, relationships, practices, individuality, situatedness. While it has involved a shift in focus from 'belief' to action and experience, it has not merely been about looking at what religious people 'do'. Nor has it only been about taking account of 'ordinary' people as opposed to focusing on ritual specialists and religious 'virtuosos'. It has also involved the problematizing of a perceived distinction between 'religious' experience and other 'life' experiences, or in other words between 'religion' and 'life'. In some quarters (Harvey 2013) it has also been about a questioning of the primacy given to 'human' experience over that of non-human animals and 'other than human persons'. Past efforts to define religion by distilling it from other aspects of experience has in many quarters dissipated under benign pressure from anthropology, ethnology and cultural studies and interest is now much more firmly embedded in the (social, political, cognitive and affective) totality of people's lives.

This volume reflects such trends as many of its contributors prioritize subjective life-experience over academic abstractions – the kind exemplified in Martin Stringer's (2008) *Contemporary Western Ethnography and the Definition of Religion*. Day, Vincett and Cotter's collection of essays *Social Identities Between the Sacred and the Secular* (2013) (published, by Ashgate, after the Alternative Salvations Conference at the University of Chester, but before this volume) embodies similar priorities to our own, and usefully exposes ways in which the sacred and secular intersect in social identities to open up a space 'in between' the two. However, while several of the contributions to our debate are clearly aligned with such a model of 'betweenness', 'betweeness' by itself fails to do justice to the extensive disrupting of categories resulting from this collection.

Within Christian theology, this turn to lived experience as the starting point for shaping and reshaping discourse about God emerges in the myriad of contextual and liberation theologies developed over the past fifty or so years and in the more recent shift to employ empirical methods in theological research. Liberation theologies in their manifold diversity – Latin American, feminist, queer, disability, black, womanist and so on – take as their starting point the ordinary and so often silenced lives of those on the underside of society. For Gustavo Gutierrez, the founding figure of Latin American liberation theology, this means beginning with the concrete, historical, material realities of the poor and marginalized because it is the concrete, real-life movements of ordinary communities in Latin America as they come to experience poverty as antithetical to Christian faith which gives a theology of liberation its distinctive character (1988: 8). For Latina theologian, Ada María Isasi-Díaz, it means that *lo cotidiano* – daily life – is a primary theological source; specifically the everyday struggles of survival by Hispanic women and their daily experiences of class, gender, family, work, poverty and religion (1996: 67).

Of course, this turn to everyday experience encapsulated in liberation theologies informs many practical theologies. Scholars have observed the methodological synergies between liberation theologies and the turn to practice, noting the influence of liberationist methods on leading figures like Elaine Graham, Heather Walton, Frances Ward and Kathleen Cahalan (e.g. Turpin 2014). Most notably, perhaps, 'empirical theology' has become an important branch of practical theology, defined by Andrew Village as a theology 'that takes seriously the need to investigate the contexts of religious belief, drawing on the methods of social and psychological science where necessary' (2015). Prominent figures like Pete Ward (2012), Leslie Francis (2009), Andrew Todd (2013), Jeff Astley (2002, 2013), Nicola Slee (2004, 2013), Mark Cartledge (2010) and others have employed a number of empirical research methods to investigate ecclesial practices, pastoral care, the ministry and the relationship between spirituality and personal experiences. Such trends are reflected in this volume as a number of theological contributions utilize empirical methods to investigate 'alternative' narratives of salvation. Similarly, authors draw on lived experience to interrogate and sometimes trouble established theological meanings.

An Invitation to the Reader

Many of these chapters present traditions as radical sources of transformation as well as dangerous sites in need of transformation themselves. Our hope is that this volume will contribute to a wider discussion about the place of religion and spirituality in contemporary society, helping to explore questions about how religious orthodoxies might function to drive social change, about how they might be troubled in light of ordinary experience and contemporary concerns, and about the illuminative value of reflecting on ordinary life using religious metaphors. We invite the reader to explore with the volume's authors creative disruptions to traditional soteriologies and the emergence of vibrant salvation narratives in unexpected settings.

Part I

Contemporary Salvation Narratives

Chapter 1

Only We Can Save Ourselves: An Atheist's 'Salvation'

Thomas J. Coleman III and Robert B. Arrowood

In 1973, Paul Kurtz and Edwin H. Wilson, who were humanists and non-theists, drafted the second Humanist Manifesto. It outlined a malleable but clear affirmation of guiding life aims and principals that could foster 'a secular society on a planetary scale' (Kurtz and Wilson 1973) and were not grounded with reference to, or authority vested in, any transcendent deity. Indeed, it was made clear that '*no deity will save us; we must save ourselves*' (Ibid. [emphasis added]). Ask any atheist you meet where 'salvation' lies for themselves and others, and the meaning of these words will surely be conveyed in his or her answer. For those who live life outside of a religio-spiritual framework, 'salvation', prosperity, meaning and hope lie not in an ethereal realm only to be accessed through prayer or an afterlife, but can emerge from careful reflection of the natural world that surrounds us in the present (Goodenough 1998). For the atheist, 'salvation' may be found in the here and now, and it is from this that any future realization of a secular 'salvation' must proceed. However, before 'secular salvation' can be explored, we must understand the building blocks of a traditionally theological concept of salvation. Does salvation have any relevance for those who are godless?

The traditional binaries utilized in the study of religion, such as the distinction between the sacred and the profane (Eliade 1959), have permeated the academic study of it for much of the twentieth century. This distinction situated religion as something sui generis, and helped to established religious studies departments as autonomous from other disciplines (McCutcheon 1997), while serving to protect the 'specialness' of religious experience as something that was only available to the religiously inclined (Taves 2009). However, the reality of lived experience is seldom reflected in such a crude either/or dichotomy (Coleman and Hood 2015; Feyerabend 1999). Therefore, is the concept of 'salvation' available only in the realm of the sacred? That is to say, can salvation be conceived of outside of its historically theological roots, and what might it look like for the atheist?[1]

In this chapter, we begin by deconstructing the notion of 'salvation' utilizing a building-block approach that allows us to compare *constructs* that may have *features* in common (Taves 2009). Secondly, we situate the building blocks of 'salvation' into the pragmatic framework of horizontal and vertical transcendence (HVT) that makes it available to the believer and non-believer alike (Streib and Hood 2013; Coleman, Silver and Hood in press) and understands 'religion' as a natural phenomenon. Thirdly, we introduce a series of vignettes gathered from two previous studies (Silver et al. 2014; Streib and Hood, in press), in which atheists were asked about beliefs, values and commitments that were currently important to them.[2] Our intent is not to simply tack the label of 'secular' in front of 'salvation' and think that any concept with a theological basis must have a secular counterpart. However, there is no, prima facie reason why an atheist and theist might experience the natural world differently. It is only their interpretation of it that may differ. While the participants were not directly asked about 'salvation', these examples serve as starting points for interpreting and understanding a naturalized conception of 'salvation' as something available in the here and now, based on one's beliefs and behaviours.

Pieces of Salvation: A Building-Block Approach

The Building Blocks

Does 'salvation' denote something that falls into some inherently religious realm? Can it be understood apart from its traditionally theological and vertically transcendent cynosure? The answer, we argue, is: 'absolutely'. In conceptualizing 'salvation' as a lived experience that is available to all – regardless of personal ontology – we embrace a building-block approach that will allow us to identify its constituent parts for the purposes of identifying these pieces in a secular, non-religious context. This framework has been elucidated best by Taves (2009) and emphasizes that, 'rather than attempt to characterize the abstract nouns religion or spirituality, some theorists [such as Taves herself] have argued for a building block approach that conceives of religions and spiritualities as disparate wholes made up of parts, such as *beliefs and practices*' (2013: 139 [emphasis added]). Thus, in order to avoid the presupposition that salvic experience is somehow sui generis, we embrace Taves' 'ascriptive approach', which 'frees us to compare things that have features in common, whether they are deemed *religious or not*' (2009: 19 [emphasis added]). Here, the notion of 'specialness' is of particular importance, as Taves draws from Durkheim's (1912/95) concept of the 'sacred' – things set apart – and 'generate[s] a second-order concept of "specialness"' (2009: 27). This analytical term, 'specialness', can beg the question if we cannot determine the conditions under which such specialness is acknowledged. Classic theoretical approaches allow us to identify deeply moving, important, meaningful and transcendent experiences that one may be 'ultimately concerned' with (Tillich 1958) as perhaps the best exemplar of specialness. Importantly, individuals need not deem these experiences religious, nor do they need to be deemed such by researchers in order to be studied.

The Building Blocks of Salvation

Historically speaking, salvation has been a theological concept that sought to free the *soul* from its inherent sinfulness through the profession of faith in a deity, and by adherence to associated rituals in the Judeo-Christian tradition and doctrinal religions of the East (Boyer 2003). In Christianity, there is a focus on one's individual relationship with, and belief in, God. Salvic notions of an afterlife and a better place begin with this self-professed belief: 'Whoever believes and is baptized will be saved, but whoever does not believe will be condemned' (Mk 16.16 ESV). First and foremost, salvation, at least in Christianity, begins with belief in God and His Son as the only and necessary means to salvation, which is not secular by the very claim that it is for 'eternity'. However, and as the reading demonstrated, there is a ritual-action orientated component as well, notably for this passage, the ritual of baptism. Other rituals and actions that are to be carried out extend to 'spreading the good news of God's love', and the Eucharist, to name only a few. For example, in the Christian serpent handling traditions of Appalachia, who take Mark 16:17-18 ('these signs will follow them that believe'),[3] to be a literal directive from God, the ritual and tradition of handling serpents is not a direct means to salvation, but an act of obedience without which salvation is impossible (Hood and Williamson 2008). In Christianity, salvation has been variously conceived, ranging from the predestination of Calvin to the grace of Luther. However, the combination of belief in God and action signalling such sincerity of belief seems to characterize much of the diverse salvational beliefs of Christians. These components, and combined output, can be represented in the prayer of the Catholic Saint, Thomas Aquinas (Aquinas and Clark 2000: 435). He writes: 'Grant me, O Lord my God, a mind to know you, a heart to seek you, wisdom to find you, conduct pleasing to you, faithful perseverance in waiting for you, and a hope of finally embracing you.'

Using Saint Thomas' prayer as a representative heuristic for the path to salvation, we can identify two broad building blocks to salvation.

1. We can identify the *cognitive component*: belief. Belief is represented in being open to an exchange of knowledge, 'a mind to know you', a will to uncover such knowledge, 'a heart to seek you', and the ability to locate an end point for the search once it has begun, 'wisdom to find you'. Thus, salvation can be said to have, first and foremost, a cognitive component that entails being open to learning, desiring to learn, and wisdom to recognize what one seeks.
2. We can also identify a *behavioural component*: actions/deeds. The action component is represented in one's conduct and behaviour, 'conduct pleasing to you', and in the determination and steadfastness of one's behaviour, 'faithful perseverance in waiting for you'. Thus, while belief is important, the behavioural component is necessary for salvation as well. One must behave accordingly in hopes that said actions and deeds produce a positive effect in bringing salvation to fruition and in maintaining it while alive.

The two components combine to produce the possibility of 'salvation itself': a better place, if only held by the distinctive religious concepts of faith. Once belief has been professed, and one's positive behaviour has been expressed, salvation is available: 'a hope of finally embracing you', perhaps now held onto firmly in faith that exceeds either belief or action. In this sense, faith is non-falsifiable, as is 'salvation' for Christians. This is quite problematic for science.

Broadly speaking, we have identified building blocks of 'salvation' that can be used to locate and identify a secular 'salvation': a belief component that holds ultimate knowledge and an action-orientated component that brings such belief and knowledge to fruition and maintains them, ultimately leading to 'salvation'.

At this point, one might ask, 'But where is God in your salvation?' The French Emperor, Napoléon, posed a similar question in the eighteenth century to the mathematician Laplace when he presented his model of the planetary orbits to the emperor (de Morgan 2008). Upon Laplace detailing his model, Napoléon asked him why he had not factored the creator into his equation, to which he famously responded, 'I had no need of that hypothesis.' Laplace's point wasn't that there was no God, only that the postulation of such a thing did not contribute to his scientific investigation. Similarly, and for our present purposes, we have no need to situate 'salvation' as something that can be only experienced at the hand of the divine. A building-block approach that embraces the category of 'specialness' over notions of sui generis will do just fine. However, and as the next section will briefly detail, God is not ruled out of the equation, He is only an option.

Horizontal and Vertical Transcendence: A Framework for Religious Studies

One approach that led the sociology of religion for much of the twentieth century was that of methodological atheism. This idea, most noticeably taken up by Peter Berger in *The Sacred Canopy* (1967), called for ruling out the possibility of the Transcendent a priori in social scientific explanation (Hood 2012). However, one important question in the social scientific study of religion is what one may be responding to (Ibid.). The methodological atheism of the twentieth century denied the investigation into a 'what' before it could even be asked. Conversely, many religious studies, psychological, and cognitive approaches merely affirm the notion that religion is inherently special, easily defined (although each scholar has a different definition!), and assign the label of 'religion' not only to the self-professed believer, but most unfortunately, the non-believer as well (e.g. Barrett and Lanman 2008; Streib and Hood 2013). Thus, two ways of approaching human experience in general, and 'religious' experience in particular, have been at war, both within, and across disciplines. One merely affirms the category of religion (and belief in god/spirits/the Transcendent) applying it to almost anything, while the other simply denies that such an object could ever exist. What is a scholar to do?

One approach that has sought to embrace this problem (between affirming and rejecting the Transcendent), and not sidestep it, has been the framework of horizontal and vertical transcendence (HVT). Here, HVT is best suited for inquiry into domains of religious and/or 'special' experiences as it is methodologically agnostic (Coleman, Silver and Hood in press). In short, this approach allows for human experience to function along a continuum: epistemologically speaking, any experience that can be had can be had by anyone.[4] However, what is unique about HVT is that it is based on taking seriously the personal ontological framework of the individual(s). Is the worldview of the subject framed with reference to a vertically Transcendent reality (God, Ahura Mazda, Allah) or does the individual find all the meaningful, special and awe-inspiring experiences in the here and now, having no need for a point of reference that posits a 'culturally postulated superhuman agent' (McCauley and Lawson 2002: x)? By positioning the acceptance or rejection of a superhuman deity-agent at the centre of our inquiry, and allowing for the possibility that experiences can be had by anyone and that it is only the label 'religion' that is traded in public discourse, we can ask meaningful questions that do not rule out the possibility that one group can have experiences that the other can't. The framing of experience is important, and the terms we use to do so matter. Just as James (1902/85: 33) saw the dispute over what he called 'personal religion' as a 'dispute about names' and even subtitled his *Varieties of Religious Experience* as 'a study of human nature', applying the label of 'religion' – implicitly or explicitly – was merely a decision bounded by language. However, even with this essentialist claim, the interpretation of experience as 'religious' is largely a political decision and, as such, deserves to be politicized as any other social institution (Guevara 2000). 'Salvation' can surely be had by the atheist, but the terms used to denote 'salvation' (the very term itself) and the baggage those terms may carry must be put aside in order for the experience to be realized in non-religious populations. While a typical response from the theist might be 'anyone can have salvation, but only after they have been "saved"', this is a theological statement, and not an empirical one. Given the prevalence of religious language used by theists to characterize important experiences throughout history, the secularists confrontation with this language may be necessary in order to express experiences that are 'special', however not in a specifically religious sense in a world inhabited by gods or God.

If 'salvation' can be broadly considered to relate to ultimately meaningful beliefs and behaviours, then we must look to atheist's themselves to tell us what beliefs, values and commitments are meaningful to them. In the next section, we present several vignettes that centre on the idea that the world can be a better place and that it is one's responsibility to make it so through one's actions. Madeline and Lily's vignettes embody the Enlightenment ideal of contributing to and bettering humanity through participation in scientific and educational endeavours. Harold and Joey's vignettes further contribute to this ideal, suggesting that the limiting of pain and the promotion of flourishing of all conscious creatures is a 'basic belief'. Finally, Jill's excerpt draws attention to the role of responsibility in effectuating this ideal, which some atheist's may see as an imperative once we realize that only we can save ourselves.

Secular 'Salvation': Beliefs in Action

Madeline's Symbolic Immortality as 'Salvation'

One central notion of 'salvation' is that it traditionally implies an afterlife – a 'better place' beyond our current world where such a 'salvation' and improvement of the human condition (the individual) can be located, and which can be reached only after a bodily death. For the non-theist, who typically believes that an 'afterlife' rests beyond the current borders of our present knowledge and sensibility, the only way to know about whether an afterlife exists is to die. It might appear that secular salvation is limited to these same restraints. Specifically, if 'salvation' must occur after death, and the non-theist believes that nothing happens after you die (or that what does or does not occur after death is at least unknowable), can salvation still be found? That depends on whether or not one believes that the actions one has taken while alive have the ability to effectuate change long after one's death. What happens to us after we die? As 27-year-old 'Madeline', who was in a PhD science programme, says:

> Uhm well the person is just gone but uhm the idea of the person like lives with those who lived with them, remember them; are affected by their decisions or affected by their lives many, many years later and that's amazing their impression lives is in our thoughts and our thoughts in thoughts; thoughts within thoughts. So it would be; we do in fact carry memories with us and how real and how actual those memories are depends but if I were to die right now the memory of me would carry with the people who know me and if I had any impact on science and later on the scientist, they might have a memory of not me, but my contribution to science.

Here we can see that even after death, regardless of whether there is an afterlife, one's very actions (or inactions) while one is alive – that is, in the here and now – have great power to 'live on' and affect change long after the individual is gone. This is certainly not a new idea by any stretch; the notion of symbolic immortality (Hood and Morris 1983), and generativity has been around for a long time. Madeline wants to be remembered not merely as an individual, but as someone who contributed to knowledge that will benefit humanity. What is important to note is that she sees the possibility that the very actions she takes in the here and now have great potential to cause positive change long after she is gone and is no longer 'here', in the 'now'. If 'salvation' is thought of as a better place that can be had by positive beliefs that are put into action, and Madeline is able to make an impact on the world around her through the production of scientific knowledge, she might have 'salvation' – a secular version.

Knowledge as 'Salvation'

To the Christian, salvation *cannot* occur with the explicit rejection of God once revealed to the knower. While grace is always a theological option, for the person to find his or her place in God's presence, one has to value and seek knowledge of transcendence that is vertically connected with a belief in God or gods. However, for the atheist, with a natural ontological worldview, knowledge of God is not only misdirected, but also fails to cultivate a 'better place' in the here and now. Just as Madeline's vignette above alluded to, one way to make 'salvation' in the here and now is by valuing knowledge and education.

Thirty-two-year-old Lily is a happily married practising psychologist with two children. She cites the 'American Psychological Association, the National Association of School Psychologists, and other groups promoting education' as key groups that she identifies with, and belongs to. These groups participate in producing scientific and applied knowledge that makes the world a better place, and Lily is a part of that mission. Education is important to her. She says that 'knowledge is power', in fact 'it's more powerful than … it's more powerful than money'. To further emphasize the importance and value she places on knowledge: 'Education is not something that you can have taken away from you. … I think that it's as essential as food.' Lily believes 'children are precious and deserve to be put first in our lives. I believe in education, especially public education and I also firmly believe in science.' To fit the previous motif again, children can also be viewed as a way to achieve immortality; by instilling in them the essence of who you are (Baumeister 1991; Arrowood and Pope 2014) would help us in achieving this. In line with the idea that if 'salvation' is the emancipation from one's current state of suffering, thus leading to a better place, Lily values education because 'education sets you free'.

'Salvation' as Human Flourishing

One of the limitations with most theistic conceptualizations of 'salvation' is that they are primarily concerned with the individual and not concerned with humans in general in the here and now. If a god can only offer salvation, then one's actions and beliefs that do take place in the here and now are largely directed only at that deity, and for a purpose that can only be realized after death. However, for the atheist, the focus on beliefs and action are purposeful purely in this life, and if 'this life' is to continue to exist, and is all one knows, then the greatest good can be found in supporting the flourishing of all sentient creatures and in the limiting of pain. Such a theme has been expanded upon from the Enlightenment onwards and in the present-day by the book, *The Moral Landscape* (Harris 2010). However, such an idea is not merely the popularized product of 'New Atheist' discourse, and is alive and well in the 'average' atheist who doesn't make the headlines for speaking out against religion. As Harold, age fifty-four, explains:

> I think the primary belief that I've come up with, actually thinking about this for some years, is the basic belief I think is that suffering is something that should be avoided in oneself, and to what extent you can in other *'feeling'* [conscious] beings. That's kind of the basis of everything I try to *believe in*. Other than that, I would think, and of course the converse of that is that pleasure is a good to be pursued in yourself, and for others when possible.

If 'salvation' is the antithesis of suffering, then Harold is clearly 'seeking' it for not only himself, but others as well. Important to note is that he considers this idea of human flourishing as a 'basic belief'. This is to say that he conceives making the world a better place and easing the pain that accompanies our existence as something that is rather straightforward. After careful reflection over a number of years, Harold believes that not only is human flourishing the greatest good, but also that it is extended to all conscious beings.

Joey, a 27-year-old college student living in southern United States, also shares Harold's belief that all sentient creatures have the right to flourish. As a social activist involved in advocating for the rights of minority religious groups and atheist's, Joey *believes* that he can make the world a better place through his actions. He understands belief as 'a certain position ... something you hold, feel, or many times know'. He identifies himself as a 'secular humanist', and Joey's core set of beliefs, as they relate to his self-identification, highlight something of ultimate concern for him: 'pro-human flourishing ... pro flourishing of all conscious creatures, and a limiting of pain, struggle, and suffering' in the world. Joey believes that 'we should naturally be concerned with the human condition', and pleads for all religious and non-religious people to 'concern ourselves with making things better'.

Once a person either deconverts from belief in God (Fazzino 2014), or simply realizes their own lack of belief from a young age (Coleman, Silver and Hood, in press), the realization that there is no God or gods to make things better entails then, perhaps, that it is up to us and us alone. This was precisely the sentiment expressed by 37-year-old Jill. She states: 'I don't believe there's any ... I don't think anything happens for any reason, just [you know, no God guiding] things. ... *I think it's our responsibility to make the world the way we want it to be* and I don't think the way the world is now is a very good picture.' She expresses commitments to 'environmental causes, environmental activism and ... feminist causes', and declares that 'social-economic ... equality is a big issue for' her. Interestingly, Jill seems to view some religious frameworks as providing an excuse for not taking action to make the world a better place – this criticism is quite understandable if most theistic notions of salvation are understood as being primarily concerned with an eternal 'real' life beyond the very short one we know. As she says, 'One of the objections I have to faith is, I think it's the way people lie to themselves to escape responsibility.' However, she goes on to add that someone with 'mature faith I suppose would … try not to do that, try not to lie to yourself about your responsibilities'. This is a very telling statement as it can elucidate the concept of a naturalized, horizontal 'salvation'. In understanding Jill's words, we can see that one's responsibility to make the world a better place and ease suffering is a concept and goal that is *god optional*. It can be believed in, and acted out by all individuals, if they choose, regardless of their ontological stance.

Eschatology: The End is Near, or is it?

A secular, naturalized 'salvation' *naturally* has implications for the direction of humanity as a whole. Post Enlightenment, and with the rise of natural epistemologies, a theistic understanding of humans and their environment was no longer needed to navigate within it. Science supplanted religious frameworks and understandings and elevated a focus on the human condition in the here and now (whether or not science chooses to recognize this is a separate matter [Feyerabend 2011]). It would appear, based on the brief narrative segments presented in this chapter speaking to what *we might* term an 'atheist's salvation', that if a common element of theistic 'salvations' begins with a belief in the ultimate, and that it is the individual's behaviour that leads to the experience or realization of a union with this ultimate, then an atheist salvation is not only possible, but has been underway since the Enlightenment. However, and to the extent that we are bound by the limits of language, it does little good to attach any 'religious' or Transcendent significance to this 'salvation'. Thus, this is where viewing these vignettes through the framework of horizontal transcendence is of particular importance. The ideals and beliefs presented here may take on a 'religious-like' significance, or perhaps an even greater significance; however, the category of religion does not control the discourse. There is no 'implicit religion' to be discussed as secular experience can be realized and understood on its own terms. Pragmatically speaking, what is of particular interest here – the idea of an ultimate better place, and the actions to get there – is ill suited to a very limited understanding of 'salvation' as something purely religious.

The polar ice caps are melting, deforestation is occurring on a global level, children and adults suffer from poverty not only in 'undeveloped' nations, but also in 'developed' nations. This list could go on and on, but the picture should be clear that there is a lot worth *saving* that can be located in the here and now, and this is precisely what the presented narratives demonstrate. While such a concern for improving the human condition appears almost an imperative for the atheist, it is also available to the theist. For example, Hood, Hill and Spilka write that 'S. M. Taylor (2007) has demonstrated in her study of Catholic nuns involved in the environmental movement [that] there can be a simultaneous affirmation of both vertical and horizontal transcendence' (2009: 282). Clearly, a secularized 'salvation' can be realized by individuals regardless of an individual's ontological worldview, and can be identified by scholars for further exploration. However, a conceptualization of 'salvation' that purely limits itself to a distant realm beyond the clouds contributes little to the shifting religious and non-religious landscape the world over.

From the position of the atheist, the mantra 'only we can save ourselves' is a normative one that may form an imperative for those who do not believe in a God. This mantra is often *believed in* by atheist's, and many times *acted upon* as they take to the task of making the world a better place through social and humanitarian action (Silver et al. 2014). Therefore, some simple building blocks that can guide further investigation and comparison between competing ontologies in the study of 'salvation' can be found to have cognitive (ultimate beliefs) and behavioural (acting on beliefs) components that combine to produce the effect (one hopes) of a 'better place'. This better place is comparable to theistic 'salvations' and deserves continued study.

One way to further this endeavour is to take a 'building block' or 'ascriptive' approach (Taves 2009) in order to locate shared commonalties of the atheist and theist in order to begin exploration. However, such an approach is still in need of an overall theoretical framework that takes ontology seriously, and avoids affirming theism over atheism and vice versa. Here, the distinction between a frame of meaning that operates on a horizontal level and one that operates on a vertical level has much to offer (Coleman, Silver and Hood in press; Streib and Hood 2013). A 'salvation' that is available to the theist and atheist alike can be found by utilizing this framework.

'The End' may or may not be near; however, if a secular 'salvation' can be sustained, it will only be sustained by the belief in a better place and by the belief that such a place is, at least in principal, attainable through one's actions. This belief-action trajectory of a 'secular salvation' is embodied in the words of social justice activist, poet and front man for the popular 1990s' rap-metal band Rage Against the Machine, Zach De la Rocha (1999/2014), who captures the notion of a 'secular salvation' when he writes, 'It has to start somewhere It has to start sometime, what better place than here, what better time than now?' A 'secular salvation' has been growing since the Enlightenment, and is available to the believer and non-believer alike.

Chapter 2

REFLECTIONS ON THE LANGUAGE OF SALVATION IN TWELVE-STEP RECOVERY

Wendy Dossett

In return for a bottle and a hangover we have been given the Keys to the Kingdom.[1]

A growing and visible Recovery Movement[2] in the UK seeks to give voice to, mobilize and organize those in recovery from substance use disorders (SUDs); mental health issues; physical, sexual and emotional abuse; and social exclusion. The language used to express these experiences of recovery is modulated by numerous vocabularies of political, social and economic empowerment, by the transformative power of self-narratives (for tellers and hearers), and by notions of religious and spiritual liberation. The focus of this chapter is on the experiences and language of people who go through the process of recovery from SUDs through a particular method – namely, the Twelve Steps – and examines the apparently salvific language in which this enterprise is often expressed.

The notion of 'salvation' implies a state from which a person must be saved or rescued. Active addiction[3] is described by practitioners of the Twelve Steps as a desperate condition from which, unless it is faced, there is little hope of escape. Yet, escape is achieved by a significant proportion of those who adopt the discipline of the Steps and take the support of Twelve-Step mutual aid groups such as Alcoholics Anonymous (AA) and Narcotics Anonymous (NA) and/or the support of treatment centres and programmes which use the Steps. Those who use this approach (which is one recovery methodology among several) often claim that the profound transformation of recovery from this hopeless and terminal condition can be understood only by reference to a power beyond the self – a higher power. This power is described by some practitioners as a transcendent being although others offer other possible interpretations. Thus, abstinent recovery is understood to be 'spiritual' in nature. In fact, 'Step Twelve' of the programme describes it as a 'spiritual awakening' (Alcoholics Anonymous World Services [1939] 2001: 60). The condition of active addiction is also described in Twelve-Step contexts as being rooted in a 'spiritual malady' (64), which must be continually addressed if recovery is to develop.

In a volume which widens and interrogates discourse around 'salvation', this chapter explores the meanings and use of some of the soteriological language used within the framework of Twelve-Step recovery. It asks whether this language is best understood as descriptive and reflective or as normative and didactic. In considering the implications of such a distinction, it reflects on the apparently shaming terms 'addict' and 'alcoholic' in the context of the remarkable transformation experienced by, and evidenced in, the lives of those that describe themselves this way. The chapter draws on some case studies from the Higher Power Project, a qualitative study of spirituality, and Twelve-Step recovery undertaken at the University of Chester in order to respond to these questions.

Context: Twelve-Step Mutual Aid

The Twelve-Step mutual aid movement of today began with the founding of the first Twelve-Step fellowship, Alcoholics Anonymous. The co-founders of AA, William Wilson and Dr Robert Smith (known within the fellowships as 'Bill W.' and 'Dr Bob'),[4] both recovering alcoholics,[5] and associated with the Oxford Group, met during the Great Depression in Akron, Ohio. Despite Dr Bob's piety and Bill W.'s own dramatic religious experience, they were, they say, only able to stay abstinent through their contact with each other and their work with other alcoholics. Together, and with the early members, they developed the Twelve Steps[6] – namely the 'programme' of AA, which was adopted by Narcotics Anonymous and the dozens of other Twelve-Step fellowships worldwide. The Oxford Group, which provided some of the inspiration for the development of the Steps, founded by preacher Frank Buchman, was individualistic American prosperity-gospel-style evangelism which appealed to the educated and wealthy. While early AA took forward some features of Oxford Group belief and practice, doubts began to emerge about the utility of simply adopting religious rhetoric when dealing with 'street drunks'. The early movement quickly abandoned formal connections with 'Groupers' and explored a variety of other sources, in particular the work of William James, Carl Jung and several writers influenced by New Thought Religion (Kurtz 1979; Pittman 1993). Minority voices within Alcoholics Anonymous continue to assert that the purpose of the fellowship is, as it always has been, to bring about an essential and beneficial conversion to Christianity. They claim that agnostic and atheist viewpoints dominated the small group writing the authoritative 'Big Book',[7] thus watering down what could and should have been a 'First-century Christian' message (Dick B 1992). Other voices note this development as one of the reasons why the Twelve Steps have been able to save so many lives, regardless of the religious or secular affiliations of those that use them (Kurtz 1979; Travis 2009). The original bifurcation, which is sometimes characterized in the United States as that between 'Akron' and 'New York' AA,[8] continues to function at various levels in AA worldwide. Particular meetings, areas and even whole movements are associated with different 'brands', all of which increasingly use digital and social media to generate and maintain their respective orthodoxies. Notable in the UK are the 'Road to Recovery' (members of which are known as 'Roadies') in Plymouth, and the more widely geographically distributed 'Joy of Recovery', both of which claim influence from the charismatic AA speaker, Clancy I,[9] and promote an 'on your knees' brand of spiritual discipline (Aldo 2013). There are other strong voices highlighting the authority assigned, in the early literature, to individuals to develop their own notion of higher power and their own daily programme of recovery. Most of these voices occupy the mainstream of AA, but an increasingly vocal minority argue that this freedom should be more actively defended. These voices are organized in America under the banners of *Agnostics and Atheists in AA* and the larger *AA Agnostica*, and similar groups are beginning to emerge in the UK (Core 2013). Observing their activity online and on Facebook, it is evident that even in these groups, diversity prevails. Voices seeking to defend the freedom for personal interpretations of higher power are matched by voices seeking to mount a secularist critique of the 'incoherent' and 'irrational' higher-power language of others.

Classing AA as 'religious' may be legitimate if selective appeals are made to aspects of its early history. However, its self-description is consistently 'spiritual rather than religious' and the Preamble read at every meeting[10] declares independence from any 'sect' or 'denomination'. The legitimacy of the 'spiritual' understanding of addiction and recovery rests in part[11] on the concept of powerlessness. The Twelve Steps understand sufferers to be powerless over the substance(s) or behaviour which cause(s) them and/or their loved ones harm. Addiction cannot, in this model, be understood as a failure or weakness of will power because the condition is *beyond all reach* of personal will power. This condition is what distinguishes an 'alcoholic'/'addict' from a heavy drinker or user. If personal will power is ineffective, then some other power is, necessarily, required. For the AAs in Akron in the late 1930s this power was inevitably the Creator of the Universe, the God of the Bible, and the language was normative, but the wider fellowship was multi-vocal on this subject from the very start.

Naming, Shaming and Claiming

The use of terms such as 'alcoholic' and 'addict' to describe people suffering from substance use disorders is being increasingly challenged (Winerman 2014; Broyles et al. 2014). The practice equates the person with the problem, and thus obscures the person. It also contributes to stigma because there is no stable sense of what 'recovering alcoholic or addict' means. For those in Twelve-Step programmes, these terms usually indicate their abstinence from at least the primary substance to which they are addicted (and usually from all mind-altering substances); they may, in fact, mean 'more than abstinent' – they may imply that they are working on a programme of recovery, that they are committed to self-improvement and signify ongoing change. This is perhaps not clearly understood by outsiders.

Furthermore, the wider Recovery Movement lobbies, rightly, for understandings of recovery that are more inclusive than the understanding of recovery advanced by the Twelve-Step model. Thus, someone who has reduced their substance use to below harmful levels, or has desisted from substance-related crime, may be described as 'in recovery'. While being (importantly) encouraging and inclusive for those engaging in 'harm reduction' short of abstinence, this does mean there is no stable or shared definition of recovery. An unintended consequence is that the adjective 'recovering' attached to 'addict' or 'alcoholic' may mean very little in a public discourse shaped by celebrity recovery failures and addiction-related violent crime. As a result recovering people are mistrusted and remain stigmatized.

While it is, on the one hand, problematic for outsiders to use the terms 'alcoholic' and 'addict' for these reasons, it should, on the other, be recognized that the act of naming themselves in this way is central to the practices of people in Twelve-Step programmes. From the perspective of the latter, the admission and acceptance of what many consider to be their 'nature' as addicts and alcoholics is the first step towards building recovery. It is equivalent to the admission of powerlessness. Without this admission, agency will be attributed (erroneously, according to this model) to the individual, and recovery may not develop.

In the context of an exploration of salvific language, it may seem an obvious strategy to equate the language of 'alcoholism' and the naming of the 'addict' with the Christian language of 'sin' and 'sinner'. The Twelve-Step programme itself, with its suggestion of the need for 'removal' of 'defects of character',[12] offers further legitimacy for this kind of reading. Linda Mercadante's (1996) *Victims & Sinners: Spiritual Roots of Addiction and Recovery* and Chris Cook's (2006) *Alcohol, Addiction and Christian Ethics* both offer sustained engagements with putative relationships between addiction and sin. Mercadante points out, 'The sin-and-salvation paradigm has ample room within it for a[n] … addiction and recovery metaphor' (27).

However, among other possible objections[13] to the simplistic elision of 'sin' and 'addiction', is the important point that members of Twelve-Step fellowships do not define each other as addicts or alcoholics. A newcomer to a meeting will not be told that they are 'classed' as such. Thus, there is no totalizing language of sin, nor even of addiction. There are only individuals speaking for themselves. From a Twelve-Step perspective there is no point in anyone other than the individual concerned engaging in the process of self-identification. Many report that they were accused of addiction or alcoholism repeatedly by family, friends, doctors, criminal justice professionals, but until they understood their own problematic usage in these terms, no real change was possible. In fact the personal owning by the individual of their identification as an addict/alcoholic is considered by them to be foundational and necessary to their recovery. This 'claiming' of apparently degrading terms is significant and empowering within this context, in a way which is sometimes overlooked in the important wider discourse, in which it is sought to overcome stigma and avoid shaming language.

Contemporary Twelve-Step Language

The Higher Power Project is a large qualitative research project, based in the Department of Theology and Religious Studies at the University of Chester and undertaken by the author and a small team, among people who describe themselves as addicts and/or alcoholics and who attribute their sustained abstinence[14] to their practice of the Twelve Steps and a concept of a higher power. Inevitably, the accounts and insights offered by those with whom we have spoken are open to analysis from a great range of perspectives. Two clear themes discernible in the accounts will be explored here, in order to respond to the question with which this chapter opened, about whether the salvific language used is best understood as being authoritative, propositional and normative, or as being primarily descriptive.

The first clear theme is the striking nature of the transformation reported by those in recovery from a previously seemingly hopeless condition. Arguably, there appears to be a natural tendency to reach for religious imagery and terminology to communicate its impact in their lives and the lives of their loved ones and communities. Such a reading of these experiences rests on a constructivist understanding of the use of religious language. When someone describes their recovery as 'a miracle', there is no need to assume this is meant merely metaphorically, nor is there a need to assume its valence requires an epistemology consistent with a religious worldview.

The second theme is the evidence for the personal 'negotiation' of the concept of higher power by people seeking to use it in their construction of a recovery self-narrative. It is patently clear that the language of higher power in the 'approved' literature is theistic and patriarchal, and refers to an interventionist God who cares about the sobriety of the individual. A key passage in the 'Big Book' known as 'The Three Pertinent Ideas' states:

> Our description of the alcoholic, the chapter to the agnostic, and our personal adventures before and after make clear three pertinent ideas:
>
> (a) That we were alcoholic and could not manage our own lives.
> (b) That probably no human power could have relieved our alcoholism.
> (c) That God could and would if He were sought. (60)

The use of the third person, 'reporting' the experiences of the early members of AA, is typical. The 'Big Book' itself describes the programme as 'suggestive': always reporting how the early members, 'we', achieved lasting abstinence. That being said, this passage is strongly theistic, promoting a clear concept of an interventionist God, not only able, but *certain* to achieve what human power cannot. There is a normative and directive tone here. The person (potentially struggling desperately with all the consequences of active addiction) reading this literature would undoubtedly receive the message that unless an interventionist God is sought and found, no recovery is possible. However, the evidence from our research shows recovering people 'grappling' with that presentation, accepting it in some cases, rejecting it in others, but most often interpreting it in terms that are both palatable and 'functional' from their perspective.

'Beyond my wildest dreams' – The Language of Transformation

Abstinence from the substance which had wreaked havoc in their lives and over which they were previously powerless is not considered by people in Twelve-Step recovery to be a mere 'lifestyle adjustment', but a radical transformation of the whole person. The new life experienced in recovery is described as 'beyond my wildest dreams', 'a miracle'. While it is possible to detect narratives of personal continuity between the using and the abstinent individual in some of the accounts, the majority speak of major upheavals in values, priorities and behaviour which go way beyond the daily commitment to abstinence. Unsurprisingly, language freighted with religious meaning is chosen by many participants to describe this transformation. This language is not selected in a vacuum of course. The interpretative community of the fellowships collectively use this language. The notable feature is that even those with non- or even anti-theistic notions of higher power still use it. Some of this language sounds notes of gratitude, some is used to denote the extreme or sudden nature of the change. The word 'saved' is used by several. For example, at the end of his interview, Sam was asked if there was anything else he'd like to say.

> Erm, well, apart from the fact I believe the Twelve Step programme is amazing. It does save people, erm, thank god for people like you who are actually talking to people and actually believe what we might be saying because, you know, if I tried to take this into a normal conversation I'd probably be s ..., s ... you know, erm, locked up or something for being a madman. Err, I, I just fully believe that erm, there's something going on and none of us understand and if we look for it, we find it, but I would never knock AA, it's saved my life, it's saved millions of people's lives.

Here 'saved' is used to describe 'lives saved' in the physical sense, and does not necessarily refer to a transformation from a state of sin, to a state of grace or purity. However, the phrase 'there's something going on and none of us understand' sounds a note of wonderment perhaps associated with spirituality.

Along with 'saved', 'miracle' is a frequently used term. Sarina (who describes herself as not religious) talked about a sudden transformation. 'I went from a using addict to a non-user overnight. A miracle!' For Maureen there was a slower transformation but she, too, uses the term 'miracle'. Here she explains an experience at a meeting:

> But I do remember, err, an experience of being, err, at a rather large meeting ... when I realized that I was, I was, err, in a room full of living miracles. There were

people who were sober, who were calling themselves alcoholics, but, who were, err, certainly for that day free from, free from alcohol.

Morgan R,[15] in a written questionnaire response, touches on gratitude and purpose, and talks of both slow 'spiritual awakenings' and more dramatic experiences.

There have been so many spiritual awakenings over the years, I have lost count. My spiritual awakenings have made me more human, they have kept me Clean, and allowed me to carry a message of Recovery to those still-suffering. They have made me useful, given me purpose, filled me with gratitude. Sometimes they have been slow and gradual, and others have been like an explosion in my life.

It is tempting to psychologize the selection of religiously freighted terminology. The transformations in the lives of these interviewees have been so extreme, seemingly appearing to have originated from a source outside of their own capabilities, that it is perhaps inevitable that these interviewees, in order to describe their experiences, reach for the most effective lexicon of powerful language, namely, that of religion. To dismiss the language as 'merely metaphorical', however, would be to ignore the force of Janet Soskice's axiom that 'no metaphor is completely reducible to a literal equivalent without consequent loss of content' (1985: 95).

On the Personal 'negotiation' of Higher-Power Language

The written and oral discourses of Twelve-Step mutual aid are pegged with strong poles of authority. Not only is 'Conference Approved' literature assigned such high status that it is unlikely ever to be substantially altered (i.e. there is no prospect of less sexist versions of key texts, let alone the removal of other offensive language[16]), but meetings are in large part rehearsals of powerful performative utterances, handed down from one generation of recovering people to the next, and repeated with liturgical regularity. 'Newcomers' who 'stick around' first hear and then internalize the format for 'sharing', which involves detailing 'what it was like, what happened and what it is like now' (this phrase is based on a phrase that appears on page 58 of the fourth edition of the Big Book). The shared material is littered with both formal and less formal repeated phrases. Some of this language is standard throughout Twelve-Step fellowships worldwide. Some might be fellowship-specific, and some might reflect regional variations, or meeting-style variations. There are women's meetings, LGBTQ meetings and agnostics and atheists meetings, all of these differentiated in style by their members' language, as well as meetings that are often orientated towards different aspects of recovery, such as 'Living Sober'. In a 'Step meeting', the Steps may be considered consecutively each week. A 'theme meeting' might focus on recovery themes such as 'a day at a time', 'gratitude', 'acceptance', 'resentments', 'powerlessness', 'prayer and meditation', 'service', 'sponsorship' and 'the Traditions'. At a 'speaker meeting', someone considered established in recovery might share 'experience, strength and hope' for twenty minutes or so to set the tone for the meeting. There is an informal and implicit 'script' for every meeting, whatever its nature. Norms are strong, and are reinforced not only by repetition, but also by the assumed authority of those whose abstinence and recovery have been of a longer duration. Some of the language is 'sloganized'. Slogans – 'Live and Let Live', 'Think, Think, Think', 'Let Go, Let God', 'Easy Does It', 'First Things First', 'One Day at a Time' – are often posted (sometimes framed) on walls. Other standard phrases – 'it's an action programme', 'there but for the grace of God go I', 'without this fellowship/programme I would be dead', 'what you put in front of your recovery, you lose, along with your recovery', 'poor me, poor me, pour me a drink', 'I was looking down on people from the gutter', 'my best thinking got me here' – appear frequently in shares (a 'share' is when a member speaks, uninterrupted, for a few minutes, about their experience). The combination of, on the one hand, this powerful formal language, unchangeable and unassailable literature, charismatic authority of long-time abstinent members and, on the other, the usually vulnerable and desolate state of newcomers sets up a site that is marked by a troubling power inequity as well as by an extraordinarily transformative potential. During the Higher Power Project research we spoke with a hundred Twelve-Step practitioners about their engagement with this powerful language. It became very clear that even when it was broadly accepted, there was always some interpretation. While this sometimes accorded with the norms of the interpretative community, there was also evidence of highly personal interpretative autonomy, sometimes resulting from some initial cognitive dissonance. Lynden's recovery, for example, started with a strong reaction against the perceived Christian nature of the Steps – 'I don't want to be saved, thank you' – but she now describes a power greater than herself as 'an ongoing creativity which is infinite'. Keith, thirty-five years sober, writes about his practice of the Twelve Steps as an atheist and his relationship with his religious sponsors:

> I use an adapted version of the 12 steps which does not mention God. I have two
> sponsors, one a devout practising Roman Catholic and the other a high-church
> Anglican; both of them accept my views and do not love me any the less.

Here we see evidence of the pluralism of belief and worldview which appears to characterize most Twelve-Step communities. This is also an account of mutual respect, which accords with AA's Third Tradition: 'The only requirement for membership is desire to stop drinking,' a corollary of which is that there is no requirement for 'correct belief'.

Project participants also offered evidence of reflection on and rejection of some of the language used in the 'rooms'.[17] The phrase 'there but for the Grace of God go I' is often heard, especially when meeting members hear of a relapse, hospitalization, drink-drive conviction, imprisonment or death of a fellow member. Usually its utterance communicates both gratitude – for not being 'in that place' – and humility – in its implicit admission that, in normal circumstances, without the support of the fellowship and programme, the speaker would be capable of the same behaviour. However, here Jennifer, a participant, engages (theologically) with what she sees as weaknesses in this, as well as other notions, rejecting them as part of her own development of her higher power concept:

> I don't consider a Higher Power to be a personal being – anthropomorphic – nor an intelligent puppeteer in the sky directing the show. I do not conceive of HP as a santa god who rewards the good and punishes the naughty. Neither do I see this force as working for some and not others as in 'There but for the Grace of God go I'.

We also see project participants grappling with the patriarchal language of the literature, and in some cases rejecting it. Ben explains: 'I describe God in the feminine because my concept of "life-giver" is purported to the feminine of all species I know of.' Jennifer, similarly, writes: 'I toss out the personal god language or the maleness ... and replace those words with GRACE or LOVE.' While there are plenty of accounts of participants seeing themselves as coming to realize the 'truths' that they perceive as being offered by the programme, there are also accounts of the rejection of apparently fixed ideas and the personal negotiation with and reshaping of the language to make it salient to their particular life experience, embodiment and worldviews. Here, Sophia describes the value to her of her experience of disagreeing with fellow members:

> The people in the fellowship have had a huge influence over my version of a HP, mainly by me not agreeing (for me) with a lot of HP versions I hear in AA. So by defining what my HP is NOT it has helped me define what it IS.

This work of interpretation, undertaken by individuals in crisis, facing often huge personal, social, family and economic challenges, appears to be central to the establishment of sustainable recovery. Shadd Maruna's exploration of the self-narratives of desisting criminals in his prize-winning study (2001) *Making Good: how ex-convicts reform and rebuild their lives* describes this interpretative work and the development of coherent self-narratives as the writing of a 'redemption script'. This is strongly religious terminology that seems neither out of place nor overstated in his thesis. For Maruna, a key feature in the development of these self-narratives is that, although they might find support, only the individuals themselves can do this interpretative work (7,163). The evidence from the Higher Power Project suggests that individual fellowship members engage in this very work of interpretation, negotiating with each other's stories, the formal literature and the oral tradition of the fellowships, among many other sources of inspiration, in order to write their own 'redemption script', and to 'own it' in a way that feels authentic to them.

Alternative Salvations

Keys to the Kingdom?

The experience of active addiction is described universally by project participants as wretched, destructive and unwanted, and the transformative experience of recovery is described in language marked by joy and gratitude, frequently expressed in identifiably religious terms. I have argued that the 'naturalness' of religious language used in this context emerges from (a) the history of the Twelve-Step programme, rooted as it is in part, in an explicitly Christian worldview and (b) the extreme nature of the transformation experienced and the search for language to communicate its force and significance. A narrow focus on the literature and on origins would suggest a propositional reading of statements about God and Higher Power, and of the epigraph of this chapter 'In return for a bottle and a hangover, we have been given the Keys to the Kingdom'. However, accounts of practitioners themselves often offer a far more complex picture in which the language of salvation is not so much 'theological' as 'phenomenological'. A religious/secular dichotomy proves, as is shown many times in this volume, to be unhelpful as an analytical frame for understanding a discourse that has common features for people who do not have common identities, for example, theists, non-theists and anti-theists. The dichotomy drives a tendency to see salvation in 'real' terms for religious people, and in 'metaphorical' terms for non-religious people, when there appears to be no experiential basis upon which to make such a distinction.

Chapter 3

PUBLIC POLICY DIALOGUE AS A SALVATION PRACTICE FOR WOMEN AND YOUTH LIVING WITH HIV IN KENYA

Irene Ayallo

This chapter argues for a transformative view of salvation. It presents a historical overview of the social exclusion of women and youth living with HIV in Kenya, and then draws on public policy dialogue to suggest that participation by those previously marginalized from policy processes constitutes an important step towards holistic transformation. It presents public policy dialogue as a salvation practice. Discussing a model of public policy dialogue developed in 2012 with six groups of women and youth living with HIV in Kenya, it argues that this process nurtures critical consciousness, validates 'local' knowledge and increases agency (Ayallo 2012).

Public policy dialogue was formed against a historical context where women and youth living with HIV have been marginalized. Particularly, these people have been excluded from decision-making processes which address issues affecting them. Notably, discussions about HIV-AIDS have been limited to elite circles and institutions, government institutions and government-approved gatherings. The model was developed through a process of dialogue, which enabled women and youth living with HIV to examine, understand and analyse their experiences of marginalization in order to transform them. Additionally, this process enabled these people to view their local public spheres as 'legitimate' forums for discussing issues affecting them, because they are the sites where socialization takes place, identities are constructed, deconstructed and reconstructed (Pateman 1970: 31). Therefore, public policy dialogue is presented as a salvific practice because it restores, to women and youth living with HIV in Kenya, the power to name issues affecting them and develop contextual ways for addressing these issues, thus encouraging their emancipation, reflexivity and transformation. Such dialogue not only takes place between these individuals, but also between them and other stakeholders. These include people or groups directly affected by HIV-AIDS or those who might be interested in learning more about HIV-AIDS, such as families, health professionals, religious institutions, NGOs and regulatory bodies like the Kenyan National AIDS Control Council. In this chapter, the role of the Anglican Church of Kenya will be highlighted.

The presentation here begins with a description of the research process within which public policy dialogue was developed. This is followed by a historical overview of the social exclusion of women and youth living with HIV, and then an explanation of the 'salvific' nature of public policy dialogue.

Developing Public Policy Dialogue

Research Process

This model of participation was developed during a doctoral project completed in 2012. The study investigated the exclusion of women and youth living with HIV in Kenya from HIV-AIDS policymaking processes and how institutions and organizations working with these people could nurture critical consciousness. The doctoral thesis argued that to address issues facing youth and women living with HIV in Kenya, there is a need for a model of participation which enables and empowers such people to view themselves as active participants in their own transformation.

The study conducted six 'dialogic workshops' with a sample of sixty women and youth living with HIV to examine their understanding of and role in decision-making processes concerning HIV-AIDS in Kenya. They preferred to be called Post-Testing (Post-T) groups, which meant that they had accepted their HIV serostatus, and were determined to live positively with the virus. During these workshops, the researcher was positioned as a 'facilitator', and used a range of problem-solving techniques to enable participants to engage in meaningful dialogue (Freire 1970: 57; Kamberelis and Dimitriadis 2005: 890). Notably, rather than asking questions in turn, participants were encouraged to talk to one another, exchange stories and comment on each other's experiences and points of view. The findings showed that these groups valued participation through dialogue. This approach was named 'public policy dialogue'. Dialogue is a social action and process which provides a framework that advocates the hearing of many voices and experiences before decisions are made, particularly the perspectives of those directly affected by these decisions.

Public policy dialogue is simply *public dialogue about public policy issues*. It is a social action because of its emphasis on people taking action, directing their own behaviour and giving meaning to their situations. Women and youth in my doctoral study described the process of public policy dialogue as 'sitting down together' and 'coming together to talk about issues affecting them'. As such, public policy dialogue creates opportunities for these people to have real conversations about the problems they face and how best to address them.

Why Women and Youth Living HIV Require a Salvation Practice

AIDS-related deaths in Kenya have fallen by almost one-third since 2007. Statistics released by the National AIDS Control Council in 2012 estimated the national HIV prevalence to be 5.6 per cent among Kenyans aged fifteen to sixty-four years, which was significantly lower than the HIV prevalence estimate in 2007, which was reported at 7.2 per cent. The report attributes the trend to a combination of factors. In this chapter, I attribute the decline to the change in Kenya's HIV-AIDS policy environment. Although still lacking, major changes have taken place since 1980. The need for greater public involvement was felt soon after the government of Kenya declared HIV-AIDS as a national disaster in 1999. In 2000 the government put in place a comprehensive multi-sectoral strategy to guide the various stakeholders in their participation in their campaign against HIV-AIDS.

The struggle to include non-government institutions and non-health officials in HIV-AIDS debates in Kenya began in about 1985. At this time, although HIV was spreading rapidly, the issues related to the disease were only thought to concern health and government officials and institutions. Ordinary people's participation, particularly the opinions and interests of people living with HIV, was conspicuously missing. In 1994, the government began to see AIDS as a development issue, which meant that it did not only concern health professionals. As a result, it included AIDS in its 1994 National Development Program for the first time. This was a significant move because it was the beginning of the realization that HIV-AIDS arises from social, economic, cultural, religious and biological conditions. For instance, women were at a higher risk than men of being infected by HIV because of their anatomy. The Development Plan also recognized the burden society placed on women in providing and caring for AIDS patients (Stillwaggon 2006).

This awareness stirred calls for greater public participation in HIV and AIDS debates and dialogues. The campaign was spearheaded by a consortium of NGOs who solicited views of local constituents through a series of policy workshops documented by Bill Rau (1994, 1996). Some of the views from these workshops were recorded in the first comprehensive Kenya HIV-AIDS policy which was made public in 1996 and initiated in 1997. This document was the first to suggest the establishment of the multi-sectoral HIV-AIDS approach National AIDS Control Council – commonly known as NACC. The advocacy by NGOs also led to the administration of the first AIDS Policy Environment Score (APES) in 1998. Since then, the number of NGOs in Kenya working to reduce the prevalence of HIV has been astounding. They exist at all levels of society, are more likely to report community-level interventions, and are most likely to direct their attention to the general public as well as to the chosen target group. These NGOs have provided forums where people living with HIV can discuss issues affecting them. However, as Benotsch et al. (2004) observe, the forums created by NGOs are endangered by the fact that most NGOs face severe operational issues, including limited infrastructure (Kobia 2003: 144) and government opposition (Orvis 2003: 249).

HIV and AIDS remain a real threat to the very existence of the Kenyan nation. Many people have died and many are living with the virus. It has been observed that the suffering is particularly considerable among poor and marginalized groups such as women, youth and people with disabilities (Gill 2010; Fox et al. 2004; Datta and Njuguna 2009; Wambuii 2006), whose views, opinions, interests and needs are often ignored in processes addressing HIV-AIDS in the country.

Traditionally, these individuals and groups have been socially excluded. Because of their marginalization, they have limited access to resources, vital information and knowledge, and processes of decision-making. The exclusion of women and youth living with HIV is reflected in lower incomes, poor job opportunities, lower education attainment rates, poorer health and under-representation in political and policymaking processes. This disparity is comprehensively documented in other literature (Datta and Njuguna 2009; Adar and Munyae 2001; Kirui 2009; Mwaura 2008).

The need for a salvation practice among women and youth living with HIV in Kenya is also real at other levels. First, their lives and bodies are constantly subjected to beliefs that render them 'less valuable' and inferior to those considered to be the embodiment of 'normality'. Particularly, the majority of people still associate the HIV-AIDS epidemic with immorality, curse, punishment and sin (Frederiks 2008: 4–22). This view contributes to stigma and discrimination, in the process intensifying marginal experiences through social isolation, rejection, fear and powerlessness. For instance, while describing her experience, a participant in one of the workshops conducted during my research stated:

> People assume that because you are HIV positive you will die tomorrow … and that you are sick because you have sinned, you have been sleeping around with many men, and you are a person without morals … so you are a waste of space and resources and should just be left to die. Our families are rejected and abused too because of our condition (Workshop 1).

A second burden borne by this demographic relates to their gender and age. The patriarchal nature of Kenyan society is well documented. Notably, women's participation in all spheres is hindered by the unequal position of women in society. This disparity is reinforced by ideologies of male superiority and the normative relegation of issues directly affecting women to the 'private' spheres (Njoroge 2006; Ayallo 2004). According to the Kenya Central Bureau of Statistics (2009), women account for slightly more than half of the total population and comprise a large voting population in Kenya, but are under-represented in strategic decision-making processes and in the civil service. Glaring gender gaps exist in access to and control of resources and socio-economic opportunities, even after explicit formal processes and structures have been developed (Ayallo 2012).

Similarly, youth form a majority of the total Kenyan population but a majority of them are unemployed (Kenya Central Bureau of Statistics 2009). Burgess (2005), Kirui (2009), Kagwanja (2005a, b) and Abbink (2005) rightly observe that youth in Kenya experience little or no representation in sociopolitical processes and decision-making bodies. Consequently, the majority resort to risky activities such as rebellious movements and to criminal activities, to which they are easily recruited. Youth exclusion continues even with the development of policies and programmes seeking to address their needs. This is because youth input in these processes is often limited, and participation, where it exists, is often confined to an urban elite, thus marginalizing poorer young people and those in rural and remote areas (Janneh 2009: 1–9).

Participants in my research expressed their experiences of the burden of gender and age. One person stated that 'men and older people are heads of everything. A woman or a young person has no place. So to be woman and young is almost like a curse' (Workshop 6). In Workshop 4, participants mentioned that they preferred not to attend public meetings, and when asked why one participant replied, 'What is the point going when because you are a woman and young, nobody will listen to you anyway, and you will just be seated at the back? We would rather stay home.'

The exclusion of women and youth living with HIV in Kenya from public dialogue underlines the urgent need for a salvation practice. Such a practice should nurture 'critical consciousnesses' as a first step towards transforming their livelihood. Anchored in the work of Paulo Freire (1973, 2002, 2005), 'critical consciousness' implies the ability of individuals to perceive the existence of disparities, ask why they exist and acquire skills to enable their transformation.

Public Policy Dialogue as Salvation Practice

Salvation is at the heart of Christian teaching, often perceived in the majority of theological literature as the 'making whole' and maintenance and restoration of authentic life (Davidson and Rae 2010; Sobrino 2008). Salvation, as understood here, has the widest scope, including in it the healing of individuals and social groups, transformation of institutions and structures and the conservation and protection of the environment. Consequently, salvation will be practised and expressed differently in different places. Public policy dialogue as a salvific practice is first and foremost grounded in justice.

Justice from a sociopolitical perspective is about 'centring the margins', looking for ways that go against the grain of dominant voices to engage individuals and groups who have been previously marginalized. An important part of this process is naming the issues causing the marginalization and finding contextual and accessible ways of addressing them. Public policy dialogue enabled research participants to name causes of their exclusion. These included sociocultural and political factors such as age, gender and lack of formal academic qualifications. For instance, asked to explore some issues hindering their participation, participants in Workshop 3 stated that 'our participation is limited because we are only women and such roles are mostly reserved for men. Women's role is said to belong within the household.' In Workshop 1, participants said that 'we do not have the money or the status ... we are not rich'. While participants in Workshop 1 stated that 'the majority of us have no formal academic qualifications, or we have no university degrees ... and we cannot speak English, the language often used in important decision-making bodies', generally, participants also observed that they did not know or understand the nature and processes of decision-making in the country.

Therefore, the process of salvation takes place in defiance of structures and institutions of oppression and marginalization, and seeks transformation (Erasmus 2005; Steuernagel 2008). In this light, 'salvation' sees the involvement of women and youth in the discussion of issues affecting them as justice building and as a means of cultivating wholeness and authentic lives. Research participants did not only name issues affecting them but also explored ways of addressing these matters. For instance, some participants stated that 'we should be educated on processes of decision-making, their key components and concepts' (Workshop 6), because 'some of us do not participate because we do not know how these processes work' (Workshop 6). These participants further indicated that 'such education will not only help us but also we can teach our children these things … such as their rights, to enable them to control their own destinies' (Workshop 6). One participant stated:

> We really liked this process of dialogue. It has enabled us to see and explore things in a natural and collaborative manner, to express our feelings and share our views. It is a model worth sharing with other stakeholders, so they know we have so much to teach them as well as learn from them.

As an expression of salvation, justice has to be about addressing concrete and substantive issues of injustice, such as those named by women and youth living with HIV in Kenya. This view recognizes that it may not be possible to eliminate all inequalities but to open up discursive terrains to all, particularly to those with the least resources. Justice as centring the margins involves an ongoing transformation of structures and behaviours by ensuring people from across different strata of society participate in the making of decisions which affect them. It is not about shifting the power centres, but making sure that many centres (represented by the social cleavages in society) are recognized, including those with little resources such as women and youth living with HIV.

Justice from a theological perspective is best captured in the notion, 'option for the margins', which I developed from Latin American liberation theology's concept of 'preferential option for the poor' (Boff 1992; Petrella 2004; West 2009; Gutierrez 1999). This perspective of justice privileges the epistemological view and experiences of individuals and groups traditionally marginalized. From a theological and hermeneutical point of view, it does not mean that God loves people at the margins more than the 'dominant'. Instead, it means solidarity with and the accompaniment of people at the margins. Marshall (2001: 93–4) argued for options for people at the margins on the basis of scripture, stating that the struggle for justice must be biased in favour of certain parties because some groups more frequently experience injustice more than others, and because the experiences of people at the margins violates God's intention for creation. Since understanding this transformative (or salvific) nature of God's justice is crucial for my argument, I quote Marshall at length:

> God's justice is as (is) a redemptive power that breaks into situations of oppression or need in order to put right what is wrong and restore relationships to their proper condition. Paul speaks of ... the death and resurrection of Christ as a comprehensive work of justice-making that liberates oppressed humanity from the power of sin and death and from the guilt of actual transgression, and brings peace with God and reconciliation between former enemies. Jesus speaks of the in-breaking of divine justice as the coming of God's kingdom, which starts to put right what is wrong on earth, establishes a relationship of new intimacy between God and humanity, and calls into being a new community to live a transformed way of life in the midst of the old order. (Marshall 2001: 93–4)

In my view, the starting point for 'putting right what is wrong' is enabling people who have been wronged to name the sources of injustices and critically discuss ways of engaging with these. Public policy dialogue, beginning at the local spheres, creates such opportunities. For instance, in Workshop 3, a participant observed:

> The feeling of being part of making decisions concerning our livelihood is empowering. At the moment, we cannot help but feel dependent when all decisions are made for us. The dependent feeling is what results from the culture of hand-outs ... being part of the decision-making processes through public dialogue helps us deal with the rampant dependency syndrome and powerlessness. Surely we do not want to be fed. Most of us are well capable of providing for ourselves. All we need is access to proper information and tools. Give us the skills ... 'miwa tol' (give us the fishing net – not the fish). (Workshop 3)

Dialogue was thus transformative because sharing experiences and reasons encouraged women and youth living with HIV to a new understanding of issues affecting them and how these could be addressed within and outside their local spheres. Moreover, as participants in Workshop 3 observed, it is freeing for people at the margins to get a chance to share their interests, perspectives and social locations.

Opting for the margins is not to 'romanticize and essentialize' people at the margins. As an alternative, I believe people at the margins have privileged knowledge of their circumstances. Their experiences of marginalization become their strengths and assets. Dialogue among women and youth living with HIV therefore begins from this 'position of experience', and not from a 'position of privilege'. People at the margins know how they have coped with marginalization, thus they are better placed to know what is appropriate, what works and what does not work. Therefore, it is important to have a process for hearing their voices and opinions and for creating avenues to encourage them to influence policymaking.

As a salvation practice, public policy dialogue as an 'option for the margins' signals the possibility of a different world. This is a world where people at the margins are enabled to take control over their lives and change their livelihoods, which begins with the ability to critically engage with the roots of their marginalization. Parallel to Castillo's (2004: 35) argument, if we are convinced that a 'different world' is possible and really want this 'different world' to become a reality, our first and most indispensable action has to be to regain a utopian consciousness. We need this because utopia represents on the one hand a critique of what exists, the different forms of injustices facing people at the margins, and on the other a proposal for what should exist.

> If we neither criticize the world we have nor make proposals for the world that should exist – that is, if our lives and plans are not guided by 'utopian reason' and its corresponding state of mind and way of thinking and of feeling – it will become clear that we are happy as we are, that we are satisfied with the present 'order' … and then logically people satisfied with what they have cannot … produce any sort of change. (Castillo 2004: 35)

Therefore, the utopian reasoning which is enabled through the process of public policy dialogue is linked to hope which stems from salvation. A society without a form of utopia in the face of marginalization and exclusion is a society without hope. And this makes it a society in which the privileged focus their aspirations upon holding on to what they have, while the great majority, those excluded and marginalized, cannot get beyond the desperate desire for survival. Thus, a perspective of utopianism provides alternate visions of society, humanity, institutional structures and orders of knowing which are brought into play.

The commitment to a better world will involve a series of steps. The first of these will include a careful analysis of the situation of the group in question to name the basic sources of injustice. It will also create the need for careful planning, together with those affected, and taking concrete actions at every level of society and within all spheres in order to challenge forms of injustice. Finally, it triggers a need for concrete practical alternatives to the unjust structures and institutions which are being challenged, and to begin the process of bringing these alternatives into being. Public policy dialogue is a step towards a better world as it is a process which enables women and youth living with HIV in Kenya to begin the 'naming' process.

Public policy dialogue, as a salvific practice, is a process of conscientization whereby women and youth living with HIV gain skills, knowledge and capabilities to define their needs and assess ways of addressing them. The opposite of empowerment is dependency and powerlessness. Public policy dialogue is educative. It constitutes an informal school of citizenship which recognizes that learning takes place in spheres outside formal education systems (Schugurensky 2004: 607). The educative process consists of sharing experiences, asking questions; for those involved in the workshops, it involved clarifying their own thoughts, broadening their outlook and making connections between personal issues and public policies. In the end, public policy dialogue processes give access to new and refined information tantamount to salvation as renewal and 'making whole'.

At the end of each workshop, participants were encouraged to draft short- and long-term plans of action. Short-term plans included how they would continue with the dialogue after the research period; and long-term plans included ways of networking with other stakeholders to share issues discussed in their local spheres, and how they would make sure that their discussions influenced actual policies.

As part of the short-term goals, women and youth living with HIV discussed ways in which their discussions at the local level will be shared with other stakeholders. A common statement from all workshops was that 'once we have understood what is going on, how things work, in our own ways, then we will seek to network with other stakeholders'. Participants across workshops mentioned a number of stakeholders, including health officials, church leaders (including the Anglican Church of Kenya), opinion leaders, politicians, NGOs and community and faith-based organizations.

As Putnam (1995: 61) observes, the more groups, organizations, institutions and communities connect with each other, the more they build their capacities and become better placed to influence actual policies because of their collective power. Because of my role as a leader and priest in the Anglican Church of Kenya (ACK), I (together with the participants) explored ACK's contribution to the process of public policy dialogue.

The Anglican church is advantageously located in Kenya. Structurally, it is present at all levels of society and so in touch with Kenyans from different strata of society. It is also ethnically diverse. It therefore reflects the nature of Kenyan society (Sabar 1997, 2002). As one participant noted, 'The Anglican Church as an institution is widely spread ... both in rural and urban areas. ... It reaches people of all kinds, the educated, uneducated, rich and poor ... and therefore is in a position to mobilise us ... in small and big gatherings ... to tell our stories' (Workshop 3). Moreover, the Anglican church has in the past provided social welfare services such as education and health facilities to complement those offered by the state. Participants generally observed that this long history of service gives the ACK credibility in advocating for the welfare of youth and women living with HIV. One participant stated that 'the Anglican Church has played a big role in society ... providing education services ... ministered health facilities such as dispensaries ... and therefore have reserved seats in several major decision-making bodies at all levels of society' (Workshop 1). Parallel to these responses, I see two tasks for the ACK.

First, women and youth living with HIV lack skills of influence, particularly those that would enable them to dialogue with groups and organizations at higher levels of society. One way of developing these skills is organizing people into communities. Their voices are more likely to be heard and their demands met when in organized communities. The Anglican church must discover the public spheres where socialization takes place, where identities are constructed, are deconstructed and are reconstructed. It is in a position to encourage the formation of local fora (such as women's groups and youth groups) and encourage people at the margins to participate at these local public spheres. The Anglican church must help to validate these fora by working with the government and related decision-making bodies.

Second, informed people are better equipped to take advantage of opportunities, access services, exercise their rights, negotiate effectively and hold 'traditional' stakeholders accountable. Without information that is relevant, timely and presented in forms that can be understood, it is impossible for marginalized people such as Post-T groups to take effective action. Information dissemination does not stop with the written word, but also includes localized forms such as group discussions, poetry storytelling and debates. All these provide an enabling environment for the emergence of informed citizen action. Because of its position of power, the ACK is able to access and disseminate information.

In summary, public policy dialogue as a salvific practice creates opportunities for women and youth living with HIV to share their views, interests and opinions which is an important step towards nurturing critical consciousness. Critical skills enable these people to change their situation, and knowing that they hold knowledge that is not readily accessible to 'expert' policymakers positions women and youth living with HIV as agents in their own transformation (Sakamoto and Pitner 2005: 442).

Chapter 4

Dieting for Salvation: Becoming God by Weighing Less?

Hannah Bacon

The quasi-religious and salvific nature of weight loss dieting has long since captured the attention of feminist scholars. In the late 1980s, Roberta Seid argued that cultural obsessions with weight, diets and fitness have taken on the form of traditional religion, supplying a wellness ethic which promises salvation through 'a now-invisible aesthetic and moral structure'; one that assumes weight loss and exercise to be 'healthy' and capable of making women happier, more beautiful and more virtuous (1989: 10). The wellness ethic, she suggests, not only promises psychological, physical and emotional transformation, but the birth of a more successful, happier self who has the ability to overcome professional and personal problems. Others have similarly argued that the thinness epidemic, with its emphasis on goodness, purity and beauty, fills the gap left by traditional religion (e.g. Wolf 1991; Lelwica 1999, 2009, 2010). Wolf sees 'the beauty myth' as 'the gospel of a new religion' (1991: 86) and suggests that the comparison between religion and an 'obsession' with weight loss dieting is no mere metaphor. 'The rituals of the beauty backlash do not simply echo traditional religions and cults but *functionally supplant them*,' she argues. 'They are literally reconstituting out of old faiths a new one, *literally* drawing on traditional techniques of mystifications and thought control, to alter women's minds as sweepingly as any past evangelical wave' (1991: 88). The 'Rites of Beauty', she holds, have taken the place of traditional religion, policing women's appetites and desires even more successfully.

My concern in this chapter is not to debate the extent to which weight loss dieting takes the place of traditional religion, but to show that secular forms of weight loss dieting continue various theological discourses about salvation, exposing theological systems as integral to the patriarchal hegemony that produces the thin ideal. Feminist reflections rightly discern a malign and insidious agenda at work in the fight against fat as marketers and health professionals promote weight loss as life-saving and self-making. Rooted in fat phobic attitudes, capitalist economics and the hetero-patriarchal urge to control and contain female bodies, such an insistence that fat must be re-formed and ameliorated is suspect.

However, the historical legacy of suspicion towards the body, time and material existence forwarded in classical theology also lurks behind contemporary cultural assumptions about weight.[1]

Drawing on the experiences of dieting women inside one UK secular commercial weight loss group, this chapter argues that ancient theological understandings of salvation as a quest for perfection and hope for a future in which the body is reconditioned resurface in this secular context as women seek a similar future where their bodies do not take up so much space. Rendered theologically, salvation, I argue, emerges as a spurious form of *theosis* as women's efforts to remove their weight and freeze their bodies in time forge their bodies in the image of the phallic God. Attending mainly to the difficulties with such salvation narratives, the chapter ends by suggesting that a theological rooting of hope within the crucible of history has the potential to invest women's present bodies with soteriological value.

Listening to Women's Stories

In 2009 I spent fifteen months inside a popular UK commercial weight loss organization. This organization has 10,000 groups nationwide and 3,500 trained consultants. I joined the group as a researcher and as a dieter, committed to losing weight and conducting ethnographic research. Like other feminist women researching fat, I was aware of the 'fraught standpoint' I embodied (Heyes 2006: 127), caught between my feminist convictions and a personal desire to lose weight (cf. Bordo 1993; Longhurst 2012; Stinson 2001; Heyes 2006). Convinced that I could not deny my own wishes for weight loss or my entanglement within the very systems and processes I wanted to explore and question (cf. Throsby and Gimlin 2010: 106–7), I included myself in the research as a participant.

During my time inside the group, I chatted informally with members and conducted thirteen semi-structured interviews with volunteers; twelve women and one man. Most defined themselves as 'Christian', although none raised faith or religion as a motivation for weight loss. Meetings took place in the hall of a local evangelical Anglican church, ironically suggestive of the theological meanings this organization resurrects, and lasted for ninety minutes. Members varied in age but the group comprised of mostly women with only two male members, neither of whom came regularly. While it is possible that other men joined but chose not to attend (cf. Bell and McNaughton 2007), the products and services of this organization were clearly marketed at women.[2] Weekly attendance averaged at around fifteen to twenty members and the majority of the group were middle class, reflecting the affluent social location of the meeting and members' ability to afford the weekly fee of £4.95. Hevala was the only non-white, non-British woman in the group. She moved from Kurdistan to the UK when she was three years old.

The consultant, Louise, appeared to be in her mid to late thirties and was involved with most aspects of the meetings, receiving members' weekly subscriptions, weighing members and speaking to new recruits about the weight loss plan. She always led the formal meeting which would routinely begin with her welcoming new members and presenting awards to those who had reached significant 'targets'. She would invite each individual to give an account of their weight gain, weight loss or weight maintenance that week, and would often intersperse such profiling with a game or talk. The meeting would always end with a raffle and with Louise commissioning the group to 'go forth and shrink!'

Salvation Through Weight Loss

Members do not use the language of 'salvation' to speak about weight loss. They do, however, associate weight loss with the creation of a new, transformed self; with happiness, self-fulfilment and positive self-change. In one meeting, Jane was presented with the 'Woman of the Year' award in recognition of her weight loss achievements. She had lost over five stone and told the group that weight loss had changed her life. When she was 'large' and carrying her 'horrible weight' she was unhappy, forced to shop for clothes in special shops because of her size. Now she could shop anywhere; now she actually enjoyed shopping. Invited by Louise to show the group the skirt she used to wear when she was larger, Jane stepped inside the garment, stretching out the elastic waistband as if to emphasize the smallness of her re-formed body. She told us that she used to fill the skirt and was overjoyed with her thinner self.

Jane's 'witness' to the life-changing nature of weight loss is not unlike other stories of conversion within this group or detailed in other ethnographic studies (e.g. Stinson 2001). Members identify weight loss with increased freedom, choice, youthfulness and with a strong sense of personal achievement and pride. They also commonly associate a thinner self with improved health, appearance and self-confidence. As Granberg (2006) observes in her empirical research, so in this group women are motivated by the expectation of an alternative 'possible self' and by the future benefits they believe this will bring. Sarah wishes to lose weight to be in a 'healthier position'; Joy joins the group 'partly to feel better in clothes'; Lisa purchases a size 12 pair of jeans and tells me 'this is the aim now, to get them on'. For others, the motivation for weight loss is to avoid certain future events or experiences: to avoid feelings of dread when viewing photographs, to mitigate certain 'ailments' that, according to Joy, 'creep in … as you get older'. For some, like Jane and Kerry, who have attained their 'target',[3] the realization of self-change allows them to experience the benefits of weight loss in the present. Jane can now run down the street without being out of breath; Kerry no longer has the 'awful bloated feeling' she used to experience when she was larger. However, members who reach their 'target' often feel anxious about the possibility of regaining weight they have lost. 'I don't want to go back to how I was, to how I looked, to how I felt' says Kerry as a 'target member'.[4]

Within traditional Christianity, notions of ultimate fulfilment, wholeness and well-being are closely aligned with the concept of 'salvation'. The Latin *salus*, from which the English 'salvation' is taken, denotes health, wholeness, welfare, well-being and healing, in keeping with the Greek *sōterion* (salvation) and *sōzō* (to save). To speak about weight loss as 'salvation' thus is to utilize the term as a hermeneutical lens for understanding narratives of self-change which emerge within this group. It is applied here, not as an imposition, but because the organization already displays a close relationship with dominant Christian thought through its adoption of the Christian moral language of sin (spelt Syn by the organization) to speak about food.[5] It is thus my contention that women's alignment of weight loss with improved well-being, fullness and positive self-change to some extent recycles traditional Christian meanings of salvation extending this close alliance and continuing the legacy of Christian thought. Indeed, members' depiction of salvation as now and not yet is continuous with dominant theological tradition which typically depicts ultimate wholeness and fulfilment as past event, present reality and future hope. Believers are already saved by grace from their transgressions, says Paul (Eph. 2.1; 2.8-9; 5), but 'now is the day of salvation' (2 Cor. 6.2), although glory is progressive because believers are being transformed from 'one degree of glory to another' (2 Cor. 3.18).

Despite reflecting these tensions, however, members predominantly conjure salvation as a future event. Joy explains, 'I was 9.12 when I started. I've managed to get eight and a half pounds off, but now I'm back up ... seven altogether I've got off. So ideally I'm still not there personally.' Lucy remarks, 'I don't know what my target is ... cos I'll probably never get there the way I am because I'm putting it on one week and it's off the next.' 'Getting there' is suggestive of a destination ahead of time and yet many acknowledge that they are not 'there' yet. Some women, like Lucy, refuse to set a 'target' for fear that this will simply invite failure. Others muse about reaching their target but admit at the same time that they do not know what their target is. Members thus hold in tension a belief that salvation is coming and an uncertainty about their ability to achieve it. The implication of this is that salvation is always delayed but without deterring members from its pursuit.

Dominant theological tradition has tended to stress a similar preference for the future often instructing that one must discipline the body in the present in anticipation of the 'resurrected' future to come. 'Now while we live in time, we must abstain and fast from all joy in time, for the sake of that eternity in which we wish to live,' advises Augustine (n.d. II.16.25, 29). Expressing a posture of longing for the future, he reflects, 'We haven't yet arrived, but we are already on the way; we aren't yet enjoying things there, but we are already sighing for them here' (1995: 400.2, 473). Aquinas similarly teaches that perfect happiness will only be realized in heaven, 'for then, by a single, uninterrupted and continuous act our minds will be united with God' (2006: Ia2ae.3, 2, 65). Members too mitigate the dissatisfaction and struggle they experience in the present with the belief that there may be something better ahead. Helen tells me that she joined the group to lose weight for her wedding and that there was a 'vague aim' that she could 'lose loads of weight'. She remembers thinking that 'it will be perfect by the time we get there'. 'Getting there', although a 'vague aim', signals for Helen arrival at a place of completion and perfection. This goal, however, becomes increasingly elusive as she continues to pursue weight loss even after reaching her 'target'. Still dissatisfied with her thinner body, she admits that she now looks at her wedding photographs and sees 'rolls of fat' she wishes weren't there. She lowers her target to accommodate further weight loss and admits that she worries there may never be an 'end' to her search for self-improvement: 'It seems to be the smaller I am, the happier I am which is worrying.'

Worrying as Helen's words are, they signal how the future functions to direct members towards the persistent pursuit of weight loss even in the light of unmet expectations. The belief that there is always *more* weight to lose, communicated by Louise's indiscriminate commissioning of the group to 'go forth and shrink', guarantees members will never feel satisfied while always ensuring hope is not entirely lost.

The Body in Exile: Salvation as Escape from Fat[6]

Helen's assumption that *increased* happiness and perfection require a *decreasing* body is, however, reminiscent of ancient theological depictions of the body and the Greek philosophical systems that often informed them. Augustine taught that lightness of body fattened the soul making it more like the resurrected body which would rise 'without blemish, without deformity, without mortality, without being a burden or a *weight*' (1993: 240.3, 66–7; emphasis mine). Not unlike Helen, he considered that controlling one's appetite for food was a way of extending the self towards future perfection. The mind, in 'tending upward', was 'held back by weight' (1995: 400.2, 473) and the body literally dragged down to earth/mortality by its hefty flesh. Basil, in rendering sensory delight as foolishness and pleasure as harmful, considered that 'leanness of body and the pallor produced by the exercise of continency mark the Christian, for he is the true athlete of the commandments of Christ' (1962: Q. 17, 273). John Chrysostom similarly contended that those who became fat through 'luxurious living' were like animals. In being 'lovers of their bodies' they were 'enemies of the Cross' (1889: 13).

Early Christians operating within the world of late antiquity, considered that a lifestyle of detachment from and resistance to the systems of the present material world prefigured the age to come. Ascetic disciplines (like fasting) trained the body in withdrawing its energies from the deadly drag of material existence so that one could focus on eternal life (Ruether 1987: 233). Tertullian thus contended that the resurrected body would be free of the need for nourishment, drinking and eating as well as the necessity for sex since these were burdens of the flesh associated to the toil of labour and reproduction and made necessary only because of death (1963: LXII, 593). Ascetic practices which accustomed the body not to feel a need for sex or food anticipated the resurrection where believers would become like the angels, 'not having to yield to any like necessity of our bodily state' (1963: LXII, 593). The heavenly future would be a future without bodily needs and without the corruption of the senses. No wonder that Christian thinkers then often considered fat representative of the corruptible world they wished to flee and weightlessness as symbolic of a God without need or fault. In his sermon on Easter day in 1626, John Donne recycles the words of the fourth-century theologian, Jerome, advising his congregation that 'the attenuation, the slenderness, the deliverance of the body from the encumbrance of much flesh gives us some conformity to God and His angels'. Enlarging the body caused the immortal soul to become buried by mortal flesh, he claimed, thus one became more like the eternal, heavenly, weightless God by disciplining one's eating and weighing less (Donne 1839: 314).

Of course, women in this group do not envisage a future free from bodily needs but they do envisage a future where the mind governs the unruly desire for sensual pleasure. For many, successful weight loss in the future is all about making the right decision: 'What do I want more? Do I want to lose a pound or have a glass of wine?' asks Suzanne; 'If you want to do it, if you've got enough will to do it, you'll do it,' asserts Jane. However, in a way reminiscent of Jerome, Augustine, Tertullian and others, it is getting rid of the 'weight' perceived as a drag on self-actualization which is deemed essential by the group. For most members, fat is conceived as a 'thing' they carry which must be abandoned. It is morally repulsive and a 'drag' on their self-becoming. Reflecting on her previously larger self, Jane remarks that 'carrying another four stone around' made her feel like she did not want to go out. 'You couldn't pick it up now,' she told me, 'and I was walking round with it'. Louise similarly reassures Hevala in one meeting that the group will help her 'get rid' of any 'excess baggage' when she returns from holiday. In both cases, additional weight – what Kerry defines as 'the horrible weight' that made her feel 'grotesque' – is like repulsive baggage we carry around unnecessarily and must be discarded if members are to feel happy with themselves and confident in public. Excess weight is deemed sufficiently separate from members for them to choose to 'get rid' of 'it'; a process of material detachment and abstractionism which assumes an individual can step outside their body long enough to view and respond to it objectively (Stinson 2001: 208; Bordo 1993: 2–5).

As well as reflecting theological opinions of fat as repulsive and in need of escape, this continues a well-established theological tradition of seeing the body as an impediment from which the soul must be freed. Augustine's vision of the resurrection, although embodied, captures the heavenly city of God as a spiritual city where time and space are distended and humanity become spiritual, even in their flesh. Like other early Christians influenced by Platonic thought, at times he depicts the body as hindrance to the soul.

> The things of sense must be abandoned, and the greatest caution must be used, so long as we carry about this body, lest some adhesive impediment of sense should clog our wings, whose task, when whole and perfect, it is to bear us upward away from these shadows to that higher Light, which it befits not to disclose itself to those shut up in this cave, unless they shall have been such, that, when they escape, their prison either being rent asunder or decayed away, they shall be able to mount up to their native atmosphere. (2011: XIV.24, 41–2)

Although rejecting this metaphor in later work, he presents the body here as a cave and prison from which the soul must take 'flight'. The senses must be abandoned and, in keeping with Louise's advice, the body that is 'carried around' as seemingly separate, left behind to enable self-growth. Just as Suzanne considers her desire for wine as a barrier to forging her better/thinner self, so Augustine contended that food only compounded the soul's captivity, dragging the soul down to earth by a lust for pleasure.

Purging the Body of Time: Salvation as Escape from the Female

Such a theological insistence that God-likeness is next to weightlessness and that the body must be contained for the sake of 'fattening' the soul is, however, thoroughly gendered. Associations emerging in this group between women's bodies and a need to contain excess by employing the mind not only recycle the body/mind dualism and traditional theological complexes of association between fat, immorality and the need for escape, but re-establish an unbreakable bond between women, sin, bodiliness and the need to escape all of these. Indeed, it is escape from the trappings of female embodiment which many women ultimately seek. Lucy told me that her breasts made her look fat and this caused her to 'hate' them. 'It doesn't matter how much weight you lose, you still look bigger because you've got big boobs. ... I could be the lightest or the smallest size clothes but I still look the fattest because I've got massive boobs.' She wondered how much her breasts weighed and resented them for jeopardizing her attempts to form a thinner self. Helen similarly recalled how the size of her breasts informed her decision to join the group:

> That Christmas I saw photos from the last Christmas works do and a night out with the girls and I was just in tears cos I just looked vulgar, it is disgusting. I mean there's one picture and I'm like ... I'm sitting down and my boobs are just like, expanding over the table. There's another picture and my stomach is so large I do look like I'm pregnant. And I was just so shocked by that. It wasn't what I thought I was seeing when I was looking at myself. And I ... so I said to Sarah, you know I'm really unhappy.

Helen's size makes her unhappy because her body expands beyond conventional limits without her permission. It is Helen's breasts which protrude across the table; it is her breasts which are 'disgusting' and 'vulgar'. Helen's stomach is also offensive to her because she looks 'pregnant'. It is the sprawling nature of her *female* body then which is so 'disgusting'; its inability to stay within fixed boundaries. Her breasts are invasive, breaching the border of the table; her stomach in appearing pregnant breaches the border between self and other.

Feminist theologians have argued that the legacy of the dualism between body and mind inherent within Western philosophy and borne out in Christian thought establishes women specifically as symbolic of unmodified indulgence and desire and thus as a place from which the soul must escape. Ruether, for example, suggests that integral to many historic forms of Christian asceticism was a compulsion to escape the corporeal, extricate mind from matter and to symbolize women as the bearers of death from which the male spirit must take flight (1983: 79–80). A similar logic emerges here as women seek to 'restructure' their female bodies by erasing their female sexual characteristics, removing their softness and displacing their fat (Hartley 2001: 61). Such restructuring is premised on the need for women to maintain rigid control over the boundaries of their bodies so as to prevent them from becoming large (Hartley 2001: 63). This serves to symbolically construct femaleness and maternality as an *excess* that breaches the boundaries of decency and as an excess that must be purged. Tracy echoes this when she talks about her desire to 'get rid' of her baby weight:

> I think I was quite um, not heavy with Joseph's baby weight but you do have extra with baby weight and I didn't really do anything after he was born to sort of get rid of that, you know. [You] just get used to wearing the clothes you're wearing don't you and then I started back at work in the September 2008 and ... but then it still took me another year, near enough another year to do something about it from there.

Baby weight here is imaged as an 'extra' that she must do something about.

Women though also consider weight loss to reverse the signs of ageing. Hevala told me that a health check at work showed that her waist measurement and fat percentage were creeping up which made her think that she was getting old. Ruth, a retired teacher, also considered that weight loss could fend off the ageing process. She was experiencing more aches and pains but this, she said, was not an inevitable part of the ageing process, just a consequence of her excess weight and 'bad' foodways. Such an identification of salvation with regained youthfulness, however, is reflective of dominant strands of eschatological thought. Augustine insisted that 'by the passage of time we are taught this very lesson of despising time and seeking eternity' (n.d. II.15.25, 29). In his sermon on Matthew's Gospel, he describes the world as come of age, much like an ageing man who 'grows up' and 'grows old': 'The world is aging, the world is going to pieces, with the labored, wheezy, breathing of old age' (1991: 81.8, 365). Christ comes to renew an ailing world, he says, and his advice is to become 'young in Christ'.

Members similarly see the future as a return to the past and in some ways reflect a protological conjuring of salvation within which controlled eating is the vehicle for a return to paradise lost. In reversing the signs of ageing and seeking a pre-mature, pre-adolescent body (with smaller breasts) and a pre-pregnancy body members associate future perfection with their ability to resist what Raphael defines as their 'unruly naturalness' and 'propensity to change' (1996: 98). The saved and sacred female body is thus a reconditioned body – a body that has purged itself of the excesses and uncontainability of femaleness, maternality and age, and for Jane this means her body becomes utterly unrecognizable. Having lost over five stone, she tells me that a man she used to date failed to recognize her in the supermarket: 'He did not know me, and I'd worked with him for ... four years or more, and gone out with him for a couple of years and he didn't know me.' Her body had become a stranger. Although a source of joy for Jane, her body symbolizes the political and cultural message that women must *lose* (their bodies/weight/space) if they are to *gain* (happiness/selfhood).

Becoming God by Weighing Less

This requirement for women to become other, to resist and undo their femaleness, to 'freeze' their bodies in time (Raphael 1996: 101), when framed theologically, I propose, casts salvation as a spurious form of *theosis* – that is, as a process whereby women *become God* by forging weightless bodies (much like Donne, Jerome and Augustine imply) and by exercising reason, moral will and cultivating transcendence.

According to Orthodox theologies, deification or *theosis* takes place through participation in the divine energies and through union with the divine image (Kärkkäinen 2004: 20, 30). This process is actualized through 'synergy': the 'co-operation of man with God' (Lossky 1976: 196) and thus by effort.[7] According to Lossky, it is only through the intentional transformation of the 'corruptible and depraved nature' (1976: 196) and by willingly cooperating with divine grace that persons become divine. Salvation, however, takes a similar trajectory in this group as women work at transforming their wayward bodies and desires. Beginning in the present and stretching out towards the future (even where the future is framed as a return to the past), women work hard to 'get rid' of their weight and in so doing, reflect the image of a timeless, immutable, bodiless (male) God.

This God, according to James Nelson and Carter Heyward is, however, a projection of patriarchal ideals: for Nelson a projection of the genital sexual values of 'big, hard and up' (1992: 94) which depicts perfection in terms of self-sufficiency and completeness; for Heyward a 'destructive controlling-device, manufactured in the minds of men' to immortalize the values of changeless Truth, deathless Life, pure Spirit and perfect Reason (2010: 7). Both contend that the erotic is lost in this production as divine love is imaged as standing in need of nothing and God, like the human person who becomes like 'him', is disassociated from the physical, tangible, sexual, painful world.

Seen theologically, women become like the hard upright God by erecting harder edges to contain their hardening bodies. The danger, as Lisa Isherwood rightly warns, is that 'once this god is projected into the sky he works his way back to earth and influences what we understand as acceptable humanness' (2007: 21), and the danger specifically in this weight loss group is that women learn and confirm that acceptable humanness means getting rid of all signs of time, fluidity and female physical maturity. Reflective of a theological landscape which confirms women's bodies as symbolic of mutability, temporality, death and need, the compulsion for women to become increasingly weightless and to lose or contain their fuller breasts, rounded hips and soft stomachs communicates a similar distaste for the processes of time and change which the female body has come to symbolize within patriarchal theology. The risk is that the abundant fleshiness of women gets straight jacketed such that it is 'born again' into a tighter space and reconditioned in conformity to patriarchal cultural ideals, such that female bodies become unrecognizable, just like Jane's.

Conclusion: Attending to Time and Earthing Hope in Bodies

I have argued that the discourses of salvation among women in this group continue harmful historical features of Christian thought, in particular the desire to flee the body and all things female in pursuit of a new self untainted by the tribulations and temptations of the flesh. As well as exposing this group's narrative of salvation as an attempt to contain the changing, liminal, abject body of women, this evokes weight loss as a spurious form of *theosis* since, rendered theologically, we might say that women become like the phallic God by leaving their weight behind.

Brock and Parker accuse Western Christianity of making humanity's location in time and space a problem. Western theology, they contend, has removed paradise from today and placed salvation beyond, behind and ahead of us and this has encouraged human persons to feel 'lost' in the here and now and anxious for 'home' (2008: 417). I have argued that similar difficulties emerge in this weight loss group as salvation is deferred to another place in the hope of attaining a perfect body free from the trappings of time, change and female embodiment. The significance of the present is caught up with 'getting there' and this prevents women from living *fully* in their bodies in the here and now. Time also comes to be viewed in linear terms as progress towards a goal, although for many women in this group, this constitutes an indeterminate end. Time is hijacked as the expanding female body is 'conquered' by the force of reason and by the capitalist demand for her pounds of flesh. Yet, if theological renderings of the body, desire and time collude to frame female embodiment as corrupt, dangerous and in need of escape, and if such theological accounts cohere with and support the narrations of salvation within this group, then these aspects of eschatology may themselves be in need of saving.

Liberation theologians often claim that it is the dislocation of the future from the pulse of history which must be challenged. God's promise for salvation unfolds within the crucible of history and in the committed action of the faith community towards the marginalized. It is this rendering of salvation as material and historical – fulfilled ultimately in the saving work of Christ (cf. Gutierrez 1988: 176–7) – which has the capacity to invest women's *present weighty* bodies with theological significance. Considered in light of a feminist analysis of the experiences of women inside this group, an alternative salvation identifies as 'salvific work' the transformation of political, economic and theological systems which conspire to demonize fat and vilify women who refuse to eradicate their perceived excess. Such an alternative, however, also casts salvation as personal conversion; as the difficult erotic daily 'work' of women (and men) as we learn to live fully in our *present* bodies and to encourage fullness in the bodies of others to whom we relate. If such work is salvific, then the *time* for salvation is *now*.

Chapter 5

SPONTANEOUS TRANSCENDENT AND TRANSFORMATIVE EXPERIENCES IN EVERYDAY LIFE

Madeleine Castro

Contemporary or post-Christian spirituality[1] appears at first glance to be a fragmented phenomenon. Characterized as 'New Age' (Sutcliffe and Bowman 2000), it often appears to refer to a rather loose characterization of beliefs, practices, rituals and ideas lacking any real structure or identifiable roots. The New Age arose out of the countercultural revolution of the 1960s, which became increasingly mainstream from the 1980s onwards (van Otterloo 1999). However, this fragmentation has been articulately challenged by some who argue that there *is* an identifiable and coherent cultural, historical and ideological trajectory to these ideas (e.g. Campbell 2007; Lynch 2007). Furthermore, others suggest at the very least that the extent of fragmentation is exaggerated (Houtman and Aupers 2007). Nonetheless, contemporary spirituality is persistently characterized in a derisory form as an inchoate, 'pick-and-mix religion' (Hamilton 2000), defined by consumer choice (Carrette and King 2005), selected from a wide array of choices likened to a 'spiritual supermarket' (Lyon 2000). From this perspective contemporary spirituality is quite easily characterized as 'alternative'[2] in a lesser sense to more traditional forms of religion. However, in Britain, traditional formal religion (viz. Christianity[3]) is in decline, at least as far as church attendance (Brierley 2006, 2008) and self-identification as 'Christian' is concerned, illustrated by the 2011 census (Voas 2012). While there is no consensus on the extent to which contemporary spiritual developments are definitive evidence of an ongoing or 'new' relationship with some form of the sacred (see, for example, Heelas 2007; Voas and Bruce 2007), there is increasing acknowledgement that there is something 'out there' to be investigated (e.g. Heelas and Woodhead 2005).

One such phenomenon that is little understood and little investigated outside of traditional religious contexts are mystical or religious experiences. Historically the preserve of holy or mystical individuals, they are also reported by ordinary people outside of a religious context with no formal framework to understand them. Many people report dramatic life transformations and notably profound after-effects as a result of these experiences, (sometimes called

Transcendent Experiences, TEs) which intimate a connection with something spiritual (Castro 2009).

Drawing on both existing literature on the subject and the data from Castro (2009), TEs and the concept of personal transformation are reviewed to consider how they can inform a discussion regarding contemporary spirituality and salvation. This chapter will include an exploration of the concept of 'transcendence', an acknowledgement of its trajectory within traditional religious texts, and a clarification of its use here. Thus I seek to

- consider how reported 'life transformations' outside of religious contexts might be considered spiritual
- explore how these transformations might contribute to a form of 'alternative spiritual salvation' and
- consider how they shape people's contemporary lives.

Defining and Discussing Transcendence

TEs can be defined as experiences which go beyond our everyday habitual experience. The term transcendent has been deployed by Charles Tart (1999) as '1a: exceeding usual limits: SURPASSING b: extending or lying beyond the limits of ordinary experience. ... 3: transcending the universe of material existence' (*Webster's New Collegiate Dictionary*, 1980: 1230). TEs are informed by experiences traditionally referred to as mystical, spiritual or religious (James [1901–2] 1982), but have also been labelled as an 'oceanic feeling' (Freud 1962), cosmic consciousness (Bucke 1905) and peak (Maslow [1964]1976), transpersonal (Grof 1972) or ecstatic experiences (Laski 1961). Others have also used the label TEs (e.g. Williams and Harvey 2001; Levin and Steele 2005; Tart 1999) or Exceptional Human Experiences (White 1990). While it is important to recognize that these experiences are sometimes identified as discreet, or distinguished between as different in the literature, there is often some overlap in the accounts that are reported and experients themselves are not necessarily as quick to make such radical distinctions (Castro 2009). These experiences are often viewed as elusive and transient, which are reputedly ineffable or difficult to describe (James [1901–2] 1982). This presents a potential challenge for scholarly definition and categorization. Indeed, Greeley (1975) points out the absurdity of attempting to neatly categorize experiences so reputedly profound. Nonetheless, it is possible to identify some core characteristics that are shared by these experiences. They include a strong positive emotional affect; dramatic alterations in perceptions of space, time and self; and a sense of connection, unity or oneness with something higher or greater (for instance spirit, nature, the universe or the divine).

It is illustrative to consider an example here. There are many varied examples from mystics' accounts that could have been selected but it is instructive to see a more informal and contemporary account from an 'ordinary' individual, submitted to Tart's (1999) online archive of Scientist's Transcendent Experiences (TASTE).

> I was listening to the music and looking through the open window at a tree in the garden, when something strange happened. I felt that I had left my body and had become one with the tree in the garden, with the pebbles on the garden paths and with everything else in the universe. I felt some mild amusement seeing my body sitting there in the living room. I had a feeling of indescribable bliss, a feeling that everything was, is, and forever will be as it should be, and could not be any other way, and that time did not pass, that the future was contained in the past and the past contained in the future, and there was only one time, time present.
>
> (Determinist 2000)

Determinist (a self-selected pseudonym) mentions a union with nature, positive affect and a sense of timelessness, showing the core elements of TEs.

When discussing and defining transcendence, it is important to acknowledge and discuss the historic use of the term transcendent within a religious scholarly context, not least because the definition I employ is a departure from this. 'Transcendent' has been used within traditional religious texts to describe something *beyond* the self and therefore, by definition, something explicitly *external*. For example, Heelas and Woodhead (2005) argue that because of this historic understanding, the concept of transcendence ought to remain within the bounds of an externally focused religion. However, we might want to question this; primarily because there are different conceptualizations of transcendence.

> For the religious, this [transcendence] may be conceived of as union with God or the Divine. Western religious tradition, decidedly monotheistic, usually conceives of a divine power or creator that is at least partly separate from its created beings and has dominion over them. Eastern religious traditions, by contrast, more typically identify divinity as an aspect of all living things, which are instilled with properties of vitality and meaning. For individuals who are not formally religious, sacred union may manifest as being one with the universe or all life or with the experience of beauty, love, or nature.
>
> (Levin and Steele 2005: 90)

Because transcendence is perceived as signifying something 'higher' than the self in the core Abrahamic traditions, this is understood as outside of, and to a degree distinct from, the self. However, transcendence in Buddhism, by contrast, concerns breaking down the illusion of dualities or dichotomies (e.g. between body and mind, or between the individual and the world). Such a conception is echoed in the mystical traditions associated with Christianity, Judaism and Islam, where the divine can be accessed through the body and is not considered wholly distinct from the self. Sometimes termed non-dual awareness or pure consciousness, this describes a state where this illusion can be directly experienced (as opposed to merely 'known') (Wilber 1999). This is a contradictory state where someone experiences being both an individual and simultaneously being indivisible from the world around them. Additionally, as Levin and Steele (2005) – and others – have identified, the transcendent is increasingly reported in relation to aspects not necessarily considered religious (see, for example, Tart (1999) for an expansive definition of transcendent). In order to understand how these experiences and any related transformative aspects are potentially spiritual, social and/or concern salvation, it is important to review the concept of transformation in the literature and review the data.

Transformation

One of the most commonly reported effects of TEs is transformation. This covers changes in people's beliefs, attitudes and their outlook on life and includes aspects such as a decreased fear of death, increased well-being, ability to better cope with hardship, heightened spirituality, improved relationships, feeling more compassionate or empathetic, role or career change and changed perspective or priorities (Bucke 1905; James [1901–2] 1982; Palmer and Braud 2002; Smith 2006; Wulff 2000). As Wulff (2000: 403) suggests, 'Some experients report feeling an intensified love and compassion for others, and many say that life as a whole has taken on new meaning.' These changes are sometimes suggestive of dramatic alterations to identity, personality or psychology. They are not perceived as transient by those that report them, but instead as long-term transformations. The way in which they are reported differs, as does the idiosyncratic detail. Nonetheless, as we will see, they are united by various concepts[4] which link to broader social concerns.

The Data[5]

John's experiences started when he was recovering from a heart transplant in hospital. Still seriously ill, he experienced a comforting vision (centred on a female face and voice), which reassured him. He subsequently experienced this face and/ or voice at times of difficulty in life. This extract picks up as John talks about how he understands his experiences. He talks here[6] about what has changed for him here regarding his beliefs/spirituality.

> And erm that's it basically so what it what a – I think what I think is really nice about the whole thing is it it proved to me that erm we do people often talk about spirit guides and guardian angels but I just feel now that err I've had the kind of proof that you need to kind of believe in it and er when it's a personal experience erm erm it's really con – it's really quite convincing and so I feel as if

I know now that there is a a guardian angel and I don't know to what extent they can intervene in your life to prevent you following certain course of action or to guide you in a particular way but what I do know is that they can reassure at different times when they feel you need to be reassured so it's a kind of a passive presence rather than er like a proactive kind of a presence you know but it is there when you need it.

John discusses how his personal experience can be interpreted as 'proof'. He alludes to his personal experience affirming some pre-existing spiritual ideas ('spirit guides' and 'guardian angels') and that he trusts this as a valid source of knowledge and authority. The highly valued nature of both personal experience and experiential knowledge reflects two things:

1. a commonly held, commonsensical belief about how some things must be experienced first-hand to be truly understood
2. a contemporary predilection for personal experience to be treated as a trusted route to valid knowledge.

His trust in the authority and authenticity of his own experience foregrounds the dramatic changes that his life and outlook have undergone. John's 'guardian angel' is a resource for reassurance and reputedly boosts John's coping ability. His transformation is repeatedly grounded in the detail of his material existence while simultaneously referencing metaphysical preoccupations. He presents a reasonable admission of the limitations of his metaphysical knowledge (e.g. the extent to which guardian angels can intervene in life), in order to strike a chord of credibility.

Other accounts equally demonstrate these aspects: trusting one's own experience; grounding the profound in the everyday and displaying a concern with credibility. For instance, Alice reports an experience in Africa where she has a sudden and spontaneous sense of interconnectedness with the natural world. She reports a vivid stillness, extremely positive feelings and a distortion of ordinary space and time. Following on from this experience, she reports these changes.

And ever since then I I dunno I've been able I've found that I'm a different person I found that I've always been had problems coping with situations and I've always had a lot of emotional issues but ever since that's happened to me I've found that I can cope with pretty much anythink that life throws at me I'm a much calmer much more organized person and I've found that things that I never thought I could achieve I'm I've actually been able to achieve. … I suppose it is quite a spiritual experience. … And I don't know it's changed the way I think about my subject as well being a scientist and there was a time when everything was evolution nothing really had a point except to pass on its its genetic genetic programming and material but now that I've realized that you know the more I think about it the more I realize that obviously evolution it couldn't just be some grand accident but it is part of something and I don't know what that is but it's just wonderful.

Her account equally suggests that she trusts her experience and values the changes it has brought. Her inner experience appears to take precedence over her intellectual life and identity (though she does not abandon her former scientific self, but instead works to integrate her experience into her pre-existing identity orienting to the presentation of a credible self). However, she does not, for instance, question the nature of the experience or dismiss it as irrational or 'delusional'. She sees it as the trigger for a better version of herself (someone better able to handle life). There is a sense in which these changes are based on what is conveyed as a profound experience. Yet simultaneously, many of these changes are rooted in an everyday existence (the idea of being more organized, with improved coping abilities).

This trust seemingly arises in different ways; illustrated by Lyn's account. Lyn's experiences all happen in the context of the death of her close friend Alex. She reports experiences that suggest the interaction or intervention of 'spirit' with physical reality. For example, Alex's favourite song playing repeatedly on two different CD players; a deleted answerphone recording of Alex's voice reappearing during Alex's wake (and only while Alex's body was in the house); a completely unexpected torrential downpour which appears to focus solely around the grave during burial; and a profound experience with a spirit medium. Lyn interprets these experiences as after death communication from Alex.

So to me it's been to me it it's erm it's like I've been told it's not a question of belief it's a question of knowing that there is life after death and I mean that might sound really sort of arrogant but I just feel because of the way it's come from I mean it came from Alex that it's real and it's sent me off on this sort of spiritual quest for the last five years you know erm sort of exploring different religions and erm trying to find out what it is that that I would feel comfortable with you know and erm I mean at the present time I feel it's Buddhism that I'm comfortable with erm but I do – haven't really sort of signed up to anything I'm still sort of you know finding my way through but that's the big impact that it's had on my life and it's made me see everything differently and erm it makes me see life differently and I mean I'm not saying that this is a hundred percent of the time (she laughs) you know I'm afraid it's er it's not that effective.

Lyn talks about her definitive personal knowledge of 'life after death' as a direct result of her experiences. Akin to the others, she reports trusting this intuitive sense, reflecting the high value placed on personal experience as a trusted and authoritative route to knowledge. The significance of the experience is conveyed by reference to the transformations and the subsequent search for spirituality and/ or meaning. As such it is therefore clear that the experience is both meaningful and profound, yet she also provides a realistic assessment of the limitations of dramatic transformation (which are tempered by everyday reality). Thus credibility is also clearly important. This also serves to locate the profound change in the sphere of her real, everyday existence.

More explicitly, Sunset directly references the importance of her own experiences when she is talking about the effects of her precognitive dream experience. She has a very intense dream, which she later interprets as a premonition of the outbreak of foot and mouth in cattle in 2001 (National Audit Office 2002). She also reports viewing it as a prompt to act upon her perceived 'abilities' in connecting with and communicating with spirit. This extract picks up when she is talking about having pursued mediumship development as a result.

> But I enjoyed it and it was good to meet other as I say like-minded people some bits of it were too extreme for me some of the old erm photos and things that are held up as evidence in the light [chair squeaks] of more advanced technology I'd be extremely sceptical of but er y – I think you have to trust your own experiences and then after that I came back and joined in a sort of a loose way a local Spiritualist church to continue a mediumship development and I have actually done a very small bit of of work as a medium and I have unpredictable abilities I would say er which is what's one of the things that I find quite frightening about it that I don't have the degree of control I should have although I have to say it's rarely erm disturbing.

Here she talks about trusting one's own experiences with direct reference to being sceptical of phenomena such as 'old photos', by which she is referring to spirit photos.[7] So she positions herself as possessing critical thinking abilities (concerned with credibility) while simultaneously affording precedence to her inner experiences. These experiences are not questioned nor are they subject to the same kind of scepticism applied to the external phenomena. The inner is trusted as a source of knowledge and reliable guidance. Following this she details her transformation, which represents quite a dramatic identity shift – to spirit medium. This is tempered however, by her admission to not being quite up to scratch as yet. She intimates then, that not only is extensive training and practice required in order to hone her 'abilities' but additionally, that this is an incremental transformation rather than an overnight one.

Discussion

The data effectively demonstrates the ways in which these reported experiences transform and shape people's lives. Equally, however, the participants articulate two concepts which resonate with ideas located in the literature on post-Christian spiritualities. These concepts can help us to consider the ways in which these reported life transformations might also be perceived as spiritual. The first idea concerns personal experience as a trusted route to or source of knowledge, which is covered by the concept of *gnosis* (Hanegraaff 1996), and closely related to this idea are notions of *authenticity* and the 'self'. The latter is often placed at the heart of post-Christian spirituality (Houtman and Aupers 2007). The second concerns the idea of the everyday. The literature characterizes post-Christian spirituality as couched within the material and earthly limits of contemporary society. As we saw earlier, this is often characterized in consumer and individualistic terms (e.g. Carrette and King 2005).

Reviewing the concepts of gnosis and authenticity within the data, authenticity is reached via TEs, as a trigger for transformation which is constructed as real and valued. These inner experiences are presented as trusted forms of knowledge and wisdom. The sense in which the experiential is valued prizes personal authority (intuition) over more generally held and accepted Western forms of knowledge (e.g. scientific reason or religious knowledge). This form of knowledge is akin to *gnosis*, which is conceived of as mystical, inner, intuitive and experiential knowledge. Gnosis is reputedly seen as an authoritative route to truth, revelation, insight and 'enlightenment' (e.g. Hanegraaff 1996). From this perspective the self is at the heart of post-Christian spirituality and it is the inner experience or intuitive sense of this true self that is valued and prioritized. Indeed, Houtman and Aupers (2007: 305) suggest that post-Christian spirituality can be 'characterized by a sacralization of the self'. In this sense, the self is perceived as a form of inner spirituality (Heelas 1996); the self is divine. What is evident from such commentary is that the perceived centrality of the self is frowned upon and contemporary spirituality is equated with a sort of worship of the self.

However, my data raises questions regarding the exclusive centrality of the self in contemporary spirituality. Authenticity tends to be an implicit aspect and while the self, and changes to the self, are present in these descriptions, talk regarding the self is not exclusively the focus. Participants talk about transformed identities in relation to other aspects of their lives and these changes are often concerned with life's meaning, coping better, treating others well and even 'serving others' (the healer and the medium). It is certainly plausible that post-Christian spirituality might arise from 'problems of meaning & identity'; whereby in response to modern society's alienating influence, contemporary spirituality prioritizes 'self-discovery' (Houtman and Aupers 2007: 316). Taking this view the spontaneous reported TEs could be treated as a disruptive force regarding the individual's concept of self (and worldview) and their subsequent reflections convey an exploration of life's meaning and personal identity. However, concerns with relationships, considering other people and serving others run counter to the notion that a journey of self-discovery is *the* only purpose of post-Christian spirituality.

The second idea concerns the notion found in some of the post-Christian spirituality literature suggesting that contemporary spirituality is *merely* material and earthbound (e.g. Bruce 2002; Hanegraaff 1996; Heelas 2008). This idea locates the spiritual in a purely secular context and has given rise to a predominantly cynical analysis of all forms of contemporary spirituality as merely about personal choices and self-obsession and reflective of consumerism in a global marketplace (Carrette and King 2005). However, while this may be one aspect of new ageism permeating the cultural mainstream, this neglects the nuances and the social dimension of those who ground dramatic transformation in their ordinary lives. As the data demonstrates, their concern with the everyday is, in the first instance, an immediate interactional concern with credibility in the presentation of self (a very social phenomenon). This reflects tacit awareness of the social context that both constrains and constructs experience. Discussions of transformation hinge upon profound change. However, instantaneous change outside of traditionally religious contexts (e.g. conversions) tends to be viewed suspiciously and thus change is grounded in everyday lives. Furthermore, popular conceptions of the self tend to be fairly fixed at the core (Gergen 1999), so fundamental change is likely to threaten an individual's credibility unless handled carefully. This is managed by recourse to a level of continuity in personal identity (their 'selves') and/or talk of change is tempered by realistic assessments or detailed limitations regarding any changed characteristics. The way in which the participants negotiate these issues regarding dramatic transformation and how this might be received, demonstrates the ways in which the social shapes people's lives regardless of transformation.

Furthermore, as MacKian (2011, 2012) has noted in her work,[8] references to extraordinary or 'otherworldly' phenomena are numerous. How can we understand this in terms of an earthbound and consumer-orientated spirituality? She suggests that these references are instead quite the opposite; indicative of spirit. In my data this includes manifestations of spirit, the presence of angels (though this is also traditionally Christian), apparitions (of unknown persons and deceased relatives), special forms of dreaming (precognitive) and non-religious sacred or divine presences (e.g. the source, the light or energies). There is a need therefore for a way of understanding these elements, which tend to be overlooked by the religious studies literature. In this respect MacKian's (2011, 2012) work is an attempt to shine light on this omission. Her research focuses on contemporary forms of spirituality she calls 'everyday spirituality'.[9] This approach puts the concept of 'spirit' at the heart of spiritual experience and practice. She also takes seriously and treats sensitively the sense of 'otherworldliness' conveyed by many of these spiritualities and experiences, which she suggests are 'characterized by an interest in more esoteric, otherworldly ways of touching the divine, and a desire to establish direct contact with spirit' (MacKian 2011: 62). In this way she begins to articulate one of the aspects that is at times missing from some discussions of post-Christian spirituality; the spiritual.

Salvation, Spirituality and TEs

At the outset, this chapter sought to explore how life transformations outside of religious contexts might be considered spiritual while considering one of the ways in which 'alternative spiritual salvation' shapes people's contemporary lives. This exploration has raised questions and invites some tentative conclusions.

In the accounts of reported transformation, there are aspects of post-Christian *and* everyday spirituality without an explicit subscription to spirituality per se. So, are these TEs and transformative accounts spiritual? As I have suggested elsewhere (Castro 2009), if we accept some of the more recent formulations of the spiritual (as potentially aesthetic, humanist and/or secular (Varga 2007), insofar as reference to traditionally religious aspects are not required), then a broader and more contemporary definition of spirituality can be seen as 'the search for meaning' (Holmes 2007: 27). Indeed, the very transformative nature of these experiences allows us to see how people communicate the spiritual profundity of experiences we might not naturally categorize as spiritual ourselves. However, this is not universally accepted and there are various examples of highly critical voices regarding the diffuse nature of the concept of 'the spiritual'. Interestingly, these perspectives are increasingly discoverable within the cultural mainstream (see, for instance, de Castella 2013, for a recent consideration of this in the British media). Indeed, van Otterloo, Aupers and Houtman (2012) suggest it is the very cultural availability of these ideas, beliefs and practices that affords the opportunities for their use in sense-making, in a way quite distinct from the original New Agers.

> It is, however, quite unlikely that this second generation's turn to New Age spirituality has been driven by anti-institutional rebellion and resistance against 'the system', including the Christian church and rationalized work environments. ... The values of the counter culture, in other words, have increasingly come to permeate the cultural mainstream. (van Otterloo et al. 2012: 253)

The relationship between the spiritual and the religious is evolving and these kinds of experiences are no longer viewed as the sole preserve of highly religious or mystical individuals. Indeed, they are much more widely reported by a variety of people (Back and Bourque 1970; Wulff 2000). Not all contemporary TEs can be seen to have explicitly religious connotations. Furthermore, while many are still perceived as encounters with the sacred, the way that this is understood may have changed.

> It appears that exceptional or transcendent experiences, many of which were once associated with religion, are being experienced by more people in the midst of daily life. This may be not so much because these experiences are becoming secularised, but because the sacred is being found in the midst of daily life.
> (White and Brown 2000: http://www.ehe.org/display/ehe-pageab52.html?ID=72)

So are these experiences forms of contemporary (alternative) salvation? If we accept a contemporary concept of salvation as Hanegraaff (1996) describes it; then yes. 'Personal growth can be understood as *the* shape "religious salvation" takes in the New Age movement' (Hanegraaff 1996: 46; my emphasis). But does this reflect the complete picture? Is it fair to suggest that post-Christian spirituality is *only* about the self? The self is a *part* of it. However, TEs and transformations concern the reality of people's lives, their identities and their psychologies. The experients seek to make sense of their personal experience within the social dimension. It is here that this work begins to sketch a partial picture of the socially constructed post-Christian self. Houtman and Aupers (2007) noted a lack of research concerning this. My research demonstrates how seemingly private, inner experiences and notions of personal meaning and identity are all ideas that are discursively and therefore socially constructed and conveyed in interaction.

Additionally, experients combine this 'ordinary' meaning-making, with a connection to something 'extraordinary' or otherworldly that fosters and facilitates profound transformation. This kind of data affords us an opportunity to ensure that we fairly and fully represent these non-traditional manifestations of spirituality as contemporary alternative sources of salvation. Indeed, there is room for much more soundly and empirically – grounded work on the experiential. McGuire (2008b: 215) suggests that we need 'to give attention – much more carefully researched and analytically precise attention – to the personal beliefs and practices by which individual spiritual lives are shaped and transformed, expressed and experienced, over time'. This chapter makes a small contribution to this.

Chapter 6

TIMOTHY LEARY AND ALTERNATIVE SALVATION

William Stephenson

The Harvard psychologist Timothy Leary first ate hallucinogenic mushrooms in Mexico in 1960, at the age of thirty-nine. He had an extremely powerful religious experience, which he found psychedelic, meaning 'mind-manifesting or mind-revealing' (Osmond 1999: 37). 'It was the classic visionary voyage and I came back a changed man' (Leary 1995: 34). Leary believed he had undergone a form of salvation; the trip 'left me feeling exhilarated, awed, and quite convinced that I had awakened from a long ontological sleep. This sudden flash awakening is called "turning on"' (Leary 1998: 13–14).

After this life-changing event, Leary committed himself to turning others on. During a decade-long career of writing, recordings and public appearances, he advocated drug use for the purpose of self-transformation. This caused huge controversy: 'For some, he was a pop culture and counterculture hero, for others, a drug-soaked Pied Piper leading the youth of America astray' (Seesholtz 2004: 106). From the 1960s onwards, he adapted ancient scriptures using the psychological lexicon of his academic discipline. The result was a series of hybrid, quasi-religious texts designed to promote the new forms of expanded consciousness that he believed were made possible by hallucinogenics such as LSD and psilocybin.

This is not to say that Leary accepted all aspects of religion uncritically. Until his Mexican experience, he had been a secularist: 'For 40 years I had been conditioned to respond negatively to the word "God"' (Leary n.d.: 1). He retained a strong scepticism towards dogma and priestly hierarchy, as opposed to the direct experience of religious ecstasy. Accordingly, when Leary composed his first LSD manual, *The Psychedelic Experience*, published in 1964, he set out to use its sacred source, *The Tibetan Book of the Dead* as a reservoir of tropes, a handy means of communication, rather than a truth in itself: 'I agreed to the religious posture – with conditions. There was to be no kneeling down, no dogmas, no holy men' (4).

Religion, like drugs, was a means rather than an end, a tool to serve Leary's revisions of received constructions of human identity. His project aimed to transform people by freeing them to get in touch with biological and sensory states which were largely unknown to ordinary waking consciousness, but towards which his chosen chemical and scriptural tools could point the way: 'The aim of oriental religion is to *get high*, to have an ecstasy, to tune in, to turn on, to contact incredible diversity, beauty, living, pulsating meaning of the sense organs, and the much more complicated and pleasurable and revelatory message of cellular energy' (Leary 1998: 196; emphasis in original).

The proposition that a transformative religious experience, a form of salvation, may occur through taking drugs was, to say the least, far from universally accepted. President Nixon called Leary 'the most dangerous man in America' (Higgs 2006: 276). Even among the counterculture, not everyone agreed with him. The novelist Ken Kesey and his commune the Merry Pranksters, for instance, took an anarchic approach to hallucinogenics, consuming them without religion, system or guide: 'Here were the seeds of disaster; what if the Leary doctrine that everyone could profit from LSD, provided the trips were rigorously controlled, got confused with the Prankster doctrine that no controls were necessary? What if the whole country began to freak freely?' (Stevens 1993: 324).

Leary was well aware not only that the establishment detested him but also that his doctrine was subject to competition, and that others would take radically different approaches to hallucinogenics; accordingly, he adopted techniques of persuasion borrowed from the capitalist mainstream. He walked an awkward line between prophet and advertising executive. He always had 'the ability to tell his listeners what they want to hear … a trait that has been variously described as brilliant, mesmerizing, psychopathic and manipulative' (Whitmer and VanWyngarden 2007: 15). His self-appointed role as a propagator of psychedelics led him to adopt a specious form of celebrity: 'Anyone who has read Leary knows that dissolution of the ego is a trick not in his repertory. … What acid needed was a model of self-creation, not a hastily constructed Tibetan orthodoxy. It needed an exemplary ego, not a dissolved one. It is both Leary's success and failure that he understood that' (Lenson 1995: 153–4). He positioned himself as the cynosure of the psychedelic lifestyle, tirelessly promoting himself even as he advocated the abandonment of the ego through drugs. As this blatant contradiction suggests, he may well have deceived even himself: 'The ego is the most potent configurer of imaginal spaces and, if not confronted directly, will turn even the most potent psychedelic experience into a self-serving and deceiving charade' (Boon 2002: 264).

Leary was unquestionably a manipulator and an egotist, and was possibly self-deluded, but his doctrines caught on. There was a moment in the mid-to-late twentieth century when chemically induced religious experience seemed not only possible but highly desirable to him and to thousands of his followers. One of the main reasons for this was that Leary offered a form of salvation or transcendence; he provided a reason to take drugs which rose above mere pleasure, defiance or self-indulgence. At the core of this promise was a fundamental revision of what it meant to be a human being; in effect, Leary offered hallucinogenics up as technologies which could move the user beyond the human condition to a newer, better state.

This chapter will argue for the continuing cultural significance of Leary's chemical evangelism by linking his ideas to the wider phenomenon of posthumanism. Like Leary's writing, posthumanism poses a radical challenge to the Cartesian construction of the autonomous ego. This, in itself, is not new. The received idea of the human subject had already been undermined by Karl Marx, Friedrich Nietzsche and Sigmund Freud, who made consciousness contingent upon social being, history and the unconscious (Marx and Engels 1999; Nietzsche 1994; Freud 2005). This was followed by the poststructuralist turn that situated identity as a function of language (Derrida 1990; Lacan 2001). Posthumanism extends these challenges in order to replace the human subject with another sort of being, usually characterized by a number of technological metaphors, perhaps the most common of which is the cyborg, 'a cybernetic organism, a hybrid of machine and organism, a creature of social reality as well as a creature of fiction' (Haraway 2000: 69). The posthuman subject is partly a machine; it is data, process and/or program rather than immutable essence. The Cartesian ego finds itself decentred: 'The posthuman view considers consciousness ... as an epiphenomenon, as an evolutionary upstart trying to claim that it is the whole show when in actuality it is only a minor sideshow' (Hayles 1999: 2–3).

Leary's use of hallucinogenics had made him experience identity as a flow of information, the ego as a socially conditioned delusion, the body as malleable through technologies including drugs, and the mind as a computer or sentient machine: 'It may offend some religions, but not reason, to conclude that the notion of self we enjoy is nothing more than an epiphenomenon arising as a side effect of the interaction of mental processing subsystems' (Leary and Sirius 1997: 34). Thus Leary's psychedelic salvationism, though very much bound to its countercultural moment, was not an isolated phenomenon but part of a wider posthumanist trend, a tectonic, still ongoing shift in perception involving a radical revision of subjectivity.

The Psychedelic Experience

In linking modifications of brain chemistry to religious experience, Leary was not doing anything very original. Aldous Huxley, a major influence on him, had argued that this had been the goal of medieval ascetics and mystics, who used fasting, self-mortification and meditation to alter their hormonal balance and thus gain access to 'unfamiliar aspects of Mind-at-Large (including psi phenomena, visions, and ... mystical experiences' (Huxley 1959: 120). However, Leary's popularization of this connection was daringly new. From early in his career, he formulated the link between salvation and drugs in terms of a lifestyle choice that could be promoted via the mass media. His infamous slogan, 'Turn on, tune in, drop out' (Leary 1998: 141) evolved out of a discussion with his friend, the media analyst Marshall McLuhan, who had told him he needed a jingle to sell his ideas: 'The key to your work is advertising. You're promoting a product' (cited in Greenfield 2006: 282). Huxley exhorted him only to turn on a small number of influential, gifted figures who could support and protect his project, such as 'artists, intellectuals, business leaders and politicians' (Higgs 2006: 35). Leary had no time for such elitism; he felt that salvation through drugs should be available to anyone, provided the subject was properly prepared.

On the most basic level, this preparation involved the adjustment of two key variables, set and setting: 'Set denotes the preparation of the individual, including his personality structure and his mood at the time. Setting is physical – the weather, the room's atmosphere; social – feelings of persons present towards one another; and cultural – prevailing views as to what is real' (Leary 1998: 11). This is typical of *The Psychedelic Experience* and of Leary's oeuvre, which is an odd combination of metaphysics and pragmatics, combining the florid imagery of mysticism with the plain style of the how-to book: 'LSD subjects do claim to experience revelations into the basic [spiritual] questions and to attribute life change to their visions. … We have been working on this project for the past six years, writing manuals which train subjects to recognize energy processes' (Leary 1998: 53).

When Leary made *The Tibetan Book of the Dead* the template for *The Psychedelic Experience*, he envisaged the Buddhist scripture as an aid to this practical project; a means of making the mystical comprehensible. This conceptualization of his source was, in fact, fundamental to the salvationist project he aimed to undertake. Leary points out that despite appearances *The Tibetan Book of the Dead* was not in fact intended, even by its original authors, to describe the moment of death and the subsequent experience of forty-nine days between reincarnations. This eschatological narrative was merely the exoteric framework for the hidden content that was decipherable only by initiates: 'The esoteric meaning, as it has been interpreted in this manual, is that it is death and rebirth of the ego that is described, not of the body. Lama Govinda indicates this clearly in this introduction when he writes: "It is a book for the living as well as for the dying"' (Leary, Metzner and Alpert 1995: 12).

Thus death in *The Tibetan Book of the Dead*, according to Leary's interpretation, is a metaphor for ego-death, meaning transcendence by the living subject of his/her old, fettered identity. Leary's manual, like its source, is not designed for death rites but is aimed to transform the initiate who is alive in the here and now, by giving him/her the necessary advice on how to use the powerful hallucinogenics that can make such transcendence possible: 'From the theological standpoint, everyone must discover the seven faces of God within his own body. … If you are serious about your religion, if you really wish to commit yourself to the spiritual quest, you must learn how to use psychochemicals. Drugs are the religion of the twenty-first century' (Leary 1998: 44).

Leary's vision is not one of heaven. Instead, he maps out an interior voyage, a revelation of the dizzyingly complex mechanics of the body. *The Psychedelic Experience* proposes a reconstruction of subjectivity based on a new form of consciousness in which the subject understands its own machine-like workings: 'The individual becomes aware that he is part of and surrounded by a charged field of energy, which seems almost electrical. ... The person becomes aware of physiological and biochemical processes; rhythmic pulsing activity within the body. Often this may be sensed as powerful motors or generators continuously throbbing and radiating energy' (Leary et al. 1995: 41). Leary's vocabulary of motors, generators and electricity carries a positive charge of posthumanist enthusiasm. By going deep inside the body to listen to the ancient, automatic, electrical biological activity which predates consciousness, the drug-using subject takes the first steps towards self-transcendence. In effect, one listens to the machinery of one's body in order to cease to become a singular 'one' at all. The monad becomes legion.

Leary believed that this experience was not unique or incommunicable but could be reproduced, interpreted and discussed in texts such as his own. He intended *The Psychedelic Experience* to allow for the 'practical interpretation of use in the psychedelic drug session' (Leary et al. 1995: 13). The final section of Leary's manual includes a number of instructions aimed at the drug user. These are either to be read in advance or read aloud during the session by a guide or, if the user is working solo, from a tape recording. They are subdivided into 'Some Technical Comments About Psychedelic Sessions' and 'Instructions for Use During a Psychedelic Session'. Even these pragmatic sections, though, reveal their roots in religion: 'In planning a session, the first question to be decided is "what is the goal?". Classic Hinduism suggests four possibilities' (Leary et al. 1999: 99). Leary lists these as power, duty, fun and transcendence. He does not give his Hindu source, but his aim is clear. He adds that the manual is aimed at the fourth goal, as it brings with it the three others: 'Illumination requires that the person be able to step out beyond game problems of personality, role, and professional status' (Leary et al. 1995: 99). Salvation, then, necessitates renunciation of the main prop of conventional human identity, the banal script 'of the TV stage set defined by mass-media-social-psychology-adjustment-normality' (Leary 1998: 35).

Jail Notes, The Politics of Ecstasy and *Your Brain is God*

Such a willed loss of selfhood might appear a threatening, nightmare vision; the opposite, in fact, of salvation. However, Leary was rapturously received by a young audience of seekers. It would be a huge understatement to say that his ideas were popular with the emerging constituency of mainly young, curious hippies: 'Psychedelia became effectively a new religious movement seeking to evangelise America... . As is evident in the writings from the period, it was clearly believed that humanity was on the verge of a new age of drug-provoked, Indian-influenced, expanded, mystical consciousness' (Partridge 2003: 107). Not everyone was convinced this expansion was worthwhile:

> What Leary has taught them [young people] is that getting turned on is not a kind of childish mischief; it is the sacred rite of a new age. They know, if only

vaguely, that somewhere behind the forbidden experience lie rich and exotic religious traditions, occult powers, salvation – which, of course, the adult society fails to understand, and indeed fears. (Roszak 1970: 166–7)

Theodore Roszak identified Leary's role in the then contemporary US counterculture as that of a snake-oil salesman for drugs; a charlatan spreading a bogus chemical gospel. To Roszak, Leary promised more than he could possibly deliver. Psychedelic drugs were far from a route to religious experience; they offered at best distracting fun, and at worst hospitalization, long-term mental illness, even death.

Others were as enthusiastic as Roszak was wary. In the same year, 1970, Allen Ginsberg identified Leary as fulfilling a role that was historically unavoidable. Leary was, according to Ginsberg,

faced with the task of a Messiah. Inevitable! Not merely because the whole field of mental psychology as a 'science' had arrived at biochemistry anyway. It was inevitable because the whole professional civilized world, like Dr. Leary, was already faced with the Messianic task of accelerated evolution (i.e., psychosocial Revolution) including an alteration of human consciousness leading to the immediate mutation of social & economic forms. (Ginsberg 1970: 9)

Thus along with the politically explosive, legally complicated and highly problematic programme of the evangelism for drugs that Leary was pursuing, there went another less obvious and not so well articulated mission; that of transcendence of the human subject towards an implied posthumanism. Ginsberg saw Leary as reacting against the technology that was busy 'stereotyping our consciousness & desensitizing our perceptions' (Ginsberg 1970: 9). LSD was a technological, synthetic antidote to this problem, thrown up by technology itself: 'a by-product of the technology that might, as it were by feed-back, correct the berserk machine and liberate the inventor's mind from captivity by hypnotic robots … an invaluable civilized elixir' (Ginsberg 1970: 10). The result would be 'that all humanity is about to be born in an entirely new relationship with the universe' (Buckminster Fuller, cited in Leary 1998: 29).

Leary cites approvingly Colin Wilson's contention that modern humankind was beginning the quest to transcend its condition: 'For the first time in history, men are beginning to feel stifled by their own humanity. Most of the great artists and writers of the nineteenth century are men who feel themselves trapped in their own limitations. … So … what does this indicate? Surely that man is preparing for a new evolutionary leap?' (Wilson, cited in Leary 1970: 28). Wilson was himself influenced by Nietzsche, whose philosophy carried a strong posthumanist charge: '[We are] adventurers and circumnavigators of that inner world which is called "human being" … . Here is a long ladder on whose rungs we ourselves have sat and climbed, and which we ourselves *were* at one time!' (Nietzsche 1994: 10; emphasis in original).

Leary felt impelled to develop Wilson's and Nietzsche's posthumanist projects. He makes detachment from material goods coupled with attachment to the body and the senses a pillar of his programme of human self-transformation: 'The awakening of the senses is the most basic aspect of the psychedelic experience. The open eye, the naked touch, the intensification and vivification of ear and nose and taste. This is the Zen moment of satori, the nature mystic's high' (Leary 1998: 34). He believed that salvation through sensory awakening would be of immediate philosophical benefit to the individual. Leary defines the religious experience as *'the ecstatic, incontrovertibly certain subjective discovery of answers to seven basic spiritual questions'* (1998: 19; emphasis in original). The questions range from the question of what power or energy underpins the universe to those of the nature and purpose of human being and awareness: 'Who is man? Whence did he come? What is his structure and function? Anatomy and physiology. ... How does man sense, experience, know? Epistemology, neurology' (Leary 1998: 19). It is through challenging received epistemology that Leary challenges received subjectivity. In *The Politics of Ecstasy* Leary aims to answer the questions of the nature and purpose of the self: 'Who am I? What is my spiritual, psychological, social place in the plan?' (1998: 19).

The answer to this question is far from a conventional one. Psychedelic drugs, he argues, if used thoughtfully and properly, under correct supervision and with proper preparation, are a route to *'direct awareness of the energy processes which physicists and biochemists and neurologists and psychologists and psychiatrists measure'* (Leary 1998: 21; emphasis in original). Thus they are comparable to scientific tools which measure the circuitry of the body:

> Subjects speak of ... witnessing the break-down of macroscopic objects into vibratory patterns, visual nets, and collapse of external structure into wave patterns, the awareness that everything is a dance of particles, sensing the smallness and fragility of our system, visions of the void, of world-ending explosions, of the cyclical nature of creation and dissolution, etc. (Leary 1998: 24)

This is typical of Leary's mixture of religion, psychedelia and quasi-scientific, technological posthumanism. His vision of nets, patterns, waves and explosions suggests an eruption of the dissonant, microscopic, fractal interior into the formerly harmonized, macrocosmic, stratified exterior. The human subject finds its own self-concept radically challenged by the disruption and fragmentation induced by the drug, and its surface ruptured by formerly hidden internal forces.

Psychedelic experience, if properly guided, could produce a vision of the networked complexity of the human–machine hybrid, or posthuman cyborg, meaning here not an actual fusion of the organic and machine, but a body composed ultimately of information in flux rather than a transhistorical human essence: 'The construction of the posthuman does not require the subject to be a literal cyborg. Whether or not interventions have been made on the body, new models of subjectivity emerging from fields such as cognitive science and artificial life imply that even a biologically unaltered *Homo sapiens* counts as posthuman' (Hayles 1999: 4). Leary would add psychedelic experience to Hayles's list of fields that create new subjectivities; moreover, his use of drugs for the purpose of challenging the received conception of the subject is just the sort of intervention on the body that can lead to a new model of identity. His project was to alter temporarily the perception of the subject using hallucinogenics and then record what the altered consciousness understood about itself.

The result was a revised sense of selfhood that distanced the subject from dominant humanist models: 'Identified with the rational mind, the liberal [humanist] subject *possessed* a body but was not usually represented as *being* a body. Only because the body is not identified with the self is it possible to claim for the liberal subject its notorious universality' that has been used to further oppression through erasing differences of gender, ethnicity, class and sexuality (Hayles 1999: 4; emphasis in original). Leary was, among other things, working to get the subject back into the body; or to reclaim being in a body as a necessary condition of identity. Rather than degrading or dehumanizing the subject, this would offer salvation from the limited, oppressive model of the self projected by the dominant ideology: 'The ability to turn on the senses, to escape the conditioned mind, to throb in harmony with the energies radiating on the sense organs, the skillful control of one's senses, has for thousands of years been the mark of a sage, a holy man, a radiant teacher' (Leary 1998: 34).

As Leary's recourse to traditional mysticism suggests, he was not an original religious thinker. He openly appropriated eastern sacred texts throughout his career. His project was knowingly derivative. Leary's preface to his verse translations of the *Tao Te Ching* in *Psychedelic Prayers* is typically open about his lack of scholarship. He cannot access the original Chinese of the *Tao*, so he relies on a series of translations and compares them, meditating while high on hashish in India: 'I had nine English translations of the *Tao*. ... Nine Western minds. But after hours of rereading and meditation the essence of the poem would slowly bubble up' (Leary 1997: 38). Leary then produces his own version and checks this on LSD, 'under the psychedelic microscope' (1997: 38). Only a few drafts pass inspection as resonating with the experiences of the drugged subject.

Leary's anti-establishment, countercultural credentials could be seen as phony here, because he is merely perpetuating the somewhat suspect appropriation of eastern tropes that has always plagued the Western tradition, and which postcolonialist studies have exposed as a fantasy (Said 2003; Bhabha 2004). However, the last chapters of *Your Brain is God*, with their sceptical account of the success of his earlier Buddhist-derived writings, militate somewhat against this impression. The turn to eastern religion 'worked because it was so seductive. There was a lot to learn back-East – The barefoot grace, the body-control sinuosity of yoga, the wiry elastic mind-trick of seeing everything from the standpoint of eternity. ... New, colorful, bizarre Hindu Lord's Prayers to monkey-mimic' (Leary n.d.: 99–100).

Leary acknowledges his earlier fascination with Eastern religion while distancing himself from a naïve celebration of all things oriental. The Buddhist, Hindu and Taoist East had always been mainly a storehouse of images to him, hence the pragmatic basis of his appropriation of *The Tibetan Book of the Dead* in his earlier writing. Although Leary claims patronizingly that his scriptural source was 'couched in primitive rural language' (n.d.: 55–6), he acknowledged that it best described the experiences of LSD users; so he sat down in 1962 to translate it loosely in order to produce *The Psychedelic Experience*.

In suggesting that the brain is God, Leary is reconfiguring the relationship of human and universe. Instead of locating divinity outside us, he places it inside. This is not new; the promise that the kingdom of heaven is within originates with Jesus (Lk. 17, 21). Leary, though, believed himself a creator of world-changing ideas: 'Leary was not a modest man. By now [1970] he saw himself as part of a lineage of great thinkers, such as Socrates and Galileo, whose ideas fundamentally overturned the existing model of reality' (Higgs 2006: 105). Nevertheless, when he makes everyone's brain God, he demonstrates his transpersonal ambitions; in Leary's worldview at least, the divinity of the cerebral cortex is a literal physiological fact, rather than a metaphysical truth or a metaphor. God is nothing more nor less than a cluster of neurons, but this is to be welcomed rather than seen as the end of religion.

Design for Dying

In his final book, *Design for Dying*, written in the knowledge of his impending demise from prostate cancer, Leary described what he anticipated dying would be like, and what would follow it. He did not expect heaven or reincarnation, but an experience of merging with all life: 'When consciousness leaves the body, neurological existence within a twenty-billion-cell ecstatic system becomes what we call infinite. ... Dying is a merging with the entire life process. ... Consciousness returns to the genetic code' (Leary and Sirius 1997: 133). Christopher Partridge has argued that Leary's terminology in his last book is more 'pseudo-scientific and anthropocentric' than religious or mystical (Partridge 2003: 108). However, Leary's vocabulary is close to that of his 1960s' psychedelic essays and manuals. He draws attention to the dilation of perceived time during dying, in which fifteen minutes, as timed by an observer, may last subjective aeons: 'In the psychedelic experience, the neuronaut frequently escapes time. ... The dying experience seems to take us into that same timeless eternity. In death, the object of objectivity is extinguished. The subjective experience of eternity *is* eternity!' (Leary and Sirius 1997: 138; emphasis in original).

Leary then goes on to suggest technological means by which identity might persist after death. He recommends cryogenics and other forms of post-mortem storage: 'The viewpoint that takes for granted the perishable, disposable human body-soul will soon be seen as historical barbarism. Individuals and groups will be free to reassume body-brain form, reconstructed by the appropriate sciences' (Leary and Sirius 1997: 154).

Underlying this possibility is Leary's posthumanist belief that consciousness is a form of data and is thus both storable and reproducible. He consistently refers to human identity not only in terms of its basic biological building blocks, the DNA shared with animals, but also in terms of information technology: 'The cell has an inside, an outside, and a semipermeable membrane that functions as the interface. A computer program has processing, data, and interface mechanisms that acquire the data and produce the results. In the mathematics of distinction, the self – the observer, is the distinction, the boundary between the interior and exterior universes' (Leary and Sirius 1997: 29). Thus the self can be preserved because it is reducible to code, software and data, albeit in biological form. This is a cyborg identity of the kind proposed by Donna J. Haraway: 'The cyborg appears in myth precisely where the boundary between human and animal is transgressed. ... The second leaky distinction is between animal-human (organism) and machine' (Haraway 2000: 72).

Leary's challenge to the orthodox picture of the human is to propose that we are not isolated Cartesian intelligences but are in fact networked machines and/or hived animals; the product of organic, molecular processes that can be mapped and copied, but that will inevitably wind down, as *Design for Dying* makes clear. Even as early as *The Psychedelic Experience*, Leary was using technological metaphors to describe the brain. During a religious experience, the mind roams freely, like 'a computer with unlimited access to any programs' (Leary et al. 1995: 68). After the psychedelic session, the subject should avoid thinking too much about it in the short term, as the brain 'is like a computer that has received a huge amount of new information to be assimilated' (Leary et al. 1995: 112).

Few religions envisage man as a computer. Thus the salvation Leary was evangelizing through his texts was certainly an alternative one. His project was framed in direct opposition to the non-drug-using mainstream and to orthodox theology. It was a forward-looking, posthumanist programme. Leary was not just offering the promise of religious experience through psychedelic drugs; he was participating in his culture's ongoing revision of what it meant to be human. However imperfectly, and sometimes naively and even dangerously, he was offering not only a chance to save oneself, but also a change in what the self meant, and a radical revision of its relationship to the universe and its sense of the divine. Leary was developing Nietzsche's project of urging an alternative to Christianity based on a profound recognition of the importance of the body and its workings. This alternative was to be sought through 'a *chemistry* of moral, religious, aesthetic ideas and feelings, a chemistry of all those impulses that we ourselves experience in the great and small interactions of culture and society ... . What if this chemistry might end with the conclusion that, even here, the most glorious colours are extracted from base, even despised substances?' (Nietzsche 1994: 14; emphasis in original).

Chapter 7

RELIGIOUS DOCTRINES IN GROUP DISCUSSIONS ON IDEAS OF AFTERLIFE: WHAT DO YOU THINK COMES AFTER DEATH?[1]

Kornelia Sammet

Introduction: The Adaptation of Religious Doctrines in Contemporary Images of Afterlife

In processes of modernization and globalization religious beliefs have become increasingly a matter of choice. Due to the internet and mass media, various religious doctrines are widely available for interpretation in relation to this life, as well as for the formulation of expectations of what will come after death. Based on qualitative data, this chapter explores the images of afterlife people describe when they are asked what in their opinion comes after death. It demonstrates that, even for members of Christian churches, secularized ideas, like remaining in the memory of the bereaved, are more familiar and more plausible than the belief in resurrection of the dead. As salvation, heaven and hell or Last Judgement are no longer the obvious options to answer the question of afterlife, the relation of people to the reality of death has undergone fundamental changes in modern societies.

This also applies to theological concepts of the afterlife. According to Michael Ebertz (1992), who explored Christian eschatology from St Paul through scholasticism and the age of Enlightenment to present times, constrictions of ideas of afterlife led to a 'civilisation' and transformation of heaven, hell and purgatory. While heaven in early Christian understanding, particularly as expressed by Augustine, had been seen as an exclusive place that was reserved only for minorities (i.e. the religious virtuosos), it also became accessible for the religious masses by the integration of purgatory as a transitional stage (Ebertz 1992: 164). Based on analyses of sermons of the nineteenth and twentieth centuries Ebertz argues that in the twentieth century at last hell no longer exists; instead heaven is 'given' to the people. Thus, Christian (or in this case: Catholic) concepts of afterlife appear civilized, adjusted and inclusive.

Ebertz' analysis is based on sermons; that is, on texts written by religious experts and virtuosos. My analysis of group discussions, which were carried out in different regions in Germany, focuses on the ideas and images of lay people and unbelievers, differentiated in relation to social situation and context.

Preliminary Remarks on Erlösung

At the outset it is important to clarify the meaning of the term salvation in my research. As a sociologist of religion my research question is inspired by the work of Max Weber. Central topics of his studies were 'salvation religions'; the 'salvation goods' they offer for their adherents; the promises they give believers and the ways to salvation they prescribe. Weber was especially interested in their 'attempts to satisfy the diverse ethical and intellectual needs of their adherents' (1978: 526). Therefore, with a materialist orientation, Weber was interested in the carriers of specific ideas of salvation, this-worldly as well as other-worldly salvation. He identified religious interests as originating in the needs of different social strata and as generating doctrines of salvation corresponding to those needs. This perspective was complemented with an idealistic approach, for Weber also explored the consequences that hopes for salvation have on the life conduct of their adherents. In my analysis, I focus on ideas of other-worldly salvation. This means concepts and beliefs of the afterlife, demonstrating how individuals 'pick up' the interpretational patterns offered by religious traditions, adapting and transforming them in the light of everyday life experiences. The question I explore in this chapter is: What do people fear or hope for when they talk about what will come after death?

The second preliminary remark is on the translation of the term 'salvation'. As the empirical data analysed here was collected in Germany, clarification is required on the translation of a term that is essential for the members of the church groups presented in the following. Translating the German word *Erlösung* is not straightforward. The German term Weber used was *Erlösungsreligion*, translated as 'salvation religions' in the English edition of *Economy & Society* (1978). In Christian theology, especially in St Paul's theology, salvation is conceptualized as redemption, referring to the redeemed slaves. This concept is also mentioned by Weber (1978: 485). The verb form '*erlösen*' is used in the German version of the Lord's Prayer for the deliverance from evil ('*Erlöse uns von dem Bösen*'). In everyday life, the German term *Erlösung* has also the notion of release, for example when someone says that death came as a release. In all these meanings the verb '*erlösen*' is connected with the preposition '*von*' (from); however, (especially in religious contexts) it is sometimes also used with the preposition '*zu*' (to), which points to the future and an end that is expected and hoped for, for example, as *Erlösung zum ewigen Leben* (to everlasting life). This positively connoted goal can be a place, a state or a good etc.; it can function as a reward for good deeds or as compensation for the hardships of the present life. For this aspect, the German translation of salvation could also be '*Heil*'.[2]

These examples show that *Erlösung* has a range of meanings: on the one hand, notions of liberation from present suffering or evil (like redemption or release), and on the other hand, notions that emphasize a promised good or state in the future (like heaven and paradise). The analyses of the empirical data explain which nuance is employed by the speakers.

Research Question and Methodology

The analyses presented are based on a qualitative approach in social science. In qualitative research, group discussions can be used as an instrument that allows the researcher to discern collective patterns of orientation (Bohnsack 2010) – in this case, to examine ideas of afterlife. Group discussions are conversations of three to six people sharing a similar background. They are either 'real groups' or placed together only for the purpose of research. According to Bohnsack, conversations during the group discussions should have an independent, spontaneous character (2010: 106). This means that the researcher produces as little stimuli as possible and rarely intervenes in the conversation, so that the participants may reveal what is relevant for themselves. In the interpretation of the data, these autonomous discussions are the special focus of interest, since they allow a reconstruction of not only differing orientations and common themes, but also significant conflicts.

The group discussions were conducted within the framework of two research projects: first, the Fourth Investigation of the Protestant church in Germany on Church Membership (*Vierte EKD-Erhebung über Kirchenmitgliedschaft*) and second, a project on 'Worldviews in Precarious Conditions of Life' at the University of Leipzig, funded by the '*Deutsche Forschungsgemeinschaft*' (DFG) from 2008 to 2012. For both studies, the concept of 'worldviews' ('*Weltsichten*') was prominent. Worldviews can be considered, with reference to Thomas Luckmann (1985), as subjective theories of life and the world (Wohlrab-Sahr and Sammet 2006). Religious and non-religious worldviews can be distinguished by reference to a transcendent sphere, and for this distinction the analysis of ideas about what comes after death is very informative.

The group discussions were transcribed word for word in their characteristic dialect, with all grammatical faults, with all the stuttering, the iterations and the breaking-off of sentences. The transcriptions were anonymized and then evaluated with reconstructive-hermeneutic procedures (Przyborski and Wohlrab-Sahr 2008: 240–71). For this publication the transcripts were translated into English.

In all the group discussions the participants were asked, near the end of the conversation, what, in their opinion, comes after death.[3] From the perspective of a sociology of religion, the reactions are very informative. The participants are requested to formulate ideas of an afterlife and by doing so, to deal with the distinction between immanence and transcendence (Sammet 2006). This approach has the advantage that it neither extorts clear decisions from the interviewees nor imputes that they can determine their position exactly. Rather, they are enabled to express their uncertainty and ambivalence as well as develop distinctive thoughts and opinions. In the following sections the empirical findings will be presented. First, with the aid of two examples, I show how traditional Christian doctrines are interpreted. Later, I present data where more secular notions are developed.

Adaptation of Christian Doctrines on Salvation

The first group presented here is a conversation circle of the *'Frauenhilfe'* group in a West German parish. 'Frauenhilfe' means literally, 'Women's Help' and is a conservative charity-association within the German Protestant church with a great number of local groupings. Most of the nine women engaged in the conversation were housewives and more than sixty years old. The social strata they belong to could be categorized as working class or petty bourgeoisie. For the women, religion was understood in terms of everyday practice, which included either charity initiatives to help the poor and disabled or organizing a midday meal in their respective parish for people unable to cook for themselves. These practices are indeed based on religious beliefs which are supposed to be shared by all group members, but which are rarely named by them. This formulation they leave to religious experts, especially members of the clergy.

This is the first reaction of the group to the death question:

Lilly: So, I can't, personally I cannot imagine a life after death.
Magda: No, me neither. Me neither. I actually believe in nothingness after death.
Lilly: Yes.
...
Gisela: The question is whether one gets cremated or buried.

On first reading, this answer might seem strange, especially since we are dealing with active church members. This spontaneous denial of any afterlife whatsoever could be observed very often as a reaction to the death question. It shows that even for very committed church members the belief in resurrection is not self-evident. But still during some group discussions of the research projects, ideas and images of a life after death are constructed.

The participants of the women's conversation circle slowly approach the question of afterlife in various ways. They refer to doctrines of other religions, for example, that of ancient Egypt, and to a knowledge that seems to them to be scientifically secured – for example, reports of near death experiences. But the problem remains for them that nothing can be known of afterlife, for nobody who had crossed the border and had been 'on the other side' – as they call it – has yet returned.

The proposition that one lives on in one's children and in the memory of others is an idea they agree with. After this, the concept of *Erlösung* is finally introduced

by one participant. In the following quotation, the word is kept in German in order
to preserve the nuances of the term:

> Else: This is what I also believe in [*to live on in her children*], but I also
> believe that I continue to live and I do not believe in any shape [in
> German: *Gestalt*] or in any form, but in a feeling, that I really, in that
> moment, that I really feel well and have peace, really, that there is
> nothing but a feeling, this is what I believe in somehow, that I am –
> um – relieved from everything else, just that.
> Woman: *Erlöst?* (= released)
> Else: Sure, but what does *erlöst* mean?
> Agnes: Yes, the soul.
> Lilly: So, while you are still here or on the other side already?
> Agnes: No, no, when she is dead.
> Else: Right!
> Gisela: Yes, but when are you on the other side? Now, as I have said, a
> friend of mine died and he was suffering violent pains, and after he was
> dead, there was so much peace on his face, so …
> Woman: He was *erlöst*.
> Gisela: An *Erlösung*. Well, one was able to see that.

In this passage, loose hopes for the release-connotation of *Erlösung* are formulated.
The evidence for what comes after death, and thus what death means to
the individuals, is obtained by observing the actual dying of relatives. From the
perceived difference between the suffering during the process of dying and the
expression on the dead person's face, the participants draw conclusions on how
it feels to be dead. Their descriptions start with the terms 'feeling' ('*Gefühl*') and
'peace' ('*Frieden*'), move to 'relief' ('*befreit*') through to the terms 'soul' ('*Seele*')
and *Erlösung*. In this case, *Erlösung* refers to their sorrow and concerns about
terminally ill relatives who were in need of care and for whom death meant the
end of their suffering.

The course of this discussion is an informative example of what I regard as a
pragmatic adaptation of religious doctrine. Even though the women's first reaction
is a very rationalistic one, this does not mean that they could not also express
hopes and wishes for what they call *Erlösung* and in doing so affiliate themselves
with Christian doctrines that were taught and promised to them.

In the course of the discussion they refer to the concept of Last Judgement and
discuss the question, if this is what they believe in. They come to the conclusion that
in Lutheran doctrine not human deeds but the grace of God matters. A question
that seems very important to some participants is discussed below:

> Magda: Do you, do you see your relatives again or not?
> Agnes: Dunno, that I don't know.
> Woman: Yes, that – we always say that.

Agnes: Yes, yes, it is said that one meets again.
Ottilie: One meets.
Woman: In another world.
Edith: Yes, that is this wishful thinking.
Charlotte: If one thinks about how many billions are already there …
Agnes: How many – what a crush must be there!
Charlotte: What an area this is. Is this then really heaven? Or where is this,
    if it is real?

This passage shows a very active and dense interaction. This involvement suggests that the question of a reunification with dead relatives is highly important for the group. In the course of the discussion they come to the conclusion that a possible afterlife existence could not be a bodily incarnation, but a feeling:

Agnes: Yes, something physical can not be any more. No, because it would
    be completely crowded then. Basically, it can only be a feeling, that what
    you call – since the soul – er – is not a part in the body, is not an organ.

The image of a disembodied afterlife is also constructed in the discussion of an East German parish. All the group members were around their mid-forties. During the discussion, they talk about the pressures they face in their daily and, especially, their professional lives. Their lives are stressful; they also criticize prevailing body standards they feel that they do not reach. They ironically lament their inability to meet these standards – 'instead of a six-pack and a wasp's waist', they have 'a racoon's belly and a bumble bee's waist'. In their reaction to the question of a possible afterlife, they refer to this description. Confronted with the question of life after death, the participants give some humorous statements; after this immediate reaction, the conversation becomes more serious:

Katja: But I am convinced that the soul will go upon another path,
    whichever one that is.
Carola: Yes.
Katja: And that'll be a surprise for me.
Carola: Exactly.
Katja: And that's why I'm curious.
Carola: Yes, that's true, yes, er. Okay I think it is, that it is – er – actually
    then, it is actually a desirable condition being dead, because according
    to Christian understanding it at first – er – continues, and
Armin: The *Erlösung*?
Carola: Ya, dunno. I wouldn't quite say *Erl – Erlösung*.
Armin: *Erlösung*?
Carola: But it is somewhere
Armin: This, this vale of tears that is life.
Carola: The soul goes there to a different world and – er – ya.
Armin: Not that it will be boring.

Elke: Exactly.

Carola: This whole nonsense here is then all gone. You don't have to bother yourself with fashion and that, the body has given over. And then ... (laughs)

Elke: Ya, you don't have to bother, er.

Markus: And make-up, ya. Make-up and perfume. You don't have to follow the trends, to keep up with the spring and the autumn fashions.

Carola: I have – er – positive expectations basically.

At the beginning of the talk, the participants do not wish to be more specific, but eventually they come to talk about the 'Christian understanding'. They suppose that it is shared by all group members. When one interviewee suggests the term *Erlösung*, it is initially rejected, yet as the conversation progresses, it is filled out more specifically. What the participants wish and hope for is that after death the pressures of daily life – expressed through the Christian phrase 'this vale of tears that is life' (in German: '*Jammertal*') – will have ended. This wish is especially relevant in the context of standards of self-presentation and beauty to which they see themselves exposed. Their ideas of an afterlife are interconnected to hopes of being released, which have their origin in their own life situations and their social position.

In both group discussions the pictures of a life-to-come painted by the participants are related to topics that are important to them in their everyday life: the experience of stressful life conditions and the suffering of seriously ill relatives. In both cases, a disembodied existence appears as something desirable and they link this concept with the Christian idea of an eternal soul. This concept also solves a problem of enormous concern for the first mentioned group: the hope for reunification with deceased relatives.

Atheistic Ideas of Afterlife

The examples of Protestant parish groups demonstrate that even for persons who consider themselves active church members the question of what comes after death is not to be answered easily. The most obvious answer is the definite end of life and the decay of the body. Thus, for the participants the main problem that has to be solved after death is what has to be done with the corpse. The discussants then approach the question of a possible afterlife very tentatively and talk about salvation as an idea taught and promised to them. During discussion between participants with decidedly secularized or atheistic attitudes, references to religious concepts can also be observed. If images of afterlife are constructed in these contexts, they are framed specifically.

In the discussion with participants introducing themselves as atheists, hopes for a reunification with beloved persons after death are also expressed, but in a very different manner and with different references (see Sammet and Erhard 2012: 440–2). This group discussion was conducted with three friends, who have completed their university studies successfully, but are not working in a position adequate to their education. In fact, two of them are working in a call centre. None of the participants belong to a church and none of them are religious at all. However, their discussion contains references to religious images.

In the first reaction to the death question, one of the participants drops in a very concrete idea of life after death, from which the further discussion unfolds:

Kata: I'll make a movie with Schlingensief.
Insa: (slight laughter)
Kata: You too?
Johannes: Well, I would do that, if I believed in meeting him again.
    Especially in meeting him again. To meet him.

One participant develops here the idea of making a movie after death, together with the German film director and performance artist Christoph Schlingensief, who died in 2010 of cancer. She turns the afterlife into an almost paradisiacal space for wishful fantasies. Thus death becomes a condition for the realization of the self, which she also applies later to her recently deceased cat:

Kata: Hey, my cat recently died.
Johannes: Yes, and it is going to, um ...
Kata: And it dances pogo with all the other cats. I find that much (laughs)
    better than saying that ...
Johannes: Well, first of all – er – I'm sorry.
Kata: Gone.

Even though the interviewee is removing the seriousness from the topic with her witty response, it is however, remarkable that she imagines the cat as still existing. The cat is just out of this world, but somewhere else, where it can exceed its earthly possibilities and thus becomes almost human. Death and afterlife form a space for the interviewee's wishes and fantasies. At the same time, self-fulfilment in the afterlife remains influenced by the subcultural identity, as the cat dances pogo and not a waltz. This concept of afterlife is legitimated by being superior to the idea of life's finiteness and death's finality.

This fantasy is answered by the other two participants with a more materialistic perspective:

Johannes: I, I, I am, I'm a hardcore atheist and – um – think that when I'm
    dead – er – I become a piece of the world, as long as the – um – coffin
    doesn't prevent me from transforming – um – into humus.
Insa: To be honest, I think that nothing at all is going to happen. (five
    seconds pause) Yes. We are dead and are eaten by worms. Or cremated.
Johannes: Which is, in my opinion, a much more romantic idea than
    somehow in in heaven.
Insa: Than stewing in eternity.

Despite the affirmation that he was a 'hardcore atheist' Johannes here transcends the sober and rationalistic explanation of the decaying body Insa adheres to. For Johannes, the transition into 'humus' allows a dead person to remain a part of the world, to be everywhere, and thus, to be close to the bereaved family, in contrast to heaven, where they would be separated forever. In the biographical interview conducted some weeks later with Johannes he talked about the death of his sister which was very hard for him. The idea that dead people are still a part of the world gives him some consolation in his grief and mourning. The German word for 'humus' or 'topsoil' used here is '*Mutterboden*', which could literally be translated as 'mother soil'. This potentially opens up association with the spiritualistic image of 'Mother Earth' and allusions to natural processes and beliefs associated with the circle of life.

In summary, this short passage is characterized by two conflicting positions: on the one hand, we have a concept of individual continuity in a transcendent sphere, which might be related to an image of a heaven or paradise as in Christian and Muslim traditions. On the other hand, there is the wish for physical continuity in this world, which is almost reminiscent of some Buddhist interpretations of death. For both perspectives, further examples can be found in the empirical data.

In many discussions, wishful fantasies of an afterlife refer not to the idea of heaven, but to the idea of reincarnation. When the concept of reincarnation is introduced by one of the participants, the others react with proposals of what they would like to be or think they will be in their next life. This is also the case in a group of young, unemployed people, who are aged between eighteen and twenty-two and who are receiving training in carpentry and gardening. One of them introduces the issue of reincarnation:

Robin: Sure, something can be after death, but it is rather that, well, somehow, that one will be reborn, it kind of could be, but dunno, what I would be after …
Florian: Then I want to become a frog.
Agata: A frog?
Florian: Yes, croak [makes the sound of frogs].
Robin: Yes, and then I become a frog heron.
Florian: Croak.
Robin: Yes, and I will have eaten you after two days.
Florian: Ugh, you eat frogs?
Robin: As a frog heron for sure.
Florian: Ugh. (Somebody laughs.)
Vincent: I want to be a penguin.
Robin: Yes.
Agata: A penguin? (laughing)
Vincent: Just relaxing all day long.
Florian: Sure. Gliding on the belly a little bit.
Robin: Hey, then I prefer to be a sloth.
…

Robin: As a sloth you are miles better, if you like to relax all day long.
Vincent: Or a lemur, dude!
Florian: Yo!
Robin: A lemur.
Vincent: Yes. Lemurs are wicked. Always nicking.
Florian: Small monkeys, dude.

The introduction of reincarnation as a catchword offers the participants the opportunity to present themselves as witty persons by mentioning funny ideas. The first idea does not seem to work well as it is countered immediately by the invention of a frog heron (in German: *Froschreiher*) which brings the reborn existence as a frog to a quick termination. The following ideas show that the reincarnations must fulfil some preconditions (beyond being funny): they have to offer a life that seems attractive to the discussants, and at the same time, they have to suit the respective participant's character. In another discussion of young men, a participant says: 'I will become such an African toad, all day long on LSD,' because he has read about an exotic toad producing a hallucinogenic substance on his skin. And in a third discussion of young, unemployed people, reincarnation as a bird is suggested: 'Then you can shit on the head of everyone you couldn't stand' (Sammet and Erhard 2012: 443). All these quotations make clear that the speakers deal with their current life when discussing the advantages of their proposals. The propositions are justified by the opportunities, comforts and pleasures the lives of these animals might offer: a lazy and relaxed life or revenge for offences experienced in this life. By referring to a possible afterlife existence, the participants imagine an immanent life that would please them, in other words: a kind of innerworldly salvation. At the same time, they present their ideas as jokes taking the seriousness out of the discussion on religious issues.

As I have already argued above, the presence of dead relatives is another issue which is for the participants connected to the question of death. Abby Day (2011) reports that many of her British interviewees talked about the experience of still feeling 'the presence of their deceased relatives' (29). It was also a topic in the discussion of East German students in our study:

Tobias: I have not thought yet what happens to me after death. I must
    so – well, I unfortunately have already experienced a few times that in
    my family someone has died. And then I have actually been actually
    always thinking – er – sure, now you can't anymore sit with him face
    to face and talk. And sometimes I have then told myself, it would be
    really nice, if that one could notice it and there I have always left a
    kind of little backdoor open and said, alas! Maybe he gets it after all.
    And I have always told my girlfriend, later on, we all will sit together
    and will really laugh our head off about it. And maybe only for myself
    as a – er – consolation. I would say, because – I think very rationally
    sometimes and tell myself – um – like you both have also said, that
    after death, yes, there won't happen anything great.

The prospect of a possible afterlife is introduced in this discussion with reference to the experience of losing relatives and mourning for them. The idea of an afterlife is characterized as a 'backdoor left open', offering consolation against one's own better understanding and self-perception as a sober, rational person. This psychological categorization of one's own behaviour allows one to think about an afterlife and to talk about it in the group. As Tobias is conscious about what he is doing, he can indulge himself. This way of dealing with ideas of afterlife is accepted by the group, if one is aware of their irrationality.

Although these fantasies are irrational for the participants, they affect their behaviour. Another group member reports that she always lights 'two candles, one for the living and one for the dead' when entering a church; and after visiting the grave of her grandmother, she touches the tombstone saying 'bye Grandma'. All these practices are ways of doing the dead 'the honour', thinking 'one sees us perhaps at the grave, looking down from heaven'.

This interviewee also gives pragmatic explanations for her irrational, inexplicable behaviour, which opens up space to discuss religious interpretations and ideas like 'heaven'. The emphasis on the better knowledge framing the talk preserves the cognitive distance from the mentioned religious concepts. The discussants note that no one has yet come back from death, so afterlife has been neither proved nor disproved. This leaves a loophole for them; as Tobias adds later, 'It can be possible, that if one dies, one meets again after all.' He applies his scepticism to all knowledge, and this includes scientific knowledge. This interpretation of rationality allows the idea of a reunion in afterlife as a speculation for him. It is not anymore a comforting self-delusion and wishful thought, but a hypothesis which has not yet been disproved.

Conclusion

These short passages taken from group discussions demonstrate how religious concepts are adapted and transformed in order to interpret one's life experience and to cope with the mortality of human beings. It is remarkable that the participants do not talk about ways to salvation, about how to achieve a possible afterlife. They take it for granted that if there is a life to come after death, it will or would be open to them.

It seems to be more important that the images of afterlife constructed – more or less seriously – by church members as well as non-believers must have subjective plausibility: on the one hand, they refer to cultural patterns of world interpretation such as religious traditions (or in other cases: to scientific mainstream knowledge). On the other hand, they are adapted to personal or milieu specific value systems. Afterlife as something which is believed in or as a space of wishful imagination has to offer a salvation good which relates to biographical and everyday experiences. In modern societies ideas of afterlife have become a matter of choice – they have to be worth believing in to even be discussed at all.

In the discussions, it can also be observed that in talking about what comes after death, about the life to come, the participants talk about their life in this world; they express what they think is of important concern in this life. They hope for release from the hardships of life in a life to come which they hope will be filled with peace, harmony and ease, and they dream of revenge for what they have experienced. They imagine a kind of self-fulfilment that appears not to be possible in this life and that transcends their earthly restrictions. The issue of utmost importance in many discussions is the hope for reunification with the dead. This hope can be understood as both a consequence and an expression of the social character of human nature.

Chapter 8

Salvation, Death and Nature as Grace

Douglas Davies

While the ancient idea of salvation became a complex variable in the modern academic study of religion, especially in the earliest twentieth century, it declined in interest for most late-twentieth- and early-twenty-first century British scholars. Alert to how intellectual styles are aligned with new academic generations, leaders and topics, we begin this chapter with this shift and with my own work which bucked that trend. From the 1960s, especially with the emergence of religious studies as a self-driving discipline vying with the slightly more established academic routes of the history of religions, phenomenology of religion, comparative religion, as well as with religion-focused aspects of anthropology, sociology and psychology, 'salvation' became increasingly marginalized as a working concept. Theology, of course, maintained its own ecclesial interest in salvation with soteriology as its demarcated field of application and liturgy its enacted domain of salvation. Various forms of critical, literary and social theory that brought new life to a variety of fatigued disciplines in the arts and humanities also conduced to different foci of interest leaving salvation aside.

Conceptual Changes

In technical terms, 'salvation' is one of those notions whose theoretical study or etic status is most fundamentally rooted in its emic status as an idea naturally occurring in world cultures, classically expressed biblically in the text, 'What must I do to be saved?'[1] As an indigenous term it has frequently undergone extensive debate within religious traditions as different schools advocated their distinctive modes of depicting and achieving salvation. This presents scholars of many disciplines with the challenge of identifying both the level of analysis and the component elements to be incorporated into their discussion of salvation. While 'salvation' as a singular noun set against many doctrinal ideas, mythic thoughts and scores of liturgical and ritual practices, tempts us to speak of salvations in the plural, this chapter will seek a unified theory of salvation.

While that simplicity may well be a naïve response to the sheer complexity of human conceptual inventiveness and behavioural cultural diversity, it will, at least, prompt its own form of critical perspective on the panorama of human being in the world.

Theoretically speaking, the notion of salvation had been of particular significance within the history, phenomenology and comparative studies of religion in the middle decades of the twentieth century, as with scholars like Brandon (1963), Werblowsky and Bleeker (1970) and Sharpe and Hinnells (1973).[2] Within the emergent UK sociology of religion, Wilson used the very theme of salvation, coupled with different means of identifying and coping with evil, to create his typology of sects (1970) for his wider non-Christian focused studies (1973) and as a general umbrella that would cover 'a wide range of items' in new religious movements (1997). This expanded his interest in Max Weber's focused commitment to the idea of the need for different types of salvation in world religions, evident in the latter's *Sociology of Religion* (1966).

However, the later (1950s and 1960s) concern for secularization detracted from notions of salvation, rendering them relatively redundant despite the rise of charismatic Christianity which attracted a mode of study all of its own. It was Weber's ideas on disenchantment, more than his concerns about salvation, that fuelled these scholarly ventures in secularization. When the later 1960s attracted research on both Charismatic Christianity and New Age phenomena, it was directed towards notions of spirituality, and salvation ceased to attract scholarly attention. Later decades detailed forms of 'alternative spirituality'[3] and the dynamics of a great variety of 'self-actualization',[4] all of which provided a different level and focus of interest from more abstract notions of salvation. To some degree, more recent interest in 'sacralization' in dialectical relationship with 'secularization' has invited the language of salvation and yet it has not, in general, been spoken as such.[5]

However, my own and by now rather unfashionable interest in salvation continued, and from the late 1960s until today 'salvation' has retained significance in my thinking and research. From approximately 1966 to 1974, my education in anthropology, the sociology of religion and theology led me to become increasingly interested in the notion of salvation for several reasons. At both Durham and Oxford Universities, anthropology's commitment to the comparative method, my research supervisor Bryan Wilson's sociological approach to sects that fostered my own study of Mormonism, and Christian theology's concerns with soteriology, coalesced in an extensive study of salvation approached in terms of the sociology of knowledge – itself then a major driver within the sociology of religion. Nottingham University appointed me in 1974, with the express task of developing the study of religion in the university; following my appointment, the 'salvation project' assumed significance in my thinking, research and teaching. Its early outcome was a 1978 paper (Davies 1978), a 1979 doctoral dissertation whose book version of 1984 we now briefly sketched before dealing with some later studies of salvation.

Meaning and Salvation in Religious Studies

Meaning and Salvation in Religious Studies, published in the monograph series accompanying the history of religions journal *NUMEN* for 1984, made minimum academic impact in the UK. I doubt if many religious studies people, let alone anthropologists or sociologists of religion read it: one negative review that included some apt criticism probably did not help.[6] Its history of religions location probably did not help either, while shifting academic interests had, as indicated above, already moved elsewhere. This was unfortunate because I think subsequent debates lost a key concept or at least a worthwhile jousting partner. However, this chapter presents an opportunity to reposition a developed notion of salvation within the study of religion as well as in the emergent innovation of 'worldview' studies (Droogers and Van Harskamp 2014). Here, then, I will briefly rehearse key theoretical issues of the 1984 volume, outline some further published developments on salvation theory before exemplifying these for Mormonism and for notions of spirituality in the UK National Health Service and in the innovation of woodland burial.

The goal of the 1984 monograph was to offer an approach to salvation through the medium of the sociology of knowledge focused in plausibility theory and not in any theological perspective. This allowed for salvation to be an analytical concept applicable to traditions that were not usually designated as salvation religions. Accordingly, the cultural life of many preliterate groups could be seen to be as much concerned with a certain transformation of insight that brings a new perspective to life as was reckoned to be the case for salvation ideals of the world's 'great' religious traditions.

That book's key question was expressed in its first sentence as – 'How does the human drive for meaning come to express itself as a need of salvation?' (1984: 1). Making the point that the period from roughly 1910 to 1960, following earlier commitments to evolutionists thought, had lacked 'any unified theory by which to approach religious phenomena', I pressed the theoretical theme of plausibility and general communication theories to argue that salvation consisted in a level of plausibility generated from a variety of subsystems in which cognitive and affective dynamics merged in conferring identity upon a person while confronting existential factors of constraint (1984: 2, 155–64). The issue of constraint was developed through 'evil' understood in terms of a descriptive phenomenology of life-negating factors. Focused in chapters on 'evil and plausibility', 'evil and witchcraft' and 'evil and salvation in Sikh religion', it drew from sources including Peter Berger, John Bowker, Paul Ricoeur, J. B. Russell, Bryan Wilson and others (Davies 1984: 28–61; 101–36) and set this essentially social scientific account of salvation within an extensive engagement with phenomena deemed radically problematic, hazardous or frustrating to the ongoing life of people.

Another sociological influence came from Hans Mol's (1976) identity theory arguing that entities conferring a sense of identity upon a person are, in turn, viewed with respect and awe, even to the point of becoming sacred; making sacrality the outcome of the social process of identity formation. Mol's work had, itself, not gained much appreciation at the time, a fact only recently redressed in an edited collection focused on his ideas.[7] Additionally, W. E. H. Stanner's profound ethnography of Australian Aboriginal life reinforced this meaning-making, identity-achieving perspective. This respected Australian scholar, influenced by study in England (though he did not find much support in the UK in later years), brought an existential understanding to bear that not only remains of considerable value to those later scholars who laboured over notions of emic and etic levels of analysis but also to a social science of humanity that embraces existential concerns.

In terms of my 1984 study, salvation could be discussed for either secular or religious contexts. It was the outcome of the drive for meaning attained through some identity conferring person, process or institution. That volume embraced ethnographic cases from Australia and Africa as well as my own studies of Mormons and, at that time, also of Sikhs. On the wider human stage, preliterate and literate groups could be viewed equally as achieving meaningfulness whose quality, in terms of sense of identity, could be regarded as sacred. The book was, in its own way, engaged in the colonial–postcolonial dialectic, and also in the clear validation of 'primitive' thought as being as equally complex as 'advanced' thought, an argument also made by Lévi-Strauss. Its burden resembled Edward Said's 1978 *Orientalism* though that was unfamiliar to me at the time.

Also integral to the original doctoral thesis[8] and ensuing 1984 publication was the desire to integrate cognitive and affective aspects of life and as part of that I tried to argue for the notion of 'social-person' as the point of encounter of both aspects of life (1984: 161–4). In retrospect that was a somewhat naïve attempt at accommodating emotion within cultural identity and in relation to what would increasingly be discussed as embodiment theory and which took sharper focus in a series of publications (Davies 1986, 2000, 2002) which were followed by the later *Emotion, Identity and Religion* (2011). With direct reference to a religious tradition this embodiment approach to salvation was also given sharp focus in *The Mormon Culture of Salvation* (2000) to which we return below.

Superplausibility

It is on the 2011 study of emotions and identity that I now focus for in it I argued for a 'transformative process of superplausibility' (2011: 212); a concept intended to highlight a feature of human religiosity that can easily pass unnoticed, in other words, the way one scheme of meaning can be superseded by another, be rendered secondary in the process, and can confer – or even impose – a powerful sense of identity upon people. In one sense that was precisely what happened in cultural terms in many colonial, revolutionary and missionary contexts involving religious conversion. Moreover, in referring to conversion I do not simply allude to the sharper forms of William James's 'twice-born' type encountered in conversionist-style groups and to Harvey Whitehouse's trauma-rooted 'imagistic' mode of religion, but also to some individuals of both James's 'once-born' and Whitehouse's 'doctrinal' mode of religion. Both of which individuals may be more slowly socialized into a religious ideological practice during the course of which significant insight of a more individual and yet 'conversion-like' form may occur.[9] For the human, capacity for creative imagination can easily be transformed into what are experienced as new ways of experiencing the world on the back of slowly learnt ideas of the world, especially when that learning also includes the symbolic acquisition of dispositions aligned with liturgical and community life. Here the role of rites of intensification become highly significant for salvation as people engage over and over again in ritual acts whose behaviours and deepening familiarity with words and ideas transform a person's worldview as life-circumstances and emotional intensities make their own impact (Chapple and Coon 1947). In other words, the emotional – cognitive resources of a tradition can be encountered in progressively developing ways as a person's situation changes over their course of life.

Hope and Reciprocity

In *Emotion, Identity, and Religion*, subtitled, *Hope, Reciprocity and Otherness*, salvation plays a significant role in a series of complementary key issues of human nature and religiosity. These are rooted in the assumption that the biological drive to survive, itself an essential factor in evolutionary development, is transformed into its cultural parallel of hope – a feature basic to the emotional dynamics of most religious, political and economic systems. Though this suggestion that hope 'as a fundamental property of social identity' is to the cultural level of life what the drive to survive is at the biological level is a relatively bold line of argument, it is inescapable when analysing the motivation behind a great deal of religious praxis (2011: 191).

For example, it is depicted in different ways both in the history cum judgement schemes of Middle-Eastern and Western traditions of Judaism, Christianity and Islam, and in the transmigration cum consciousness Eastern traditions of Hinduism, Buddhism and Sikhism. Hope gains part of its force from people's negative experiences that frustrate their immediate and longer-term goals and is vital in relation to pain and the potential it carries both for hopelessness and for a challenge to religions and their posited meaningfulness of life (2011: 81–4, 207–8, 235–6). Within Christianity hope becomes something of a relational concept grounded in the Trinitarian notion of an interpersonal deity yet, even there it soon becomes framed by the notion of 'the problem of evil' in terms of apparently inexplicable suffering. The Indian-grounded traditions have something of a lesser issue over pain and other negations of life through its notion of self as a *karma*-driven entity set amid ongoing changes in the cosmic cycles of existence whose dynamics involve the theme of merit.

Merit and Reciprocity

In Hinduism and Buddhism, then, as in the other 'great' world religions, salvation entails powerful schemes of reciprocity in which merit acquisition plays a fundamental role. Salvation is frequently depicted as a relational process in which devotees require a capital of merit to enable betterment in their future existence of a post-mortal heavenly paradise or of a reincarnation of transmigrating spirit. Merit is variously acquired by hard-won obedience to divine commandments, by martyrdom for the faith, or in receiving a gracious gift from a beneficent deity. Within Christianity, for example, even that gracious gift is posited upon the merit generated by Jesus as both the perfect law-keeper and the personal life-giver, to which Catholic traditions sometimes add the merit of the saints and martyrs that combine in a treasury of merit managed by the church. The sharp historical Protestant and Catholic divide over accessing merit – itself constituting the salvation-capital available to humans as sinners devoid of personal merit – does not render redundant the primary importance of merit in salvation. On the contrary, the high profile of merit acquisition highlights the significance of ordinary human relationships that function in terms of reciprocity. It is the very ordinariness of reciprocal relationships as integral to social life and mutual relationships that allows for an intensification of the significance of merit in the supra-normal or supernatural domain of the afterlife. In mainstream Islamic traditions the acquisition of merit in terms of submissive obedience to the deity and divine commandments is integral to the post-mortem judgement of Muslims and their subsequent punishment or experience of bliss. As for Hinduism and Buddhism, they are, classically, preoccupied within merit acquisition whether in terms of caste duties and *karma* or of a mindfully proper set of relationships with the Buddhist way of life, including gift-relationships with monks. Many ancestral traditions are also rooted in similar reciprocal acts of devotion, blessing or curse. While salvation embraces this reciprocity-grounded merit it may also embrace a 'heightening of the sense of identity' within a 'meaning metamorphosis' in life, as well as being an 'expression of the human drive to survive and flourish' amid life's constraints, not least in terms of suffering and allied forms of deliverance (Davies 2011: 24, 72, 203).

Though we cannot explore the theme here, this paradigm of merit is, occasionally, offset within religious traditions by a love – grace union motif that renders merit-language redundant or at least exists uneasily alongside it. This is an important theme for salvation and could, for example, be explored in lovegrace areas of love for Krishna in Hinduism, for the True Guru in Sikhism, for the saviour-figure in some Pure Land traditions of Buddhism, and for devotional and union with Jesus in Christianity. Such a sense of loving engagement with a divine figure reflects easily upon interpersonal human love relationships and its intensified form highlights the importance of emotions as dynamic elements within religious experience.

The Shift in Awareness

Above all, then, the 2011 'emotions book' reveals its origin in the 1984 plausibility-grounded monograph through its developed notion of superplausibility. It explains why many societies appear dissatisfied with the levels of meaning operating at ordinary levels of plausibility generation and reinforces the argument against 'any sharp divide between the "salvation religions" and other religious or cultural traditions that often involve a shift in self identity' (Davies 2011: 213). In other words, it seems that many societies have not been satisfied with 'ordinary' forms of socialization and its attendant scheme of plausibility but have instigated addition processes to intensify and transform 'ordinariness' into something extraordinary. And it is precisely the ensuing 'extra-ordinariness' that I describe as 'superplausibility' involving a transformation of perception affording its own form of salvation. This suggests why numerous traditional societies often engaged with rites of initiation that took a person's acceptance of the way things are, a sense often acquired in childhood or early youth, and transformed it through additional experience and knowledge to generate new insight into the way things really are.

For those interested in ritual studies, this is reflected in the theoretical difference between Arnold van Gennep's ([1908] 1960) original analysis of the changes in social status achieved through rites of passage and Maurice Bloch's (1992) development of that approach in his notion of rebounding conquest or rebounding violence in which the existential awareness of initiates is added to the formal changes in social status. To this we could, most certainly, refer yet again to Harvey Whitehouse's dual-mode theory of religion in which the 'imagistic mode' of ritual initiation involves traumatic experiences that conduce to revised worldviews (2004).

Stanner and Douglas

A whole anthropological generation before this Stanner (1905–81) allowed the emotional dimension and its allied insights of the Murinbata people to spell out the 'refuge and rottenness' of human existence within what he described as a 'covenant of duality' (1959)[10], a 'covenant' offering its own form of superplausibility grounded in the life experience acquired by a people and transmitted to ongoing generations in rites that foster a shift in awareness. His near contemporary, Mary Douglas (1921–2007), also attested to the power of insight aligned with ritual practice in her 1963 work on the Lele of the Kasai in Central Africa. Not only did she analyse the ritual symbolism of animal sacrifice in the Pangolin to describe how the people 'confronted ambiguity in an extreme and concentrated form' but she also interpreted this scheme of things as 'capable of inspiring a profound meditation on the nature of purity and impurity and on the limitation of human contemplation of existence' (1966: 169–70). Many other examples could be cited and, for example, lead to similar analyses for Christianity and its formative ritual events that impact upon devotees at different points in their life course.

It was precisely in this kind of ethnographic analysis of traditional societies that I saw material entirely worthy of comparison with what had so easily come to be called the great world or salvation religions. Differences resulting from literacy, elite scribal and priestly traditions, royal and state patronage of large populations, as well as from enduring architectural ritual spaces all made their contribution to the visibility of 'world religions' while it was solid anthropological attention paid to societies that had taken different social, economic and political pathways that granted access to smaller and otherwise unknown ways of being human, which also included meaning-making of both 'ordinary' and 'extraordinary' sorts. Also of relevance here is colonization and the resulting cultural impact, which saw indigenous and albeit implicit forms of 'salvation' being devalued and replaced by explicit practices and doctrines affording salvation in Christian, Islamic, Hindu, Buddhist and Communist terms. Here I will offer but one example of such supersession of plausibility, and will do so for the case of salvation and the Church of Jesus Christ of Latter-day Saints (LDS).

Mormonism: Salvation in Two Modes

My first postgraduate research, directed by sociologist Bryan Wilson, was on Mormonism and, from that beginning in 1969 until the present, I have devoted periods of study to it in what came to be a complex interplay of anthropological-sociological engagement aligned with much historical and some academically theological work. From my first paper on Mormon eschatology (1973), itself a significant subset of salvation, through to *Joseph Smith, Jesus, and Satanic Opposition* (2010) whose subtitle *Atonement, Evil and the Mormon Vision* focuses the salvation theme upon the Mormon preoccupation with atonement, the theme of the drive for meaning being metamorphosed into the need for salvation has been solidly present.

This preoccupation has also involved the alliance of salvation with notions of identity detailed in the 1984 monograph for both Mormonism and Sikhism (1984: 136–54). In terms of the Church of Jesus Christ of Latter-day Saints this perspective was invaluable, with the theoretical issue of plausibility and superplausibility being, perhaps, partially fostered because of that group's own distinction between 'salvation' and what it calls 'exaltation'. The latter is its own potential version of superplausibility. Here again we find echoes of the emic-etic interplay of description and theoretical analysis. The salvation–exaltation distinction also carries some relevance as the local Mormon church and home life on the one hand and temple activity on the other interrelate. The local 'chapel' rites resemble those of many other Christian denominations but the temple rites, accessible only to devoted and tested saints, confer endowments allowing access to a higher order of post-mortal salvation designated as exaltation. Whereas Christ's resurrection guarantees 'salvation' in the sense of ensuring a resurrection from the dead – this by divine grace – it is a person's faithful life and obedient response to the church's call to engage in temple ritual for self, family and the dead that promises 'exaltation' in eternal domains of transformed and deified family life. No other Christian denomination has gone so far in terms of specifying and providing a ritual-symbolic means, as well as an ethical-organizational code, complementing salvation with exaltation or, to use the technical terms provided earlier in this chapter, plausibility with super plausibility.

This distinction also carries its own dynamic echoes of my earlier allusion to colonial super-cessation of one ideology over another. Early Mormonism's development between its inauguration in 1830 until the first prophet's death in 1844 involved an explanation of why other pre-existing Christian groups were inadequate to the purpose of making available the real salvation accessible in the days of Jesus and his immediate apostles, but which was then lost, or rather removed by God, until its restoration through Joseph Smith Jr. The apostasy of historical Christianity and its restoration through Joseph involved an interpretation of history in direct terms of salvation history. Time itself, as with much Christian thought, now becomes an explicit medium of both plausibility-salvation and superplausibility-exaltation.

Mormonism, most certainly in its nineteenth-century mode, replicated the nature of earliest Christianity in being dependent upon its preceding Christian denominations (just as earliest Christianity had been dependent upon Judaism). Earliest Christianity's validation was so deeply rooted in its narrative of Judaism's fulfilment that the language of a 'new testament' flowed easily from that of an 'old testament' and could not be told without it. Similarly, the emergent Mormon narrative was so embedded in a complex fashion both in the 'old testament' and in the 'new testament' of denominational Christianity that its telling demanded a devaluation of the apostasy of that 'new testament' Christianity that formed itself after the days of Jesus. In analytical terms, the very fact that 'ordinary' Christianity had its own strong grammar of discourse of salvation required this new Mormon religious movement, albeit one that self-defined as a Christian 'restoration', to have its own higher-order notion of salvation; and that is what emerged in the LDS notion of 'exaltation'. In a further subtle turn, Mormonism's self-identity as a source of salvation strongly identified itself with pre-Christian Judaism (Davies 2010: 21–40).

Secularization, Spirituality and Salvation

Turning from the Mormon case, it now remains to indicate how the notion of salvation, sociologically described in terms of plausibility theory, might be applied to aspects of contemporary life apart from the many explicitly religious contexts of identifiable 'world religions' vibrantly active in many parts of the world beyond Western and northern Europe. Here I cite but two cases drawn from my own more recent research interests: the British National Health Service (NHS) and the innovative practice of woodland burial. Though these may appear oddly diverse, their very diversity will reveal the value of a plausibility approach to salvation.

National Health Service, Spirituality and Salvation

The NHS is the largest British institution dealing with the well-being of the population at large. Its creation after the 1939–45 Second World War marked part of national reconstruction after devastation. With the later twentieth-century decrease of popular engagement with denominational religion, including the Church of England, the NHS's spectrum of social care for a great majority of the population at times of personal crisis, when life's meaning and significance is open to question, is enormously significant. In other words, plausibility maintenance falls disproportionately upon the NHS; it becomes a lifeline and, in its own fashion, a means of salvation. This has become increasingly evident through the rise of the notion of what can best be called health care-spirituality. The adoption and increasing use of 'spirituality' as a term within NHS circles stresses the quality, value, depth and meaningfulness of life that is identified as an integral part of patient care, and as a wider identification of that plausibility of existence that conduces to well-being (Cassidy and Davies 2003). If we think of this in terms of a 'new spirituality' aligned with a 'new secularization', we can see the driver of the dual process as the NHS, taking the slightly tedious debate over secularization away from the standard sociological idea of established churches losing significance in the public sphere.[11]

The publication of the extensive *Oxford Textbook of Spirituality in Healthcare* in 2012 marks a developing trend in identifying spirituality as a sphere of deeply significant relevance that uses language not allied with traditional religious groups (Cobb, Puchalski and Rumbold 2012). Some years before this, in 2007, for example, The Royal College of Psychiatrists' own sub-group on spirituality produced its *Spirituality and Psychiatry* (2009: 4), itself a landmark in change of medical-psychiatric attitudes to a dimension of human experience that had not, hitherto, been given much attention. In this context the notion of spirituality touches 'certain kinds of intensely focused moral and aesthetic response, or on the search for deeper reflective awareness of the meaning of our lives and our relationship to others and to the nature of the world' (Cottingham 2005: 3). Cottingham's formulation is easily read in terms of plausibility theory. Other examples of NHS spirituality include the National Council for Palliative Care and its Dying Matters Coalition of 2009 that initiated conferences in 2010 entitled 'Finding the Missing Piece', and in 2011, 'Finding a Common Language'.

Spirituality is also a theme explicitly taken up by atheists who see it as something that is as much theirs as the possession of theists. André Comte-Sponville, for example, rehearses personal experiences of unity with the cosmos to say as an atheist: 'At last I had understood the meaning of salvation – or bliss, or eternity' (2008: 159). His experience seemed to provide its own kind of super plausibility, of awareness of his being in the world that transcended his prior awareness. His account is so like that of traditional mystics that it highlights the power of theological or ideological frameworks to define how experiences are signified and appropriated.

The NHS does not have that kind of anticipation for its patients, but sees spirituality in terms of a wider network of meaningfulness in life and relationships; something staff are required to bear in mind when dealing with patients at times of life-crisis, when plausibility is potentially most fragile. It is in this general sense the NHS becomes a means of salvation and it is as such that we might see it as enshrining core cultural values of personal worth and community care that make it a serious candidate for status as a sacred institution just when many traditional forms of sacred institutions are losing social significance. This is, perhaps, why the NHS has become a general touchstone of political sensitivity: to play with it is to play with the sacred as the guardian of core values, to harm it is to blaspheme.

But perhaps the most poignant aspect of the NHS in relation to spirituality and salvation comes in the contemporary debate over doctor-assisted death. Here the issue of human dignity pinpoints the worth of an individual as acknowledged by society, a notion highly redolent of traditional ideas of salvation lying in the worth of an individual in relation to God. Though a great deal could be said on this, as on doctors as embodiments of a society's core concern with a distinctive form of reverence for life, it will suffice to pinpoint death as the vehicle that traditional religions most often associated with ideas of salvation and which now falls into the terrain of health care-spirituality and its associated politics. As a backdrop to the major contemporary issues of human value, self-perception and social constraint, we might offer a brief formula indicating how traditional religion in Britain included its own form of spirituality alongside ethics and worship. In a more secularized context, however, we have witnessed the rise of a health care-spirituality alongside the recently formed ethics committees. So, formulaically speaking we might suggest that traditional religion consisted in its own form of spirituality combined with an ethical code and embedded in worship. By contrast, within the secular context, these alliances transform into a pursuit of an appropriate form of spirituality pursued alongside the work of an ethics committee but devoid of an overarching worship framework. These expressions carry their own implications as far as the idea of salvation is concerned so that, from a traditional religious perspective, the absence of worship might be argued as a profound loss of human relatedness to a supernatural 'other'. However, from a secular stance it could be argued that an ethically responsible framing of health care, notably end of life care, and possibly assisted death if and when deemed legal, can generate a quality of mutual relationship that satisfies the needy individual as, some would argue, is the case in the ideology and practice of hospice care. While these debates continue they benefit from plausibility theory and the notion of salvation.

Woodland Burial

One other application of salvation as plausibility might be considered in terms of the innovation of what is variously called woodland, green, ecological or natural burial. As with NHS spirituality this also reveals a potential relocation of discourse over human worth as we encounter personal choices over body burial and the placing of cremated remains in sites deemed 'natural' whose good views, beautiful settings and location offer a degree of coherence with a person's lifetime affinities. While it would be excessive to identify woodland burial too closely with people's ecological ethic, it is probably true to say that this kind of burial speaks much less of traditional Christian ideas of burying in a graveyard or cemetery and resting in peace in preparation for resurrection and more of a paradigmatic scene of salvation interpreted as a person giving themselves back 'to nature' in a place of plant, insect, bird and other animal activity. In an increasingly secular context the traditional spirituality of eschatological hope is transformed into an anticipated participation in a place relatives might visit with some positive spirit (Davies and Rumble 2012). Issues of choice of integration of lifestyle with what we can call death-style become an expression of plausibility versus implausibility of participation in religious rites and places where those styles are dissonant.

Conclusion

Salvation can be conceived as participation in a form of cultural power or social force that benefits individuals and causes them to flourish (Van der Leeuw [1933] 1999). This traditionally involved afterlife trajectories embracing saviour-figures and reciprocal schemes of merit, grace or love. Traditional schemes of plausibility were often superseded by colonial missionaries or by paradigmatic shifts in ideological perspective, including that often described as secularization. This chapter has argued that plausibility theory offers a means of descriptively interpreting the drive for meaning and its outcome in religious ideas of salvation, typified in Mormonism and secular notions of spirituality in the British National Health Service and the innovation of woodland burial.

Part II

Re-reading Traditions

Chapter 9

Whose Salvation? A Very Particular Christian Question

Jenny Daggers

Introduction: Locating 'alternative salvations'

The question of who is saved in Christ has long exercised Christian theologians, with debates reinvigorated during the Reformation following Calvin's development of the doctrine of predestination. However, European modernity with its anthropological turn to the human subject has wrong-footed this longstanding wrangle within Christian theology. Theologians may continue to debate their understandings of the reach of salvation in Christ, but as belief in traditional Christian tenets weakens in Western culture beyond the churches, those outside the churches have different preoccupations. For this thoroughly modernist constituency, the issue is a perceived attempted imposition of 'salvation in Christ' on those who repudiate Christian belief, rather than a pressing question concerning who is included and who is excluded from salvation.

In the same historical moment, as a consequence of the postcolonial 'Age of Migration' (Castles and Miller 2003: 4–5), diasporic Christian churches interrupt the succession of Euro-American denominational traditions, while believers within different and incompatible faith traditions are living and practising their faiths side by side. Within the new diversity of world Christianity, how are the parameters of Christian debates determined? How can specifically Christian debates about who is saved be meaningfully conducted in the context of interreligious living? In short, given secular or even atheistic unbelief and detraditioned spirituality (Boeve 2007: 16–24), diasporic Christian diversity, and fervent belief and practice in other religious traditions, what sense can be made, from a Christian standpoint, of the notion of 'alternative salvations'?

To add further complexity, postcolonial critique offers a different angle on 'alternative salvations'.[1] From this perspective, a genealogy can be traced, linking the notion of 'alternative salvations' with the Eurocentric generic habit that accompanied modern European colonial expansion. By generic habit, I mean a cast of thought which assumes that our own ideas, arising from our modern Euro-American contexts have a universal reach,[2] and a Eurocentric tendency to create generic categories which other traditions are invited to inhabit. This colonizing logic has a hegemonic dimension and an inclusive dimension.

The hegemonic dimension expresses Eurocentric white supremacism – the belief in the superiority of white European culture and technology, which will therefore realize a global destiny through the eventual displacement of all other cultures. Eurocentric colonialism is imbued with this form of universalizing logic in both secularized and Christian missionary forms.

In contrast, the inclusive dimension attempts to address the damage done by white supremacist thinking and aggressive Christian mission, with their inherent disrespect for other cultural traditions – and thus for other religious traditions also. In its inclusive form, the Eurocentric generic habit upholds the intrinsic value of different paths to human flourishing, whether secular or religious. The diversity of human traditions is seen as offering alternative ways of reaching the single, generic goal of human flourishing. The important point for this essay is that the generic goal has been defined exclusively by Euro-American thinkers; there is, then, a hidden hegemony even in the inclusivism that is offered as remedy. It follows that the Eurocentric generic habit is preserved, even in attempts to address the ill effects of the colonial mentality. 'Salvation' as a generic term – capable of realization through a variety of 'alternative salvations' – fits this template.[3]

This generic habit is also reflected in some of the key categories developed in Euro-American disciplines for the study of 'religion and the religions'.[4] Categories drawn from Christianity have been shaped into generic tools (leading to a Christian bias that religious studies has worked steadfastly to eliminate). This generic habit reappears in 'pluralist' approaches to Christian theology of religions (Hick and Knitter 1987). Postcolonial criticism has exposed the Eurocentric generic logic that is a fatal flaw in this courageous, committed and principled project, despite its tangible fruits in terms of building interreligious harmony and respect (Kwok 2005: 199; Surin 1990: 196–8).[5] Euro-American academic disciplines of Christian theology and religious studies alike are challenged to confront their inherited Eurocentrism; in seeking to address colonial hegemony, both have contributed to the ongoing inclusive dimension of colonizing logic.

In light of this recognition, how might scholars of colonizer heritage in Christian theology and religious studies – particularly white scholars – attend to our Eurocentrism? One way, I suggest, is to shrink our Euro-American concerns back within their local Euro-American parameters, so that insights and priorities arising in other localities can exert their due influence in directly shaping global debate. As one small step in this direction, this essay resists generic appropriation of the particular Christian theological term, 'salvation', to serve secularizing or pluralist projects. This essay thus strikes a slightly awkward note within this innovative collection on alternative salvations. Might some of the resourceful projects celebrated here as means of human flourishing be differently named in their own terms, rather than borrowing the term 'salvation' from Christianity? For Christian projects, why not speak in particular Christian terms drawn from its varied tradition, rather than in accordance with a generic pluralist remapping of Christianity as but one form of some generic category 'religion' (in the expectation that 'alternative salvations' will be discernible among its other forms)?

This argument for shrinking the reach of the term 'salvation' is written by a Christian theologian from a Christian perspective, but it is possible that participants from other discrete religious traditions may concur that the generic term 'salvation' is something of an imposition. (Given the roots of Christianity within Judaism, and the Christian borrowing of Jewish notions of God's salvation of his chosen people, Jewish – Christian interrelations are a special case here. However, Jewish notions of salvation are distinct from those developed within Christianity. The integrity of Jewish notions of salvation deserves respect, rather than Jewish traditions being viewed through a Christian lens, or judged by criteria of Christian construction.) This imposition can be avoided, and a more accurate translation can be made of the key concerns of other religious and secular traditions, if the term 'salvation' is reappropriated to Christianity, rather than used in the sense of 'alternative salvations'.

So what might it mean to shrink a Euro-American concern with 'salvation and alternative salvations' back to its local Christian context? Can local Christian traditions be hospitable to the other traditions they encounter? How can inclusivity be advanced if generic, overarching categories are shrunk back to their local origins?

Shrinking the Generic to the Local

In answer to these questions, my contention is that the postcolonial reorientation of Euro-American Christianity is helped by shrinking the generic notion 'salvation' and 'alternative salvations' back within particular Christian discourse that is rooted in Jewish notions, but distinct from these. Further, shrinking 'salvation' back to a core Christian belief enables the following: the resiting of Euro-American Christianity within postcolonial world Christianity; traditioned building of hospitable interreligious relations as an alternative to Christian 'pluralist' projects; and renewed witness in the context of Euro-American (post)modern atheism, secularism and detraditioned spirituality.

For this argument to hold good, three moves need to be in place: first, the diversity and dynamism of Euro-American local Christianity needs to be acknowledged amid the wider diversity of twenty-first century world Christianity; second, the capacity of local and traditioned forms of Euro-American Christian theology to engage in hospitable interreligious encounter needs to be demonstrated; and third, the ability of these shrunken, local and thus clarified Christian claims to bear witness to detraditioned Euro-Americans needs to be shown. In all three directions – world Christianity, religious diversity and Euro-American detraditioning – shrinking the generic back to the local allows for a renewed relevance of Christian theology in its various Euro-American traditions.

To assert the value of tradition, albeit local tradition, is to invite critique of an implied retreat within some well-defended fortress-like structure (Knitter 2002: 183; Hedges 2010: 176; Fletcher 2005: 69–77). However, tradition as conceived in this essay has an open boundary, which is a site of exchange between discrete

Christian materials and cultural materials available in the wider surrounding culture. Using Kathryn Tanner's notion of the borrowing of cultural materials for transformation to Christian use (Tanner 1997: 112), local traditions can be understood as dynamic and constantly changing in ways that reflect the cultural context, while also preserving and representing discrete Christian materials – biblical, liturgical and doctrinal – through transformation of currently available cultural materials (Daggers 2013: 159–71).

Note also that it is to be expected that Christian cultural materials will be borrowed and transformed to other cultural uses. Given the entangled nature of the relationship between Euro-American Christianity and secularizing detraditioning, it is important for Christian theology to reappropriate Christian materials that have been borrowed for other uses. As Graham Ward observes, psychological, anthropological and philosophical discourses 'attempt to colonize, appropriate and transfigure' distinct Christian theological vocabulary (Ward 1999: 48). While applying his insight to the borrowed notion of 'salvation', it is important for Christian theology to reappropriate 'salvation' as a discrete Christian material so that theological debate can work creatively with this received doctrine, transforming borrowed materials to the Christian use of proclaiming salvation in Christ, rather than allowing this discrete Christian idea to be rendered invisible in its transformation for alternative purposes.

One corollary of this move is that incommensurate differences between Christian traditions, between Christianity and other religious traditions, and between Christianity and detraditioned practices come into view. Where the generic makes visible common ground and encourages encounter around commonalities, local traditions in dialogue can risk acknowledging irreconcilable differences in the course of hospitable encounter. Rather than generic terms being laid down for interreligious exchange or for inclusivity, each local tradition that elects to take part will need to define for itself what George Lindbeck refers to as its own 'different warrants for interreligious conversation and cooperation' (2009: 40–1). Inclusivity becomes receptivity towards those who seek encounter as insiders or outsiders to a local tradition.

In this way, local Euro-American Christian traditions can be remade in a postcolonial mode to face towards diasporic Christianity, religious diversity and secular scepticism, while borrowing newly available cultural materials to resist Eurocentrism and to remake colonizing attitudes. With this aspiration in view, attention now turns to the particular Christian notion of salvation in Christ. The aim of the discussion is to investigate how available cultural materials are being transformed to Christian use in service of the church's mission within a reinvigorated world Christianity, in interreligious hospitality and in witness to detraditioned Euro-American culture.

Salvation in Christ: That Persistent Christian Question

The modern Euro-American anthropological turn prioritizes human subjectivity and agency over divine initiative. Given the stress on human self-determination, it is not surprising that pluralist notions of alternative salvations should appeal: in this perspective, by chance or by choice, human beings set themselves along one way of salvation among others. Different forms of Christian churches, different religions or different detraditioned secular or spiritual practices can be seen as presenting a plethora of alternative salvations. The generic habit insists that alternatives be viewed as equally effective paths to the same goal, so allowing all options to be included within a single project. The anthropological focus, coupled with a Euro-American cultural commitment to inclusivity, creates a cultural field that bears on Christian theology as it speaks of salvation in Christ.

On reviewing the received tradition of theological debate, it is striking that salvation is both central to Christian theology and a long-standing source of passionate disagreement. To speak of salvation is to be reminded of the nature of theology: a human discourse about God that reflects on how God has revealed God's self in the world through acts of creation and redemption. In this speaking, human life is caught up in the divine life of the triune God, in the effects of the *Missio Dei* in which the Son and the Spirit are sent to the world. To speak of salvation is to remember that our contemporary life is lived in the space between what is already achieved in Christ and the kingdom that is yet to come, or to put it differently, is lived in Christian anticipation of salvation as union with the triune God. To speak of salvation, then, is to speak eschatologically. However, the eschaton is only sensible by means of revelation, so theology, as Barth insists, is *nachdenken*, a thinking after what has already occurred; thus theological thinking comes *after* what Gerald O'Collins refers to as the 'primary divine "search" for human beings' (O'Collins 2008: 63), which is to be completed in the eschaton.

When Christian theology debates the reach of salvation, this question concerns God's intentions towards all people, as discerned by theologians. The debate that has run and run concerns the universality or particularity of salvation: this is connected with dogmatic beliefs in heaven as the single destiny for all humankind versus the double destiny of heaven or hell, which requires judgement and division. As Morwenna Ludlow shows, the Pauline statement in I Cor. 15:24, 28, that at the end 'God may be all in all', has been read to imply a universalist eschatological hope that the whole cosmos will be saved – yet, due partly to the influence of Augustine of Hippo, the dualistic stream that asserts the possibility of hell as well as heaven as eternal destiny has been more powerful from the fifth and sixth centuries (Ludlow 2000: 1). In the cultural field of a powerful imperial church, universalist views of (unconditional) salvation were seen as threats to ecclesial authority and the stability of society, and the association of universalism with immorality and social upheaval persisted into the European modern period (Ludlow 2000: 2–3). The anathematizing in 533 of universalism as *apokatostasis*, based on Origen's interpretation of the reference in Acts 3:21 to 'the time of the restoration of all things' (*apokatastaseôs pantôn*), set the baseline for subsequent orthodox understandings of salvation (Hilborn and Horrocks 2003: 220–1; Ludlow 2003: 192–3).

In contrast, the contemporary Euro-American field is more conducive to notions of universal salvation where Christianity is located as one way among others; there is pressure on Christian theologians, too, to abandon dualist commitments to a double destiny in favour of a single universal salvation. As I will show, recent eschatological thought on salvation remains divided. On the one hand, there are those who hold fast to the dual destiny. On the other, universalism is developed in response to the challenge arising from contemporary Euro-American anthropological and inclusive commitments that strongly resist any such division of humankind, and even more strongly protest the incompatibility of eternal punishment in hell with the nature of a loving God.

Contemporary divisions emerge from post-Reformation theological debate. Magisterial Protestant reformers held to the doctrine of dual destiny. For Luther, this was essential if the principle of justification by faith was to be upheld (Hillborn and Horrocks 2003: 220). Calvinists consolidated salvation through God's election alone, upholding particular redemption of the elect over against Arminian emphasis on human decision to accept or reject the universal redemption in Christ, which is available to all (Marlowe 2005). Reformation history, including English non-conformity, is riven with disputes between the orthodox centre ground, Catholic and Protestant, and a complex interrelated tangle of often sectarian groupings who formulated – often in secret – a variety of universalist-tending ideas. This marginal yet prevalent universalism was informed by theology but also reflected Renaissance humanism and – from the eighteenth century – Enlightenment egalitarianism (Ludlow 2003: 199–206; Hillborn and Horrocks 2003: 220–5). Ludlow identifies two main forms of universalist thought as evident in eighteenth- and nineteenth-century developments: 'purgational universalism' (Rowell in Ludlow 2003: 204), which maintained that the purpose of post-mortem punishment was to reconcile all people to God; and 'hyper-Calvinism', which accepted Calvinist doctrines of predestination and atonement, but insisted that all people were saved (Ludlow 2003: 205). As we will see, versions of 'purgational universalism', with an emphasis on reformative rather than retributive punishment, reappear in contemporary evangelical universalism.

Significantly, the Enlightenment academy provided an arena where universalist ideas took centre stage in public debate, initially in controversy over the eternity of hell and whether the threat of eternal hell was effective in shaping moral conduct (Ludlow 2003: 207). This is important not only because it moved the issue from the shadows of its association with radical sectarianism, but because it demonstrates the way in which Christian debates transcended the limits of Catholic and Protestant orthodoxies, to be shaped by respected proponents of rational religion, as much as by authorized Christian theologians. This shift in the arena of debate demonstrates the dynamic behind the generic habit discussed above, insofar as Christian ideas were taken up to form generic categories. One implication for Christianity is that discrete Christian materials may be borrowed for subtly different uses, without this change in use being immediately apparent.

Even while the Enlightenment academy subjected the threat of eternal hell to rationalist critique, ambivalence persisted about the moral effects of denying hell as reality. Hillborn and Horrocks note, at the same time, a growing 'moral disgust at the idea of endless divine retribution' (2003: 227). No doubt influenced by the tenor of this wider debate, as Ludlow comments, Friedrich Schleiermacher was the first major theologian to consider universalism since the Patristic period (2003: 207). Questioning how a doctrine of eternal punishment of sinners was compatible with the 'eternal fatherly love of God', and pointing out that the biblical evidence for eternal damnation is inconclusive (cited in Ludlow 2003: 207), Schleiermacher asserted the election of all humanity to salvation in Christ (Hillborn and Horrocks 2003: 227). Ludlow also finds tentative expressions of 'hope' that all will eventually be saved, in eighteenth- and nineteenth-century pietist circles in Würtenberg, and in the work of both Soren Kierkegaard and F. D. Maurice (2003: 208–9).

Universal Salvation in Christ? Renewed Contemporary Debate

In the limited space available here, the final part of this essay considers three focal points within contemporary theological debate where a case is made for the hope of universal salvation – over against an enduring Calvinist commitment to a dual destiny in the eschaton.[6] My contention is that all three may be understood as productive instances of the borrowing – for *theological* purposes – of local Euro-American cultural inclusivism. Shrinking each instance back to its Euro-American local will allow dialogue partners within world Christianity, the interreligious arena and the detraditioned secular constituency of the local Euro-American world to engage with these theologies in terms of their own choosing, rather than in imposed generic terms.

The first focal point is an unexpected surge of universalist thinking within recent evangelical theology. One significant factor here is the considerable impact of Karl Barth's 'soteriological universalism' (Kärkkäinen 2003: 16–19). Barth's universalism is consistent with his theology of revelation, with its emphasis on Christ as the 'Revealed'. It depends on the dual role Barth ascribes to Jesus Christ as both 'Electing God' and Elected Man', in whom all humankind is chosen for salvation (Kärkkäinen 2003: 18). For Tom Greggs, this hopeful assertion of 'eschatological universalism' is entirely dependent on Barth's 'christological exclusivism' (2011: 189). In other words, notions of 'alternative salvations' are firmly ruled out by Barth's identification of salvation with Christ alone. But excluding the possibility of alternative ways allows Barth to hope that all are included at the eschaton.

Read in this way, Barth opens the door to a 'hopeful universalism' as opposed to a 'dogmatic universalism' (Lincoln in Hillborn and Horrocks 2003: 236). The collection, *Universal Salvation? The Current Debate* (Parry and Partridge 2003), shows a widespread evangelical reluctance to adopt this hope.[7] Hillborn and Horrocks see reasons for this reluctance in the findings of Boyd and Eddy's 2002 study, *Across the Spectrum: Issues in Evangelical Theology* (cited in 2003: 238). Their observation that universalism is implicitly bracketed with pluralist theology of religions (2003: 238) is important for the argument of this essay: for evangelicals, Barth's 'hopeful universalism' may provide a way to new theological insight, whereas Hick and Knitter's pluralist method is firmly rejected.

The problem of hell persists for local Euro-American Christians who are drawn or challenged by cultural inclusivism. Notions of post-mortem salvation are deployed to assert a biblically based alternative to eternal torment in hell,[8] thus nudging closer together evangelicalism and a post-mortem version of universalism. For Bonhoeffer, talk of *apokostasis* (universalism) 'may be never more than the sigh of theology wherever it has to speak of faith and unfaith, election and rejection' (cited in Greggs 2010: 157, 165): this local Euro-American moment is certainly a time for such theological sighing. As an evangelical Barthian scholar who seeks to undo the binary of the dual destiny, Greggs writes:

> While we may not wish to move from a dogmatic form of separationism to a dogmatic form of universalism, to have a wider hope grounded in the graciousness of God we may ... point to the tension that exists in understanding our conversion as a response to God's undeserved free-loving kindness – a tension which sees the insider on the inside undeservedly and united to the outsider in shared sinfulness, and which thus makes us undogmatic about where the friendliness of God in Jesus Christ may be found because we are so dogmatic that the friendliness of God in Jesus Christ has found us. (2010: 157)

His words provide a good example of an evangelical openness grounded in what Paul Nimmo calls 'a highly particular [Barthian] universalism' (2010: 35); such openness is ready to bear witness to its own convinced theological stance, but is also fit for respectful engagement with world Christianity, interreligious diversity and detraditioned Euro-American secularism.

Moving to my second focal point, post-Vatican II Roman Catholicism, a parallel move is evident of a revival of debates on universal salvation from a position of traditioned openness. Catholic voices had been muted subsequent to the definitive Second Council of Constantinople in 533, but this was to change in the post-Vatican II context. Karl Rahner both shaped and reflects the spirit of Vatican II in its new openness to dialogue with those outside the Catholic Church; he exerted an influence in Catholic theology equivalent to that of Schleiermacher and then Barth in reformed theology. A strong parallel can be drawn between the path opened by Barth's 'hopeful universalism', and a reading of Rahner's (less well defined) attitude to universal salvation, informed by his anthropology and his hermeneutics.

The availability of grace to all human beings (through the supernatural existential and the *Vorgriff auf esse*) creates the hope of salvation for all. However, Rahner also retains the possibility of eternal loss, through a hermeneutic that accepts the paradox of irreconcilable scriptural tension between universal salvation and a dual destiny for humankind at the eschaton (Ludlow 2000: 241–7). As Ludlow comments, 'Rahner's view of universal salvation is coherent and attractive when expressed in terms of hope', even though there remains a difficult eschatological tension in his leaving open the possibility of hell (2000: 247). This reasserted hope resonates with the spirit of the times in Rahner's local Europe.

In the current generation, the European-centred Vatican II impetus towards dialogue connects with the imperative towards ecumenical dialogue within world Christianity, interreligious dialogue and engagement with detraditioned secularism. The authorized magisterial position on Catholic attitudes to other religious traditions has recently been clarified (Becker et al. 2010). While the possibility of other religions being upheld as alternative ways of salvation to the Catholic Church is explicitly excluded, the inmost consciousness and intrinsic meaning of other religions is respected *'from within the Christian order of salvation'* (2010: 511). Rahner's 'hope' and 'possibility' are palpable when this respect is grounded in awareness that the values and limits of other religions 'will be revealed at the *parousia*, when God will reconcile all things and be all in all' (2010: 510).

Gerald O'Collins (2008) widens the skirts of this hope by making a scriptural argument for 'the salvation of God's "other peoples"' (2008: v) and thus for 'the universal scope of God's offer of salvation' (2008: vi). O'Collins's traditioned commitment to Christ as the universal Revealer and Saviour grounds his argument about God's intended salvation of God's other peoples. I suggest he repeats the Christian theological logic that underlies Rahner's use of the term, 'anonymous Christian': to locate all human life within the scope of salvation in Christ.

The figure of Lady Wisdom, Sophia, features large in O'Collins's exposition, allowing him to envision both Christ and the Holy Spirit in the feminine terms of universal Wisdom (2008: 233, 243). Sophia creates a bridge with my third focal point – universal salvation according to liberation theologies, with particular attention to feminist theology. The biblical figure of Sophia invites all people to her feast (O'Collins 2008: 57), to an abundant table with room for all. This vision of the eschaton – of the kingdom that is not yet come – is a driving force in traditioned liberation theologies. The vision places in stark relief the unjust lack in the lives of the poor. Liberation theology's powerful new interpretation of salvation as liberation (Gutierrez 1973) generates an imperative towards realizing this heavenly vision on earth through the struggle for justice.

It is possible for this struggle to sit within a similar notion of inaugurated salvation to that assumed by both Barth and Rahner. As Ludlow puts it, an inaugurated eschatology assumes 'the grounds for the fulfilment of the universe were established in the creation and re-established in Christ after the Fall; thus a process of perfection has begun in him through the Spirit, but will not be completed until the end-times' (2000: 259). So understood, the struggle for justice is placed in the space between the already achieved and that which is to come.

The struggle for gender justice works in solidarity with other global justice struggles, including those grounded in detraditioned secular projects or in other religious traditions. The figure of Sophia in feminist theology (Fiorenza 1995; Johnson 1995; Kim 2002)[9] can be deployed to maintain a traditioned place for feminist theology. Sophia allows Christian liturgy to be re-energized by drawing on the biblical feminine divine – as engaged by O'Collins – so relieving a long-assumed maleness in the triune God (Daggers 2014). More important for the argument here is that the vision of humankind invited to Sophia's abundant table inspires a hope that all people may be included in salvation, coupled with a commitment to work for justice in these in between times. Given the sheer evil at work in the world in systematic structural injustice, and our complicity within it, the hope in universal salvation may still be tempered by the possibility of judgement.

Conclusion

In conclusion, this essay has argued that a generic category of alternative salvations reflects a modern Euro-American colonizing and universalizing tendency, where local Euro-American notions are assumed to have a global reach. In response, my contention is that 'salvation' may usefully be shrunk back to its context within the Western tradition of Christian theology. Within this local tradition, understandings of salvation have been strongly contested. A recent concern with renewed theologies of universal salvation – explored in brief in evangelical, Catholic and feminist theologies – can be seen as different forms of local Euro-American response to a local cultural concern with social inclusivism. My contention is this shrinking to the local allows traditioned voices to be open to dialogue within world Christianity, interreligious encounter and engagement with detraditioned secular Western values. If these dialogue partners choose to respond with polite bemusement or outright rejection to notions of their being within the reach of salvation in Christ, that would only point out the very local nature of this particular Christian idea. At least, traditioned openness provides a visible alternative to the aggressive Christian mission that arises from over-exuberant conviction of a dual destiny in the eschaton, wherein all hope of universal salvation is eliminated.

Chapter 10

'Unlock Paradise with your own Blood': Martyrdom and Salvation in Islam and Christianity

Paul Middleton

There was none other good enough
To pay the price of sin;
He only could unlock the gate
Of heaven and let us in.

(Cecil F. Alexander 'There is a Green Hill far away', 1847)

If you have to lay down your life for God ... it is not in gentle fevers and on soft beds, but in the sharp pains of martyrdom. You must take up the cross and bear it after your Master, as he himself instructed you. The sole key to unlock Paradise is your own life's blood.

(Tertullian, *On the Soul*, 55)

Martyrdom and Salvation in Islam

Arguably, the twenty-first century so far has been significantly shaped by the actions of fewer than twenty men, who on the morning of 11 September 2001 hijacked four planes, and flew two of them into the 'Twin Towers' of the World Trade Center, New York. As iconic as it was deadly, more than 3,000 people, including the nineteen hijackers, were killed on the day now known simply as 9/11. The attack led to the then US President George W. Bush to declare a 'War on Terror', leading to subsequent invasions of Iraq and Afghanistan. That he also called this response as a 'Crusade'[1] fuelled the 'Clash of Civilisations' narrative (cf. Huntington 1996), the effects of which continue to shape the world's political and religious landscape, particularly of the Middle East.

The attack also brought to worldwide prominence the mode of 'suicide-attacker'. However, 9/11 was by no means the first occasion such tactics had been used. Since Russian anarchists employed explosives at the beginning of the twentieth century to kill both themselves and their targets, Japanese kamikaze pilots, the Tamil Tigers, the Kurdish Workers Party, the Syrian Nationalist Party, Hezbollah, Palestinians and Chechens all deployed suicide missions to some effect against stronger enemies (Pape 2003; Gambetta 2005a). Therefore, although 'suicide bombing' is particularly associated with Islamist groups in the modern mind, it is worth noting that the majority of suicide missions have been carried out by secular groups (Gambetta 2005: 261). Nonetheless, the rhetoric used by modern 'suicide-attackers' to explain or justify their assaults have been couched specifically in terms of the Islamic martyr tradition.

For example, in June 2001, Ismail Masawabi, a well-educated Palestinian, killed himself and two Israeli soldiers in a suicide attack. From his 'martyr-video' it is clear he understands himself to stand in the long line of Muslim martyrs who die fighting for freedom and justice.

> Thanks be to God who brings about the mujahedeens' victory and the dictators' defeat. ... Dear Muslim youth the world over: I greet you with the blessed greetings of Islam; greetings that I send to all of you who fight in the name of religion and the nation; ... The wish to become a martyr dominates my life, my heart, my soul. ... We are a nation living in disgrace and under Jewish occupation. This happened to us because we didn't fight them; we didn't fight for God. (Quoted in Reuter 2004: 90–1)

Masawabi goes on to explain that inaction in the current crisis is not an option for the true Muslim, and that he prefers 'to meet God and leave humankind behind' before warning his audience that God will not forgive any who do not rise to the challenge and fight for Islam. He then expresses the belief that his actions will take him to heaven:

> My brothers and my family: I shall be in Paradise where everything will be mine. So don't be sad that you've lost me. In Paradise I shall be immortal, so you should be glad that I'm there.

While Western politicians are often at pains to resist connections between 'terrorism' and Islam, that numerous posters, murals, songs and internet sites (Bunt 2003) celebrate the actions of those who kill and die for God demonstrates that Masawabi's narrative was plausible enough to fuel the Palestinian martyr cult, which praises its *jihadi*-martyrs (Bloom 2005: 19–44).

Al-Qaeda employed a similar narrative after 9/11. Osama bin Laden set the conflict within the parameters of an apocalyptic Holy War, mirroring George W. Bush's Crusader-inspired 'clash of civilisation' ideology:

> The world has been divided into two camps: one under the banner of the cross – as the head of the infidels, Bush, has said – and one under the banner of Islam. ... Adherents of Islam, this is your day to make Islam victorious. (Quoted in Middleton 2006: 7)

It is within this potent apocalyptic context that Islamic notions of *jihad* and martyrdom meet. Yet, this is not a new development in Islamic martyrology.

Islamic martyr theology was essentially shaped by the early battles against the Meccans. Although ultimately victorious, Muslims endured military setbacks, and therefore had to account for those who died in conflict. The solution was to develop a conception of martyrdom where God would reward the fallen.

> Do not think those who have been killed in the way of Allah are dead; they are rather living with their Lord, well provided for. Rejoicing in what their Lord has given them of his bounty, and they rejoice for those who stayed behind and did not join them, knowing that they have nothing to fear and that they shall not grieve. (Qu'ran 3:169-70)

It is important to note that the very earliest traditions made little distinction between the rewards for those killed in battle and those who died in other ways (Affsaruddin 2014; Cook 2007). However, by the mid-eighth century, the battle-martyr interpretation was firmly established in exegetical tradition, along with the rewards such martyrs could expect.

> The martyr has six distinctive features in the presence of God: God forgives his sins as soon as the first drop of his blood strikes the earth; he will enjoy the vestments of faith; he will marry a dark-eyed damsel; a door to Paradise will open for him; he will be spared the torments of the grave; and finally, he will be kept safe from the greatest fear, that of the Day of Resurrection.[2]

While the seeds of Islamic martyr theology are found in conflicts with outsiders, it was developed in the foundational Sunni – Shi'a intra-community dispute, and the decisive battle at Karbala, commemorated on the Day of Ashura.

Importantly, therefore, since Islamic martyr theology developed in the context of battle, the 'martyr-killer' is *not* an incongruent concept. Furthermore, while suicide is forbidden in Islam (Qur'an 4:29), Hussein's inevitable death at Karbala provided the means by which commentators can incorporate 'suicide operations' into the sphere of martyrdom. A number of *fatwas* have declared that modern 'sacred explosions' are not suicides, but acts of sacrifice.[3] So speaking *specifically* about Palestinian suicide bombing, Egyptian scholar, Yusuf al-Qaradawi, insisted:

> It is not suicide, it is martyrdom in the name of God. Islamic theologians and jurisprudents have debated the issue, referring to it as a form of *jihad* under the title of 'jeopardising the life of the *mujaheed*'.

For al-Qaradawi and others, this form of attack, carried out for the right motives, is similar to 'plunging single-handed into the enemy with reasonable certainty of being killed'. Since this can be permitted, so too are those circumstances where the 'holy warrior's' death is certain in the attack.

The most extreme appropriation of classical martyr theology was found in the Iran–Iraq War (1980–8). After Saddam Hussein's invasion of Iran, Ayatollah Khomenei, invoking the spirit of Karbala, recruited hundreds of thousands of young men to charge the Iraqi front line in mass human suicidal waves, until either they overran the enemy or were mown down by Iraqi gunners. Banners bearing the slogan: 'Every land is Karbala ... every day is Ashura' encouraged Shia Iranians to see themselves as heirs to Hussein's martyr-army, fighting against the errant Sunni Muslim. It is widely reported – though physical evidence is lacking – that volunteers were issued with keys to be worn round their necks which would open the gates of Paradise on death. Khomenei declared, 'The tree of Islam can only grow if it's constantly fed with the blood of the martyrs' (see Reuter 1994: 33–51). Iranian soldiers were told their martyrdom would result in entry to Paradise.

These historical snapshots demonstrate widespread, though by no means universal, belief in the efficacy of martyrdom, which at least for some includes 'suicide missions'. Such actions are rooted in ancient Qur'anic exegetical traditions, in which martyrs constitute a category of 'special dead' who attract specific rewards, buy exemption from general judgement by bartering their own lives (Qur'an 4:74), effectively (whether the Iranian key story is true or not) unlocking Paradise with their own blood. While Islamic martyr theology has attracted criticism, many of these martyr-tropes are anticipated in early Christianity,[4] in which Christians could similarly win salvation by voluntarily shedding their own blood through martyrdom.

Martyrdom and Salvation in Early Christianity

In one of the earliest creedal statements preserved in the New Testament, St Paul writes:

> For I delivered to you as of first importance what I also received, that Christ died for our sins (ὑπὲρ τῶν ἁμαρτιῶν ἡμῶν) in accordance with the scriptures. (1 Cor. 15:3)

For Paul, as for all New Testament authors, the death of Jesus was a decisive salvific event through which the sins of believers could be forgiven. While there is some variation in the New Testament over the precise mechanics of atonement (e.g. Hengel 1981; Frey and Schröter 2005) the authors generally assent to Luke's affirmation that there is 'no other name under heaven by which people can be saved' (Acts 4:22), and that the shedding of Jesus' blood is the significant factor in effecting salvation. So for John, 'The blood of Jesus ... cleanses us from all sin' (1 Jn 1:7), while the author to the Hebrews insists the singular nature of Christ's atoning sacrifice: Jesus is

> a high priest, holy, blameless, unstained, separated from sinners, exalted above the Heavens [who] has no need ... to offer sacrifices daily, first for his own sins

and then for those of the people; he did this once for all when he offered up himself. (Heb. 7:26-27; cf. 9–10)

However, some early Christian texts trouble both the singularity and sufficiency of Christ's suffering and death.

In Colossians, both appear to be challenged, as Paul's suffering seems to contribute to the as yet incomplete work of salvation:

> Now I rejoice in my sufferings (ἐν τοῖς παθήμασιν) for your sake (ὑπὲρ ὑμῶν), and in my flesh I compete what is lacking (τὰ ὑστερήματα) in Christ's afflictions (θλίψεων τοῦ Χριστοῦ) for the sake of his body (ὑπὲρ τοῦ σώματος αὐτοῦ), that is, the Church. (Col. 1:24)

Whether or not the letter is by the hand of the apostle, Paul is presented as in some way making up for a perceived shortfall in Christ's suffering. Arthur Droge goes so far as to suggest Paul is here presented as 'a second Christ' (1988: 263).

A similar idea is found in 2 Corinthians 1:5-7, where Paul and his fellow-workers 'share abundantly in Christ's suffering' (τὰ παθήματα τοῦ Χριστοῦ), which is for the church's 'comfort (παράκλησις) and salvation (σωτηρία)'. In 2 Corinthians, Paul also envisages that members of the church will share in the suffering of the apostles (1:7; see Lim 2009). Paul usually presents himself as an imitator of Christ, and urges his churches to imitate him in turn (1 Thess. 1:6; 1 Cor. 11:1; 2 Cor. 1:6; Gal. 4:12; cf. 2 Thess. 3:7, 9). Moreover, Paul can even speak of himself being poured out as a sacrificial libation for the faith of his churches (Phil. 2:17; cf. 2 Tim. 4:6-7). As such, Paul's suffering is 'for' the church, and so even if the presence of any expiatory significance in Colossians 1:24 is contested, it is clear that Paul's suffering performs a vicarious service.

However, Paul is not alone in this blurring of the distinction between Christ's suffering and that of the early Christians. As believers began to die for their faith, the martyrologies that followed modelled stories of the martyrs on the death of Jesus and adopted some of the theological claims about his death. This development is already underway in the Book of Revelation.

Revelation

Martyrdom is a prominent feature of the Apocalypse.[5] In fact, Revelation contains the earliest depiction of martyrs in a post-mortem state:

> I saw under the altar the souls of those who had been slain for the word of God and for the witness they had borne; they cried out with a loud voice, 'O Sovereign Lord ... how long before you will judge and avenge our blood on those who dwell upon the earth?' Then they were each given a white robe and told to rest a little longer, until the number of their fellow servants and their brothers should be complete, who were to be killed as they themselves had been. (Rev. 6:9-11)

The judgement theme that pervades the Apocalypse is here intimately connected with the experience of the martyrs. They call for vengeance on 'the inhabitants of the earth' (6:10), a *technicus terminus* for those who worship the Beast (13:3, 8, 16). Moreover, Revelation's judgement is delayed until a certain number of martyrs are killed (6:11); martyrdom is a way in which Christians can hasten the End, by contributing to the number of those who must be killed before judgement takes place (Lee 1998; Middleton 2006: 158–71).[6]

Moreover, as well as bringing judgement forward, the martyrs – as in Islamic thought – buy themselves an exemption from the final judgement. Among the rewards reserved for the martyrs in Revelation is an exclusive early resurrection. Those 'beheaded for their testimony to Jesus and for the word of God, and who had not worshipped the beast' come to life and reign with Christ for a thousand years (20:4). Only after this are the rest of the dead raised for judgement, at which point they will be judged by what they have done (20:13-14). However, martyrs are exempted (20:6); their martyrdom saves them from judgement.

As with many early Christian accounts of suffering, John links the martyr's experience with that of Christ's. In the Apocalypse, Jesus functions as the proto-martyr (Middleton 2015); he is described as the faithful witness/martyr (ὁ μάρτυς ὁ πιστός),[7] the firstborn of the dead and the ruler of the kings of the earth (1:5). While many readers have read the death of Jesus in the Apocalypse as a model of non-violent acceptance of suffering (e.g. Bredin 2003; Blount 2005), his act of martyrdom also fully incorporates his vindication, resurrection and elevation to the position of judge, who smites the nations with a rod of iron (19:15). Martyrs in Revelation 'follow the Lamb wherever he goes' (14:4), and this includes his martryogical pattern of death, resurrection and glorification. (Middleton 2015: 232–6). The martyrs are also presented as faithful witnesses (e.g. Antipas is ὁ μάρτυς ... ὁ πιστός in 2:13); they are redeemed from the dead (14:3) and sit on Christ's throne (3:22) to reign (20:6) and judge the nations (2:26). In other words, the martyrs do what Christ does. They not only 'wash their robes and make them white in the blood of the Lamb' (7:14), but also supplement Christ's blood with their own (16:6) in order to win salvation. In Colossians and Revelation, we witness the genesis of a soteriological problem within early Christianity. As Jesus' death became a paradigmatic model of discipleship, those who followed his path of suffering and martyrdom came themselves to function in some way as 'second Christs'.

Martyrs as Alter Christi

As Christians sought to interpret experiences of persecution and suffering, they turned to the model of Christ's passion. Through developing an understanding of themselves as constituting a 'suffering body' (Perkins 1995), early Christians were able to transform experiences of suffering from hardships which had been endured (e.g. Gal. 1:4; 2 Thess. 3:1-2) into joyful opportunities to imitate Christ (e.g. Phil. 2:5-11; Mt. 5:11-12//Lk. 6:22-23; Jas. 1:2). Suffering and martyrdom became the ultimate sign of commitment to Christ, so that in the letters of Ignatius, we witness a strong link between discipleship and martyrdom.[8] Those who wish to be disciples, he writes, must imitate Jesus (Rom. 6.3) and 'voluntarily choose to die into his suffering' (*Magn* 5.2). Ultimately, for Ignatius, it was only through martyrdom that one could finally *become* a disciple:

> Let me be food for the wild beasts, through whom I can reach God. Better yet, coax the wild beasts, so that they may become my tomb and leave nothing behind. ... Then I will truly be a disciple of Jesus Christ, when the world will no longer see my body. (Rom. 4:1-2)[9]

This idea is not entirely new in early Christianity. The cross saying (Mk 8:34//Mt. 10:38//Lk. 9:27; Q14:27), especially in its Markan version, indicates that taking up the cross is a *precondition* rather than a consequence of following Jesus. 'If anyone wishes to come after me, let him [first] deny himself, [next] take up his cross, and [only then] follow me' (Mk 8:34).

Similarly, Hebrews holds up the suffering Jesus as a model to emulate:

> So Jesus also suffered outside the gate in order to sanctify the people through his own blood. Therefore, let us go forth to him outside the camp and bear the abuse he endured. (Heb. 13:12-13)

Both Mark and the author of Hebrews, therefore, create a pattern of discipleship modelled on the suffering and death of Jesus. To be a disciple of Jesus one must suffer like Jesus. As if to illustrate the point, in the earliest recorded story of Christian martyrdom, Luke creates explicit parallels between Stephen's stoning and Jesus' crucifixion (see Pervo 2009: 168): Stephen is seized, tried by the Sanhedrin, false witnesses accuse him of blasphemy and threatening the temple. In death he commits his spirit to Jesus, cries aloud and prays for his persecutors (Acts 6:8–7:60).

The idea of martyrs modelling Jesus is developed in the second- and third-century martyr acts. Some narratives explicitly pattern the deaths of the martyrs on Jesus' Passion (Moss 2010: 45–75). In the *Martyrdom of Polycarp*, there are several clear points of connection (see Dehandschutter 1982: 660–1): Polycarp predicts his death; he is betrayed by one of his household; rides into the city on a donkey; prays for the church, hears a voice from heaven; and his body is pierced. Furthermore, the martyr is a 'sharer in Christ' (Χριστοῦ κοινωνός; 6.2) to the extent that Christ is the pilot (κυβερνήτης) of his body (19.2). As well as mirroring the death of Jesus in his own sufferings, the martyr enjoys a form of mystical union with Christ (cf. Gal. 2:20; Phil. 2:13).[10] As the identities of Christ and the martyrs became intertwined in Christian martyrologies, theological accounts of Christ's death began to bleed into theologies of martyrdom. In what follows, I highlight three areas where the martyrs take on significant theological aspects generally reserved for Christ's death: the defeat of Satan, sacrifice and salvation.

Martyrdom as Overcoming Satan

In the synoptic Gospels, Jesus is portrayed as an exorcist; the 'strong man' who overcomes Satan (Mk 3:22). However, for other New Testament writers, the decisive means by which Jesus defeats Satan is his death (e.g. Jn 12:31-33; 1 Cor. 2:8; Heb. 2:14-15; 1 Jn 3:8). Christians are, as a result, able to overcome Satan through resistance (1 Pet. 5:8-9), God's help (Rom. 16:20), or importantly, as in the Apocalypse, through martyrdom (Rev. 12:11).

Early Christian accounts of martyrdom set the martyr in the midst of a cosmic conflict (Middleton 2006), where the principal enemy is Satan rather than the Roman State. After one of her prison visions, Perpetua, who had been condemned to the beasts, realizes 'that it was not with wild animals I would fight, but against the Devil' (10:14). In the *Martyrs of Lyons*, the persecution of the Christians is set in an apocalyptic context, where Satan marshals his troops against the church, 'swooped down with full force', and 'training and preparing his minions' for their battle 'against God's servants' (1:4-5). Furthermore, sadistic jailors are said to be 'aroused and filled with the Devil' (1:27), while Ignatius also attributes 'cruel tortures' to the Devil's doing (Rom. 5:3).[11]

Significantly, Satan's goal is not to cause the death of the Christians, but to tempt them away from their confession of faith.

> Those who were condemned to the beasts endured terrifying torments. ... The purpose was that, if possible, the tyrant might persuade them to deny the faith by constant torment. For many were the stratagems the Devil devised against them. But thanks be to God, he did not prevail against all of them. (*Mart. Poly.* 2:4–3:1)

However, some in the church did deny under torture. In the *Martyrs of Lyons*, those who fell away are said to be 'untrained, unprepared, and weak, unable to bear the strain of a great conflict' and 'stillborn' (1:11). They were 'ensnared by Satan' (1:14) and 'devoured by the Devil' (1:25). By contrast, those who achieved martyrdom repressed (καταπιέζω) and overwhelmed (καταργῶν) Satan (1:23, 42). Perpetua also achieves this victory, trampling on the Devil's head (*calcaui illi caput*; 4:7; 10:11; cf. Rom. 16:20), through her martyrdom. Similarly, Tertullian states:

> The Christian is snatched by faith from the jaws of the devil, but by martyrdom he fells to the ground the enemy of his salvation. By faith the Christian is delivered from the devil, by martyrdom he merits the crown of perfect glory over him. (*Scorpiace* 6)

For Tertullian, while faith is enough to save the Christian from Satan's grasp, when the martyrs follow Christ's example of suffering and death, they also share in his cosmic victory over the Devil.

Martyrdom as Sacrifice

Sacrifice is the second theological element of Christ's death attributed to martyrs (see Castelli 2004: 50–68; Moss 2010: 83–7). The sacrificial element of Christ's death is found throughout the New Testament (e.g. 1 Cor. 5:7; Eph. 5:2; Heb. 9:14, 26), as both an offering to God and for the people. As Christ became the Passover Lamb (1 Cor. 5:7), Polycarp is said to be a ram offered as a burnt offering to God:

> So they did not nail him, but tied him instead ... like a splendid ram chosen from a great flock for a sacrifice, a burnt offering prepared and acceptable to God. (*Mart. Poly.* 14:1)

This image of Polycarp invokes the *Aqeda* (Gen. 22), which was itself an important lens for early Christian interpretation of the death of Jesus. As with Christ's death, Polycarp's martyrdom benefits the Christian community. His death 'put an end to the persecution, as though he were setting his seal upon it by his martyrdom' (1:1). Polycarp's death becomes in effect a death *for* others.

Ignatius also speaks of his impending martyrdom as a beneficial sacrifice to God (Rom. 2.2; 4.2). On several occasions he states or prays that his sacrifice might be a 'ransom' (ἀντίψυχον) for the faithful (*Poly.* 2:3; 6:1; *Smyr.* 10:2; Eph. 21:1). Maturus and Sanctus are also described as sacrifices (*Mart. Lyons* 1:39). Martyrs, therefore, are found to enact the notion of discipleship as sacrifice found in the New Testament (Rom. 12:1; 1 Pet. 2:5).

Behind much of this sacrificial imagery is the presentation of Jesus in Hebrews. In this letter, Jesus functions as both high priest and sacrifice. Origen exploits this idea in writing on the martyrs:

> For just as those who served the altar according to the Law of Moses thought they were ministering forgiveness of sins to the people by the blood of goats and bulls, so also the souls of those who have been beheaded for their witness to Jesus do not serve the heavenly altar in vain and minister forgiveness of sins to those who pray.
>
> At the same time we know also that just as the High Priest Jesus Christ offered himself as a sacrifice, so also the priests of whom he is High Priest offer themselves as a sacrifice. This is why they are seen near the altar as near their own place.
>
> Moreover, blameless priests served the Godhead by offering blameless sacrifice. ... And who else is a blameless priest offering a blameless sacrifice than the person who holds fast his confession and fulfils every requirement the account of martyrdom demands? (Origen, *Exhortation to Martyrdom*, 30)[12]

Origen merges the image of Jesus as priest and victim in Hebrews with the presentation of the martyrs in Revelation as both blameless sacrifice and priests of God. Furthermore, he explicitly links the function of Christ's death with the martyrs. Just as Christ died to atone for the sins of the people in the same way as the priests of the old covenant used the blood of goats and bulls for the same purpose, the martyrs are also able to minister forgiveness by means of their own blood. Just as the high priest offered himself as a sacrifice, so also do the priests of the high priest. Christ's transaction in Hebrews works because he is a blameless priest offering a blameless offering. Similarly, martyrs, by virtue of their martyrdom, function in heaven like Christ as both blameless priests and the offering, and are thus able to forgive the sins of those who pray. Origen's theology of martyrdom clearly threatens the uniqueness of Christ's atoning sacrifice found in Hebrews.

Martyrdom and Salvation

Third, Origen's belief that the martyrs are not only sinless, but appear to be able to forgive the sins of others appears in other early Christian texts. We saw earlier that the Devil ensnared and devoured some of the Christian community in Lyons. However, successful martyrs snatch back some of those souls, so that 'the dead were restored to life through the living' (*Mart. Lyons* 1:45). Those who had previously denied saw examples of successful martyrdom and rushed back to the arena to retract their denial, and so were 'conceived and quickened again in the womb' (1:46). This is not quite the cosmic forgiveness of sin found in Origen, but it is the martyrs that provoke the repentance of the deniers, and who force Satan to 'disgorge alive all those whom he at first thought he had devoured' (2:6). However, martyrs and confessors, as those who model Christ most closely, were believed to possess the power to forgive sins and therefore grant salvation. Perpetua is able to alter the post-mortem fate of her brother, changing it from suffering to peace (*Pass. Perpetua* 7–8).

By the end of the second century a rudimentary martyr cult had developed (Brown 1980) as the status of martyrs become elevated. Relicts were collected (cf. *Mart. Poly.* 17–18) and worship was held near their graves. Moreover, martyrs and confessors came to rival the authority of the developing episcopacy (Klawiter 1980). In Saturus' prison vision, Perpetua intervenes in a dispute between a bishop and a presbyter (*Pass. Perp.* 13:1-4), suggesting – at least in some Christian circles – that martyrs outranked the offices of bishop and presbyter.

This tension between the respective authority of martyr and bishop developed through the third and fourth centuries, especially in the aftermath of the persecutions of Decius, Valerian and Diocletian when the church had to deal with the large numbers of the lapsed (see Middleton 2012). The lapsed turned to the confessors – those who modelled Christ most closely – to pardon their betrayal. Cyprian (*On the Lapsed*) and Tertullian complained about the too easy restitution offered for the lapsed, with the latter restricting the power of the martyrs to 'purging their own sin' (*On modesty* 22). This is significant. In attempting to curb the power of the martyrs, the early church fathers theologically crystallize the popular idea that those who endure martyrdom effectively save themselves. So, Tertullian asks:

> Who does not join us, and joining us, does not wish to suffer, that he may purchase for himself the whole grace of God, that he may win full pardon from God by paying his own blood for it. (Tertullian, *Apology*, 50)

Other writers, such as Origen express similar ideas, but the logic is devastatingly simple. The Book of Revelation depicts martyrs in heaven before the general resurrection, therefore martyrs must have a special status to be raised instantly. Martyrdom was considered to be a second baptism (e.g. *Pass. Perpetua* 21:2). Since baptism was the washing away of sins, martyrs were by definition sinless at the point of death, and so by baptizing themselves in their own blood, attained salvation.

Conclusion

The martyr is a controversial figure, as likely to provoke fear and suspicion as admiration and respect. The term has always been contested in both Christianity and Islam (Middleton 2014), with the suicide bomber's martyrological status being particularly contested today. While attempts have been made to distinguish between 'true' and 'false' martyrdom in both traditions (Wicker 2006), other studies have argued that even these attempts constitute nothing more than a 'martyr-making' process; martyrdom simply becomes a death of which the narrator approves (Middleton 2014). Even the so-called 'lust for death' in contemporary suicide missions can be compared to the early Christian phenomenon of 'voluntary martyrdom' (Middleton 2006, 2013; cf. Moss 2012; Buck 2012), or even what Droge (1989; Droge and Tabor 1992: 113–28) takes to be Paul's suicidal musings on whether to remain with the Philippians or go to the Lord, driven by the clear conviction 'to die is gain' (Phil. 1:23).

Martyrs display extreme acts of devotion or commitment to their cause. For early Christians, martyrs most closely re-enacted the passion of Christ and inspired devotional cultic activity. The cult of the martyrs grew into the more full-blooded Christian cult of the saints, including a concern for the collection of relics[13] that provided subsequent generations with a tangible link to both the martyr, and through him or her, Christ. Similar cultic remembrance is found in Islam through the commemoration of Karbala on the Day of Ashura, or the near cultic commemoration of modern Palestinian martyrs. Behind these celebrations is the conviction that martyrs comprise a category of 'special dead'.

In both Christianity and Islam martyrs attain rewards for their devotion. The most significant of these appears to be an exclusive reward; exemption from the normal process of eschatological judgement. Jensen insists post-mortem reward is 'a necessary part of any theology of martyrdom' (Jensen 2010: 140). However, while post-mortem punishment seems to act as a deterrent to denial in early Christian martyrologies, there is little evidence reward is the *primary* motivation in either Christian or Islamic forms of martyrdom. Nonetheless, religious reflection on martyrdom led to an exalted status of the martyrs and the practice, so that Tertullian's quip that the 'sole key to unlock Paradise is your own life's blood' could have been written for many Islamic as well as Christian contexts. Even if the report about the physical 'key to paradise' in the Iran – Iraq war should be doubted, the story resonates strongly with early Christian beliefs that martyrs can save themselves. Furthermore, in early Christianity, martyrdom constituted not only a rival locus of authority to church leaders, it also blurred the uniqueness of Christ's salvific death. In both Islam and Christianity, therefore, martyrdom becomes a potent alternative source of salvation.

Chapter 11

CHRISTIAN SALVATIONS IN A MULTI-FAITH WORLD: CHALLENGING THE CULT OF NORMALCY

Wayne Morris

Introduction

What does salvation mean for Christians and what implications have beliefs about salvation subsequently had for people of other faiths? The response to both parts of this question is multiple and complex. There is no one way in which Christianity has singularly and universally articulated what it means by 'salvation' and this has meant that the role of soteriological discourses in Christian praxes towards people of other faiths reflects this multiplicity. Nevertheless, in Western forms of Christianity, it is here argued, a particular dominant soteriological paradigm has emerged to become the principal framework that has informed and is informed by historic Christian approaches to people of other faiths. It is this dominant paradigm that so many Christian theologies of religions have wrestled with since the middle of the twentieth century when the need for alternative soteriologies began to be developed in a new religiously and spiritually complex world. By looking at this dominant paradigm of salvation through the lens of disability studies, this chapter argues that soteriological discourses have been used to reinforce a Christian 'presumption of superiority' (Suchocki 2005: 154) over people of other faiths that have led to praxes of the normalization of religious others. That being so, this chapter explores how alternative salvations from within Christianity may be useful for developing alternative praxes for a multi-faith world today, conscious that the future of the planet is largely dependent on respectful forms of human co-operation that were not necessarily observed in the past.

Intersectionality: A Methodological Approach

In recent years, the disability movement has experienced a considerable amount of fragmentation as this once, apparently homogenous political movement, became a source of oppression for some for whom it was supposed to be a force for positive transformation. Groups such as the Deaf community wished to be identified as an indigenous minority language group in the UK, akin to first language Welsh speakers (Ladd 2003: 16), while, it has been argued the civil rights and social justice agendas of many disability rights activists sought rights that people with severe intellectual disabilities could never attain: autonomy, independence, employment and the right to make decisions about one's own life (Reinders 2008). The disability movement has fragmented because the lives of the people about whom it sought to 'speak' [sic] were far more complex and diverse than a single agenda had the capacity to respond to. While this fragmentation mirrors developments in other identity and civil rights groups, increasing attention has been given more recently to the intersections between diverse oppressed peoples. Robert McRuer's *Crip Theory* (2006) is a case in point. In this work, McRuer draws on queer theory to offer insights into the complex and multiple experiences of disability. He argues that while identifying as queer and identifying as disabled are not the same experiences, many of the structures, systems and philosophies that lead to oppression are common to many marginalized groups (McRuer 2006: 2) Thus, in challenging such oppression, there is value in the intersections between identity groups being highlighted so that struggles for transformation can be realized through solidarity between oppressed groups.

While identifying as disabled and identifying with a particular religious or spiritual pathway are also not the same experience, this chapter aims to draw on disability studies and disability theologies to highlight some of the structures, systems and philosophies – and theologies – within Christianity that have been used to justify negative Christian praxes towards people of other faiths. In particular, I will draw on the principle of able-bodied praxes of normalization to highlight the ways that Christianity has developed theologies that insist that people who subscribe to its beliefs are normative and those who do not are considered both to be abnormal (not Christian) and subsequently in need of normalization (conversion). This has led to significant acts of aggression and oppression by Christian persons and nations towards people of other faiths. I do not pretend that Christianity has always been the aggressor and other religious traditions and spiritual pathways the oppressed; relations between people of faith are more complex than that. However, because this text is written from a Christian perspective, I aim to interrogate some of the traditions in which I am located in a Western (post?) Christian context through a lens of disability studies. In so doing, I seek to think about how the notion of salvation in particular has been used to justify a Christian sense of superiority over people of other faiths, and to challenge my own tradition to consider why alternative salvations are, therefore, necessary.

Disability and Normalcy

In a work on theologies of disability, Thomas Reynolds discusses what he calls 'the cult of normalcy' (Reynolds 2008: 28). By this he means the ways in which groups construct concepts of normality that become 'representative of a community's identity or sense of itself and, accordingly, functions by marking out and idealizing those attributes and capacities competent to contribute to its good' (Reynolds 2008: 48). Thus, the one with the idealized attributes and capacities is set up as normative and good while those who do not conform to such ideals are labelled as 'abnormal' and bad. Such concepts of normality are dependent on what societies consider to be of the greatest value to them. That has variously included qualities and characteristics such as capacities in economic productivity, education, physical prowess, the capacity to fight in war, to have children and so forth. Whichever of these qualities are considered to be valuable to a society become almost sacred qualities, while the bearers of them are given a privileged status.

Because different societies value diverse qualities and characteristics, Davis argues that disability is an 'unstable' and fluid category (2013: 271). There is no universal or fixed notion of what constitutes disability and, therefore, subsequently, normalcy. What normalcy serves to do, however, is provide boundaries by which those with power can reinforce their own position of superiority while labelling as 'other', 'abnormal', 'different', 'disabled', those who do not conform to such norms. As a result, because people with disabilities are often perceived to be less important to society, medicine and science have largely been orientated towards the eradication of conditions that are considered to be disabling, or else people with disabilities have been hidden away, subject to abuse, violation against their bodies and sometimes even killed. The cult of normalcy has the potential for devastating consequences for those who do not conform to its criteria.

Salvation as Normalization

Mainstream dominant Christian theologies of salvation have been developed by particular groups and institutions that have understood themselves to be normative and good so that soteriological discourses serve to justify the enforced normalization, or alienation, of those considered to be 'abnormal'. Dominant Christian understandings of salvation generally include three key parts that make a complete soteriological narrative: first, an understanding of a condition that is so wretched that it necessitates salvation; second, there is usually a description of a process or mechanism through which salvation is realized; and third, there is a construction of an end state of salvation, a utopia or vision of a better and improved reality than the one from which salvation is needed (Morris 2014: 37). For illustrative purposes, we will consider the second stage, the process or mechanism for realizing salvation, and the proposition that 'faith' is necessary for salvation to move from one state into a new and better one. However much we may wish to discuss what faith actually is, in practice, faith is generally understood to be something tested through a person's public confession and/or subscription to a set of beliefs and ideas. Therefore, it is assumed, in order to be saved, a person will normally have language and the intellectual capacities to learn a set of beliefs and make choices and decisions about them; what is assumed is able-bodied normativity (Morris 2011: 121–34). Or consider the notion that to be in a state of salvation, the third stage, is to be deified; to become God. Given that the human quality that has been understood to most closely reflect God's likeness and image has been the capacity to reason, to become like God – to enter a saved state – presupposes again not only able-bodied normativity, but male normativity too since it has been assumed that men are more rational creatures than women (see Vogt 2003: 49–59).

Dominant Model of Salvation Informing Christian Engagements with People of Other Faiths

If Christian soteriological discourses can be understood as having three key aspects to them in the way described above, what has the dominant soteriological model looked like with regard to people of other faiths? If, as Augustine argued, human beings are in a state of original sin, then this is the principal understanding of the state from which human beings need salvation. While that sin may well be expressed in human acts of evil, sin is something more than simply things that human persons say and do, it is fundamental to the human condition itself, present in us as a result of the fall. There are a number of processes by which that normalization can be realized through conversion. Baptism has been key in many Western traditions as the process by which salvation is ensured, hence the historic emphasis on infant baptism. In many Protestant traditions, a personal decision of faith has become important whereby a person is first persuaded and then declares a personal faith in Jesus that is thought to lead to their salvation. Whichever process is emphasized, salvation is achieved through a human act, the legitimacy of which is determined by those already in the churches. Another dimension to the process whereby salvation is made possible is located in the death and resurrection of Jesus Christ. Without that, it is understood, salvation would not be possible by human efforts alone. It is only that event that opens up a way for humans to be saved. Humans remain in a state of original sin, but live in confidence and hope that that sin will be removed once they enter Paradise. In the dominant understanding of salvation, the saved state can never be fully realized in this world. It can be worked towards, and human persons can engage in processes that secure their salvation, but the saved state is only fully realized in the life beyond death. While such an outline of the dominant model of salvation may appear crude and oversimplified, it is my hope that it is recognizable to most readers familiar with Christian understandings of salvation.

With regard to people of other faiths, this means that because every person is in need of salvation and because all are in a state of original sin, the transformation into a new and better reality, a saved state, is something that everyone needs. Such a position serves to justify the need for Christian persons to engage in seeking the conversion of non-Christians to Christianity. All are in a state of 'abnormality' in the sight of God, and the pathway to normalization is through conversion to the saved state, normativity, that only Christians possess. The processes by which salvation is possible are controlled by the Christian community. Only by participation in rites of passage or declarations of faith, and in conformation to Christian ideas and practices, is salvation a real possibility. Finally, because salvation is only ever fully achieved in the life beyond death, the suppression and oppression of people who do not conform to Christian norms has been justified on the understanding that salvation does not pertain to concrete acts of injustice in the here and now, but to the state of original sin, release from which is only possible in the world to come. More so, the cause of future eschatological salvation of human persons has been used to justify acts of violence, oppression and death for the purposes of achieving that salvation. Let us explore this further.

Salvation as Normalization of People of Other Faiths

This same cult of normalcy, that sets up one group as normative, and insists that salvation can only be found through conforming to those norms is at the heart of dominant Christian theologies and practices of salvation. When it comes to religious or spiritual difference too, we can find many examples of this in Christian historical engagement with people of other faiths. Sugirtharajah notes how, in the nineteenth century, Christians were encouraged to become missionaries, arguing that if Christianity could have so many benefits for Britain, then it could also have the same impact in the newly colonized lands. He cites the 1813 publication, the *Missionary Register*, to show how this case was made:

> Your own ancestors, in this very Island, once worshipped dumb idols: they offered human sacrifices; yea, their sons and their daughters unto devils: they knew not the truth: they had not heard of the name of Jesus. ... But mark now the contrast: you now are a favoured nation: your light has come: the glory of the Lord is risen upon you: all these heathen rites have ceased ... an established Christian Church lifts its venerable head: the pure Gospel is preached: ministers of the sanctuary, as heralds of salvation, proclaim mercy throughout the land. (Sugirtharajah 2001: 63)

Sugirtharajah (2001: 62) argues, 'The intention was to turn the former waywardness of the British and their present state of maritime power into an irresistible argument for the spread of the gospel.' Colonialism was thus justified as having benefits to colonized peoples, giving them the opportunity to experience temporal transformation from living in a state of 'savagery' and 'barbarity' found in their indigenous spiritualities and practices, to a new and improved state of 'civilization' and military prowess, realized because of Christianity.

George Tinker, commenting on colonial Christianity in North America, argues that the missionary message of 'salvation in Jesus alone' led to the 'unequivocal disavowal of the beliefs, experiences, ceremonies, community connectivity, and religious traditions of one's own culture' (Tinker 2008: 130). Such an understanding of salvation in Christianity is derived from and reinforced 'amereuropean Christian triumphalism' (Tinker 2008: 129), he explains. Soteriological discourses, therefore, were used to argue that spiritual pathways and expressions different to Christianity were of no value or worth, but inferior to and necessarily superseded by Christian beliefs and values. The exclusivist claim that salvation is only possible through Jesus means Christians have complete control over the normative pathway to a new and improved reality from which all people in all places need salvation.

Further, Brock and Parker have argued that Anselm's understandings of atonement and his view of the sacrificial death of Christ justified the Crusades against Jews and Muslims in three ways. First, saving souls of those who would otherwise be lost was seen as essential. Second, because Christ had died for the salvation of the world to satisfy God's honour, anyone who rejected the Crusaders' gospel affronted Christ. To satisfy God's honour was, therefore, the duty of the Crusader. Third, it was thought that sacrificing one's own life for Christ as Christ had done for humanity, provided an assurance of one's own salvation. Thus both 'killing and being killed imitated the gift of Christ's death, the anguish of his self-sacrifice, and the terror of his judgement' (Brock and Parker 2008: 270). Salvation was thus about an insistence on conforming to a particular set of beliefs that would lead to the same eschatological end for everyone. In working towards and achieving that normalization, perhaps some of the most violent and deadly acts of history have been committed in the name of Christian soteriology.

Conscious of the often devastating consequences such soteriological beliefs and practices have had in Christian history, since the 1960s, alternative theologies of salvation have begun to be developed that have sought to value other religious beliefs and spiritual pathways, but they too often succumbed to the same agendas of normalization. Take the threefold typology of Alan Race (1983), represented by pluralisms, inclusivisms and exclusivisms. Exclusivisms and inclusivisms maintain that salvation is still only possible in the life beyond death and that salvation is realized through faith in, and the actions of, Jesus Christ. Both maintain the normativity of Christian pathways to salvation while continuing to focus on the realization of a new and better reality outside of this world, often failing to address the injustices of this world and the way such theologies of salvation have been used to oppress people of other faiths. Pluralisms, on the other hand, have often taken more seriously the possibility that salvation is something that can be realized in this world, such as in the work of Paul Knitter (1985). However, they still often take Christian understandings of salvation as normative and argue that other religions, to varying degrees, either have the same discourses about salvation as Christianity (e.g. Hick 1996) or that the usefulness of religions can be measured against what are effectively Christian notions of salvation (e.g. Knitter 1985). Both proposals are problematic. What I argue here, however, is that alternative Christian salvations need to be used to displace the dominant understanding of salvation, salvations that cease to see people of other faiths as persons in need of conversion, and therefore normalization, to Christianity. Soteriologies are also needed that focus not on a future eschatological salvation that can justify or ignore all kinds of injustices in the present, but that speak of salvation as the construction of new and improved realities in this world.

A Need for Alternative Salvations

While a departure from a Christian superiority complex that views people of other faiths is needed to ensure the violence of the past is not repeated, the present makes new demands on Christianity that mean alternative salvations must be considered. Reflecting on the events of 9/11, Duncan Forrester argues that contemporary Christian theology is now confronted with the 'urgent life and death question of how to understand, discipline, channel and criticize the powerful ideological forces of religion which in fact dominate the global political scene' (Forrester 2005: 33). This, I argue, involves among other things, the Christian churches taking stock, reflecting on their history of approaches to people of other faiths and seeking to think about alternative possibilities; this is required if the future of our planet is to be secured and relations with people of other faiths in an increasingly complex and multi-faith world is to be improved. The Christian superiority complex, based on a particular understanding of Western Christian normativity, if perpetuated, will surely only lead to history being repeated whereby Christians seek to impose their norms onto others. We have already seen the kinds of consequences that this has had.

If salvation is about recognizing a condition from which salvation is necessary, a process for realizing salvation and a sense of what the end state of salvation could look like, then what resources, even within Christianity itself, might shape new attitudes and practices towards people of other faiths? In particular, I am interested to explore here how those practices might change if our soteriological gaze is orientated away from questions about whether people of faiths might be saved from some concept of original sin into a post-mortem heavenly possibility, to an understanding of salvation as dealing with concrete and systemic sins that are detrimental to human flourishing in the present, with a view to constructing alternative soteriologies that lead to transformation in this world. Such understandings of salvation, while present but historically marginalized in mainstream Western Christian traditions, provide a rich resource for reshaping Christian beliefs and praxes towards people of other faiths and spiritual pathways. Difference is not seen as something to be normalized, therefore, which might provide an alternative future paradigm for Christian relationships with those people who represent religious and spiritual difference. In the remainder of this chapter, I will outline what one such approach to salvation might look like and consider in brief what the implications of such a soteriology might mean for Christian engagements with people of other faiths and spiritual pathways.

Salvation as Healing

Perhaps the most obvious way of thinking about salvation in the Christian tradition that would be of value to the argument here is the consideration of the notion of salvation as healing. The word, often translated as 'healing' in English, is a translation of the Greek, σώζω, to save. This is the most obvious approach to salvation because this chapter seeks to think about Christian engagements with people of other faiths and spiritual pathways in light of disability theories and theologies. The notion of healing has been important in those discourses. Salvation as healing has often been interpreted in light of the dominant understanding of salvation outlined earlier, as a form of normalization. The healing narratives in the gospels have been used to argue that there is no place in the kingdom of God for the person with a disabled body and that only when their bodies conform to able-bodied normativity will they be eligible for the kingdom of God. That conformation to able-bodied normativity will happen either in this world or the next, it is supposed. If a disabled person does not conform, it is thought that this is because of either a lack of faith or unrepented sin (McCloughry and Morris 2002: 98). However, readings of these gospel texts from disability perspectives have opened up new and alternative interpretations of these texts. In the remainder of this chapter, I will consider one example of such a re-reading of a healing narrative and consider its significance for soteriological thinking and practice with regard to people of other faiths and spiritual pathways.

The story of the Deaf man in Mark 7:31-37 is one account of 'healing' that has been used to justify the conformation of a Deaf body to hearing normativity. In brief, the Deaf man is presented to Jesus by others and his companions beg Jesus to lay hands on him. Without a moment's hesitation, Jesus turns the Deaf man into a hearing person and so, by implication, is saved from his Deaf state. He has no agency over what happens to him, but rather the decision about what should happen is made on his behalf. At first glance, therefore, this does not appear to be a liberating account of salvation for Deaf people, many of whom do not see their deafness as something that is in need of cure (e.g. Hunt 1996: 24-5). Indeed, it could be interpreted as a discourse of normalization. However, Deaf readings and hermeneutics of the narrative tell a different story. I have discussed this story elsewhere and draw on fieldwork with Deaf people to inform the reading of the narrative outlined below (Morris 2008: 102-4).

A Deaf Reading of Mark 7:31-37

The following provides an account of Deaf readings of this healing narrative. In response to the friends of the Deaf man, Jesus takes the man away from the crowd. Many Deaf people have some residual hearing and crowds can be very difficult and uncomfortable places to be if there is noise. So Jesus takes the man aside and begins to communicate with him away from the place of discomfort. Jesus touches him and then begins to communicate with him. Jesus engages with the man physically by touching his ears and tongue. Many Deaf people get the attention of one another by touch, and engaging with other people in this tactile manner is 'normal' for most Deaf people (though perhaps touching their ears or tongue would be considered inappropriate). The man can only see and touch and so Jesus does not speak with him, but rather simply looks up towards heaven in a physical act. Many Deaf people have explained that this story exemplifies someone who communicates with the Deaf man in a way he would have understood. Then Jesus says the word, '*Ephphatha*' – be opened. This is a remarkable moment in the account because the words of Jesus are recorded in Aramaic in the midst of a Greek text. Deaf people have noted that the word '*Ephphatha*' can easily be lip-read in a way that the Greek, '*Dianoichtheti*', cannot (because the noises and sounds are created inside the mouth) (Davies 2002: 148–9). Jesus communicates in a way that the Deaf man can understand and, perhaps, the gospel writer deliberately records the term that Deaf people could see. The first miracle in this story, therefore, is not that the Deaf man can suddenly hear, but rather that for once there is someone who understands the life of a Deaf person and is able to communicate with him in a meaningful way.

This, for Deaf people, is the moment of healing, of salvation, when Jesus shows he has learnt the language, the means of communication of Deaf people. He has taken on their culture, their way of seeing and being in the world, and he engages with them. This is salvific because the new reality is one in which Deaf ways of inhabiting the world are honoured and this is an improved state over that of marginalization and exclusion that the Deaf man would have previously experienced. The second miracle is that, following the man's new found capacity to hear, he is also suddenly able to speak. For someone who is an adult, and who has never previously heard a language, to suddenly be able to speak that language and understand it is remarkable. It would be as remarkable as a hearing person suddenly finding they can speak another language they have never heard before. Jesus enables this because it means that the Deaf person will no longer live in the kind of isolation which many Deaf people experience on a daily basis because they cannot communicate with their neighbours. Rather, he will be able to function as a part of society and be fully in community once more.

Salvation as Healing and Christian Engagements with People of Other Faiths

Two miracles have been identified in the story above that can be understood as soteriological in that they transform the state of the Deaf man – and Jesus and the crowd – from one state into a new and better reality. On the one hand, the Deaf man is treated as a person worthy of the attention of Jesus, and Jesus engages with him on his own terms and he becomes the centre of Jesus' attention. On the other hand, the experience of being able to engage with Jesus and the crowd as an equal is liberative for the Deaf man, Jesus and the crowd. The person who was once isolated and marginalized, because he happened to be different to the rest of society, is enabled to participate fully in it to the benefit of all. This, for Deaf people is the moment of salvation in the story, not the cure of deafness, but an event that enables this marginalized person to be a part of society. While this involved the Deaf man being made hearing, it is reflective of a society that could only be inclusive in that particular way. If inclusion and participation in society is the key to the narrative, however, that could be achieved by different means today. Engaging with a person on their own terms and in their own language, and providing means through which they can participate in society are understood to be the two key salvific dimensions for all participants. So what might the significance of that be for Christian engagements with people of other faiths and spiritual pathways?

First, salvation need not necessarily involve Christians insisting, as a precondition for respectful and honourable treatment, that people of other faiths become like them. If engagement with people of other faiths is to be taken seriously, there is a need to learn the language and culture of those with whom Christian persons wish to engage and to use it in their encounters with others. That act alone can be understood to be soteriological. Indeed, rather than seeing the person of another faith as an enemy to be made like us or else persecuted, a new and better reality is realized than the one we already inhabit by engaging with people of other faiths as people whose language, culture, way of life, beliefs are honoured. Second, through this engagement, the Deaf man enters into a position of being able to participate fully in society. This second part of the narrative should not be understood as full participation being made possible only after the Deaf man is made to hear, but rather as a moment in which space is created for reciprocity. Just as Jesus had learnt and used the preferred method of communication of the Deaf man, so that man in turn discovers the language of Jesus and the crowd around him and can relate to and communicate with them. Thus a new kind of relationship of reciprocity is realized. In turn, if Christian persons can seek to understand salvation as a possibility in this world where they create new realities by engaging with people in their own terms, that reality may be further developed by the people of other faiths discovering more ways of positively engaging with members of the Christian faith.

Conclusion

Soteriological discourses matter not simply because they are matters of faith for Christians, but because how Christians think about salvation has implications for their engagement with people of other faiths. Using the lens of disability theories and theologies it has been argued that the dominant soteriological paradigm of Christianity in the West has historically assumed the rightness and superiority of Christianity over people of other faiths and spiritual pathways and subsequently considered that all are in need of normalization. Such an understanding has led to acts of marginalization, oppression, violence and death that have created mistrust between people of different faiths who often have each perceived the other as enemies. However, Christian theology has more to say about salvation than the dominant paradigm suggests. It is also concerned with this world, the ending of injustice and inequality, the creation of new and improved realities in the here and now and a Christian responsibility to foster such change. This chapter provides a brief outline of why such alternative salvations are needed and has, tentatively, explored the question of what such a soteriology would look like. It is hoped that in exploring the riches of the Christian tradition further, we can begin to rediscover more ways of thinking soteriologically that speak to the state of the world at present and provide resources to help make engagement between people of faiths better.

Chapter 12

GENDERED CONSTRUCTIONS OF SALVATION: OVERCOMING THE BINARIES

Emily Pennington

Introduction

I begin my chapter with an invitation for you to join me on a theological fence. Perhaps not the most comfortable place, but certainly the most interesting and, I hope, fruitful position from which to start our explorations. Sue O'Sullivan writes that 'sitting on a fence can be an exciting pastime. Perched, half in comfort and half scared you'll tip over, not quite sure which way to look, but with unique vantage points, it has a lot going for it' (1996: 112). Fence-sitting thus straddles two pastures; both secure and precarious. It is this perception of coexisting realities that forms the content of this chapter. The pastures upon which we will gaze are the well-known dualisms of traditional Christian thought: mind and body, spirit and flesh, life and death, future and present and, ultimately and respectively, male and female. We have been encouraged, if not implored, to dismount on the side of the first of these couplings. The choice is, however, illusory, for the fence from which we began is, in fact, an erroneous division erected by patriarchal theology. This division has served to devalue all that is associated with the female by depicting it as separate and subordinate to the male.

Many feminist theologians have responded to this by seeking to reverse the binary by prioritizing the present, embodied life. Although helpful, such perspectives are ultimately insufficient for they essentially surrender the spiritual and future dimensions of life to their patriarchal constructions. There has certainly been cause to favour the female, but what is now needed is a return to that divisive fence in order to *destroy* the fence and its pretence of value-laden separation. Thus, while I am firmly rooted in a feminist theological appreciation of material, embodied life I seek to marry this with an eschatological understanding of future, salvific existence. In so doing, I hope to illustrate how that which has been deemed inferior and inconsequential to eschatological life is *no less* integral than that which has been prioritized. Moreover, I will show how attending to these neglected and discredited dimensions of existence may even illuminate the specific nature of eschatological life. Ultimately, this means that eschatology need not be rejected by feminist theology but can instead be rethought in ways that both confirm and inform its concerns.

Identifying the Problems

On the surface, the Christian tradition seems to both appreciate and affirm embodied existence, what with the centrality of the Incarnation and the emphasis on the resurrection of the body. Further probing, however, reveals a marked suspicion of the body, and the female body in particular. Images of saved life contribute to and confirm this suspicion. In the spirit of Plato, the Christian tradition has made the masculinized spirit superior to the feminized flesh. Rosemary Radford Ruether has exposed and expounded this Platonic dichotomization of spiritual transcendence and material embodiment, and the attribution of the former to the male and the latter to the female (2002: 67). She claims that this association indicated a radical shift in mainstream thinking, as man came to be understood as partaking in 'the same transcendent status as God, outside of and above nature' (2002: 67). Platonic thought, then, introduced the dualistic idea that the male is to be associated with that which is transcendent and spiritual on account of him being the authentic incarnation of the soul. The female, on the other hand, was seen to represent the corruption (and corruptibility) of the soul, which manifested itself in her association with fluid and tumultuous materiality (Keller 1996: 102). The association of the female with the material and the male with the spiritual exposes allusions to a future 'spiritual embodiment' as being nothing more than a patriarchal hijacking of the female by the male. Ruether concurs and writes that 'redeemed life is perfected spiritual masculinity. Women can become "perfect," whole, and spiritual, only by rejecting everything about themselves that, both culturally and biologically, was identified as specifically female' (1998: 30). Such perspectives can only serve to devalue women's lives by defining their bodies as dangerous and threatening to, and therefore absent in saved existence.

These are not, however, mere inferences and allusions. The Gospel of Thomas, for example, makes this gender-conditional salvation explicit: in verse 114, Jesus is purported to equate Mary's salvation with her 'becoming male' (Stefaniw 2010: 344). The oppression of women here is twofold as Stefaniw explains that women were to be seen as male in their spiritual life and female in their social life. This meant that women were required to deny their womanhood in order to partake in redemptive communities, but simultaneously retain their 'femaleness' socially, as this pertained to the way they should be treated (Stefaniw 2010: 348). This, of course, simply reinforces the identification of the male with the infinite and redemptive, and the female with the finite and corruptible. Whether intended or inferred, be it literally or symbolically, the Christian tradition has promoted the idea that women's bodies (as women and as bodies) are not as capable as male bodies at partaking in saved existence. Such imaginings have legitimized the patriarchal vilification of women's bodies – bodies depicted as irrefutably material and mutable.

This association of women with mutability has been deemed to be located in women's embodiment of the restrictions and limitations of present life. As Miller-McLemore articulates, 'Bodily, monthly, women know life's limits' (1994: 145). Such limitations are named in terms of finitude and transience; attributes that have been greatly feared by a patriarchal theology that prizes the ability of the intellectual and the spiritual to endure forever. Most predominant and most pertinent is the fact that this fear has been manifest in the usurping of female live-giving powers. The fear rests on the belief that as women bring life, they also ensure death. This has particular relevance when thinking eschatologically, as the Christian tradition has suggested that eschatological existence requires a rebirth by and through the Father God. This rebirth supposedly remedies material restrictions that culminate in death; restrictions that have been placed on creation by the 'condition' of being born of a woman. Jantzen makes a similar observation, noting that the Christian tradition has often framed salvation in terms of a necessary reparation or correction of the 'maternal birth'. She observes the notion within the tradition that 'it is only by this rebirth, which redoes or undoes the maternal birth, that it is possible to be a "child of God," to become divine' (Jantzen 1998: 143). This devalues women's experiences of birthing and mothering and deems them inconsequential to, and even preventative of, experiencing eschatological life. Keller notes that this spiritual substitution of mothers deems them 'eschatologically expendable' (1997: 57). In addition to the association of women with materiality, then, the particular ways in which women experience this embodiment have been used to suggest that women's bodies have no place in the story of salvation or the future of creation.

Valuing the Material and Mutable

In response to this I, along with many feminist scholars, propose that we revalue rather than refute the association of women with the material and the mutable. The way forward is not to deny that women's bodies change but rather to dispel the myth that gendered, embodied change warrants vilification. Feminist theologians have often sought to do this by redirecting their attention to life in the present. Patriarchal theology has highlighted the female body's capacity to embrace both life and death. Along these lines, some feminist theologians have sought to reclaim and rename death as an integral, albeit tragic and often painful, aspect of life. Carol Christ and Grace Jantzen are most vociferous in their support of this perspective, with both suggesting that an acceptance of the limitations of life redirects our attention to the here and now and compels us to 'enjoy whatever time is left as much as possible' (Christ 2003: 124; cf. 1987: 95; Jantzen 1984: 36). It seems that death is both sobering and encouraging: it reminds us that we are indeed limited, but inspires us to seek the best possible life within these limitations. Death, then, orients us to life. This contrasts with the more traditional perspective that death (not forgetting its female mediator) is something we require saving from.

Christ and Jantzen's approach to neither deny nor become inordinately concerned with death, but instead to reconfigure it from the perspective of affirming materiality is, to be sure, a beneficial approach and one that informs my own explorations. However, I suggest that accepting death as conclusive both lacks hope and indicates an acceptance of the final obliteration of materiality by mortality. Far from an acceptance of death orientating us to an appreciation of life's fleetingness, then, it actually makes the present the sole locus of reality. In so doing, no alternatives are made available to the suffering and death we experience: the body ceases to exist at death, rather than being enabled to become more and so endure in the future. Such endurance, though, may be possible and could provide a substantial affirmation of the material. We may rethink the association of female bodies with materiality and mutability in such a way that embodied change comes to be seen as the content of both present *and* saved life.

An Embodied Eschatology

An embodied eschatological existence is, it would seem, a thoroughly biblical vision. 1 Corinthians 15:35-57, with its unequivocal emphasis on the resurrection of the body, is often quoted in support of such claims. The passage specifies that the resurrected body is characterized by imperishability and immortality (15:53). It is important to note here that this need not refer to the body being discarded and *replaced* by a different, imperishable, immortal body. Such constructions come too close to the patriarchal theological depiction of a spiritually embodied existence in the eschaton. As noted, promoting such an existence merely upholds the binary oppositions of the male and the spirit over and above the female and the material. Moreover, there is the possibility that an emphasis on transformed bodily existence undermines life as it is experienced now. Yet if we attend to and interpret the body not only as the inescapable location of our identities but also as God's intended home for us, we see that such perspectives cannot legitimately be upheld. Indeed, the affirmation of the thoroughly material body can and should be *achieved* and not *thwarted* in the eschaton. Moltmann claims that the eternal life we are to experience is not a *different* life from the one we experience now, but is rather a life that makes this life different (1997: 2). The material life endures but is made different, is 'derestricted', to quote Bauckham (1999: 16), so that it may be enabled to endure. Moltmann is emphatic about not rejecting the physicality of lived existence, as elsewhere he writes that 'it is this mortal, this lived, and this loved life which will be raised, healed, reconciled, completed, and thus find its divine destiny' (2010: 62). Here, embodied life is not rejected in favour of either a disembodied or spiritually embodied future. Rather, materiality arrives at its completion, is experienced in full and is eternally imperishable in the eschatological future.

Furthermore, change and flux may be seen as central features of this eschatological materiality, this future embodied life. We can imagine a body which is changed in the future so that embodied change may endure. Carol Christ helps our considerations here by asserting that 'not to be embodied, not to change, is not to be alive' (2003: 45). A future of enduring life that affirms embodiment must accordingly and necessarily also affirm change, lest this new life be nothing like life at all. We can assert, then, that life in the eschaton is typified by the changes that take place in the body *and nowhere else*; as Keller asserts, it is '*as body the self takes place*' (1996: 176). However, such an appreciation of enduring change is admittedly problematic, as change is often associated with limitations and, ultimately, finitude. That which changes ceases to be what it once was, and ultimately ceases to change. Conradie notes that 'the problem remains here that the sting of finitude is death' (2005: 305). Yet as we have seen, there are those who propose that that change is unproblematically founded on this finitude that embraces and enables death. It is not *finitude* that must be overcome, Jantzen writes, but rather *the desire to overcome finitude* (1998: 155). This returns us to the suggestion that death should be accepted as an inescapable and integral part of life. Keller expands on this, claiming that a 'death-free creation [is] unimaginable without *reconstituting* the very elements of which all life is made' (2003: 419). Creation, it would seem, is so accustomed to the experience of death that a cessation of death would compromise the very essence of creation. This suggests that life would not be life if it were endless; if death were not its conclusion. Thus if change is to endure in the eschatological future it seems necessary that death must also endure.

The problem is exacerbated by Hall who notes that, ecologically speaking, the lives of some members of creation, some aspects of the earth, actually *depend* on the death of others. He writes: 'The teleological end of an acorn is to become an oak; and that "transcendent" purpose is also contained within the structure and substance of the acorn. In a real sense, therefore, disintegration and integration, destruction and fulfilment, death and life are present in every organism' (2006: 31). This suggests that if death ceases to exist in the eschatological future, then the acorn endures and the oak tree can never live. The two cannot simultaneously endure. Yet what worth is there to an acorn if it only ever remains an acorn; if its existence is static and prevented from experiencing any potentiality? Change need not *require* death, but may instead be typified by the *transformation of death to life*. The acorn, in this understanding, finds its existence fulfilled in becoming an oak tree; this is, as Hessel-Robinson articulates, 'creation brought to its fullest, most abundant potential in God's future' (2010: 19). Change can thus continue to be present in future embodiment, as we are able to change *within* life as opposed to from life to death. Possessing life does not mean one day dying, but rather living with and in a changing and fluid embodied existence. Change can remain in the eschatological future, but without the tragedy of loss and decay. All shall be held together in a web of life that does not allow space for erosion or sorrow but rather weaves each change together into more and more life.

This has particular resonance with feminist theology because, as has been illustrated, women's bodies have suffered under their association with materiality and mutability. In an attempt to appreciate, rather than denigrate, women's bodily manifestations of this changeability, I now look at a specific embodied experience of women – namely, the experience of the female body as the maternal body. Such an experience epitomizes the reasons provided for the association of women with both life and death; as Mount Shoop notes, 'New life and new death are immediate in pregnancy more than in any other facet of embodiment' (2010: 67). Without wishing to homogenize or normalize certain women's experiences by claiming that all women give birth, I nevertheless affirm that these particular experiences are of theological meaning and value. We may utilize, or 'futurise', Grace Jantzen's symbolic of natality here. Jantzen argues that natality is no more to be associated with birth than mortality is with death: it may be a corollary of it but is not exhaustibly defined by it. Rather, Jantzen writes, natality communicates 'the potential for newness and for hope, the creative possibilities of beginning again that are introduced into the world by the fact that we are all natals' (2009: 8; cf. 1998: 144). Still, Jantzen is clear about claiming the specifically gendered origin that an imaginary of natality carries, as she observes that 'natality cannot be thought of without body and gender' (2009: 48; cf. 1998: 136). Indeed, there are many women who are able but choose not to give birth and/or be mothers. These women's bodies are no less indicative of the eschatological future as they still embody change and fluidity; hallmarks of embodied life. As such, Jantzen enables us to consider natality as a model for eschatological embodiment that is rooted in but is not, ultimately, limited to women's varied experiences of generating life.

Before this is possible, it is important to address the patriarchal constructions of these experiences in order to avoid reproducing them. Not only has there been a simultaneous fear and fascination with the particularly female ability to contain both life and death within her body (Christ 2011: 134), there has also been a desire for individuality and parthenogenesis which denies such origins (Braidotti 1994: 23). Jantzen's ethic of natality successfully challenges both assumptions by emphasizing and valuing these bodily origins. In addition to this though, the birthing body has also been constructed as the consummate image of female passivity; the female body a mere receptacle for and servant to male desire (Ruether 1998: 73). Aristarkhova has responded to this by reconstructing the maternal process as one which requires work. This is framed in terms of 'letting the other be, become, breathe' (Aristarkhova 2012: 175) and as such can be a model of activity which provides a space in which others can live and become living. However, the focus here is still on the female body giving itself for another. Thus it is helpful to add an ethic of mutuality to Aristarkhova's rethinking of maternity. In order to do this, I suggest we balance the giving or making of space for another with Rivera's advocacy of the importance of having a space of one's own (2007: 97). This space must be one of self-love and self-care in order that the activity of the maternal body is not understood as mere self-depletion. A simultaneous affirmation of the self and the other as embodied in maternity can then allow us to view women's bodies as worthy in, of, and for themselves and also as able to cultivate and empower worth in and for others.

In addition to reconstructing problematic constructions of maternity, it is beneficial to attend to difficult experiences of maternity. One particular experience I wish to focus on here is that of miscarriage. While this may seem an unlikely focus given its inherent tragedy, I claim it can actually communicate a specific and substantial *hopefulness*. I have been compelled to think in this direction by L. Serene Jones's article 'Hope Deferred', in which she retells and reflects on her friend's experience of suffering a miscarriage. Here, Jones's friend's womb essentially becomes a tomb, with her friend being forced to confront her realization that 'my womb is a death bed, my body a grave' (2001: 235). Jones's reflections on this provide a window of hope for the tragic experience, and enable us to think of a new model for eschatology that embraces not only women's experiences of birthing but also women's experiences of non-birthing; of having their ability to birth taken away from them. Referring to the crucifixion, Jones claims that Jesus' death occurs in the very depths of God, even in God's womb, and as such indicated God's ability to take death into God's very being (2001: 242). The experience of death within life that occurs in the woman's body as she miscarries can, in this way, be understood as mirroring God's experience of loss on the cross. This is not to romanticize or divinize the woman's suffering, nor should it subsume other women's experiences or make them pale in comparison. Rather, it indicates 'God's solidarity with them' (Jones 2001: 242); God's empathy with the embodied encountering of loss and sorrow that typify many women's experiences of miscarriage.

However, alongside this we may assert that God's engagement with creation is not exhausted at the point of empathy. Continuing with my attempt to reject dichotomous constructions and reconnect the pieces, I contend that God is able to both empathize with the experience of simultaneously embodying life and death, while remaining more than this experience. God is able to embrace and transform this death by enveloping it in God's essential life. Jones' reflections hold together God's empathy with her friend with God's ability to transform the suffering that has necessitated that empathy. She imagines her friend 'finding great solace in her solidarity with this God who has born such loss, her sense of utter aloneness melting away', and she also sees her 'looking at God and being even more amazed and comforted by the differences between herself and this God that holds her' (2001: 243). Again, then, there is a sense in which God is able to take death into Godself and transform this into life. Life in this context may simply (though certainly not ineffectually or insignificantly) pertain to a recognition of the compassion of others and of God, but it can be much more than this. If we think eschatologically, the transformation of death into life fully and finally enables the material experience of a body transformed from death into abundant and eternal life.

Resurrection as a model for new life can thus be (and, indeed, has been) central to imagining an eschatological future where death does not obtain but is, rather, transformed into new life. However, given my desire to speak specifically from and to women's experiences, more discussion is necessary. The particular resurrection narrative of Jesus provides further fuel for our discussion here, as it makes women central to the experience of new life. Hagner notes that it is to women that Jesus communicates the first message of his resurrected life (1998: 109). When the womb has become a tomb, as in Jones's friend's experience, we can look hopefully to the resurrection and see how the tomb of Jesus becomes a womb from which Jesus is birthed into new life. Furthermore, the message of new life is then transferred from the stone womb to the fleshy womb, as the women are called to birth the resurrection story to others (see Mt. 28:8, Mk 15:47, Lk. 24:9). As such, the resurrection story enables us to depict an eschatological life that does not vilify women and seek to usurp their birthing capacities; instead, it centralizes them.

There are, to be sure, issues here. Rambo notes that examples of women speaking and writing theology do not inherently or automatically mean that women were liberated in doing so. '*What* they speak', she argues, 'cannot be overshadowed by the fact *that* they speak' (2011: 40). The point being made here is that women's speech often indicates 'not the power to speak her own truth but the power to speak *the Truth*, something that comes from outside of her' (2011: 46). In the instance referred to above, it is the male Jesus who is both the enabler and the subject of the message that the women bear. Furthermore, in Mark and Luke's accounts the women's message was received with incredulity as opposed to open acceptance. Thus there are certainly problematic gender dynamics present here. However, Rambo invites us to consider an alternative perspective: she argues that women can 'inhabit traditional theological houses without being imprisoned by them' (2011: 52). The message we are concerned with here is that of an eschaton which finds its most articulate expression in the embodied lives of women. This suggests that while being conveyed within the confines of a masculine culture and context, the message borne by women *is* liberating. Indeed, Jesus' entrusting of the message to women was a radical move, particularly when some claim that it is only relatively recently that women have begun to have their voices heard (cf. Keller 2008: 907). Jesus' resurrection, then, emphasizes a life that overcomes both biological death and all of the gendered symbolism held therein, and also the institutional deaths caused by the silencing of women.

Conclusion

These considerations can cause us, albeit cautiously and considerately, to begin to articulate an eschatology that contradicts death, not merely by abolishing it but by creatively transforming it into life. This life is characterized by abundant provision and enjoyment. Moltmann articulates this particularly eloquently, as he writes: 'The fullness of God is the rapturous fullness of divine life; a life that communicates itself with inexhaustible creativity; an overbrimming life that makes what is dead and withered live; a life from which everything that lives receives its vital energies and its zest for living' (1996: 336). Such a perspective posits the life of God and the life we receive from God as the overwhelming reality and totality of creation's existence. This is not to say that the realities of death are discounted;

they continue to be experienced in the here and now and are not, as Jantzen rightly observes, anything to be ignored (2009: 48). Rather, what an eschatological interpretation of natality communicates is a God who cannot, ultimately, allow death to obtain, and who makes central the experience of life. Thus, whether we use the images of birthing, motherhood or natality, the emphasis is consistently on the centrality of women's experiences as a model for thinking about life in the eschatological future. All of these emphasize the creation of new life, 'the possibility of fresh starts, new and creative approaches that can subvert violence and destruction' (Jantzen 2009: 48). The particular violence and destruction that such an emphasis on natality and life can subvert is the patriarchal desire to construct eschatology as the final obliteration of embodiment. An embodied eschatology has the ability to affirm the complexity of women's lives and their experiences of embodiment, even if such complexity makes a comprehensive account of these experiences ultimately elusive. Nevertheless, the partiality I have operated within lends itself to aspects of specificity in which we can both ground and direct our hope. Sufferings and their transformations, whether experienced now or hoped for in the future, have propelled my explorations of what an ultimate transformation of suffering and death may look like. The retention of bodiliness and its corollary of change is a complex, though essential, aspect of eschatological existence, and its simultaneous endurance, transformation and fulfilment is what I have sought to specify here. By reclaiming materiality, we refuse to subscribe to the simultaneous vilification and marginalization of women and to the location of meaning in the present alone. Rather, we can reclaim *both* the embodied lives of women and a future that enables these embodiments to become more than they presently are. Moreover, such an image of salvific life can inform our moves to cultivate such life in the present, as alluded to in my rethinking of the maternal experience in relation to both self and others. The spiritual and the material coexist, are enabled to do so by a God who is both transcendent and immanent, and are thus no longer separated by the fence erected by patriarchal theology.

Chapter 13

ANIMALS AND UNIVERSAL REDEMPTION: ALL DOGS GO TO HEAVEN

Kris Hiuser

The purpose of this chapter is to attempt to show that the idea of animal redemption is not one that is absent in the Bible; rather, I will suggest that the case for animal redemption and restoration is one that can be highlighted through a number of means. This perspective is contrary to a common understanding of animals and their lack of redemption or presence in a redeemed state, based in no small part on the writings of Thomas Aquinas who stated that animals had no part in a redeemed creation. After noting Aquinas' dominating influence regarding a theological outlook towards animals which either actively denies their presence in a redeemed state, or which fails to discuss their presence, I will offer an alternative view. Specifically, this chapter will look at the topic of animal redemption in three ways. First, a look at the eschatological images of the future which exist showing the peaceful presence of both humans *and* animals, as illustrated in Genesis, Isaiah and Revelation. Second, I will examine verses which support the idea that all creation is involved in the redemptive purpose of Christ in Romans, Ephesians and Colossians.[1] In both of these cases, I will show that there is a surprising amount of scholarly consensus regarding the presence of animals in these eschatological and redemptive verses. Finally, I will look at various suggestions as to what this might entail, proposing ultimately a universal restoration and resurrection of all animals.

Aquinas

Thomas Aquinas is a major and influential figure in the Christian tradition, and his influence has extended to include how Christians understand animals. Three claims which Aquinas made with regard to animals were that humans had no moral duties towards them (1929: II-II 64.1), that they were not fallen (1922a: I 96.1) and that they would not be redeemed or present after God's restoration (1922b: III 91.5). Given the focus of this chapter, it is the third of these claims (and to a degree the second) which is of most significance.

In his fifth article regarding discussion into what the world will be like after the judgement by God, Aquinas examines whether plants and animals will be present, and ultimately states that neither plants nor animals will be (1922b: III 91.5). The focus here is not to engage with Aquinas' claims directly,[2] but to show that such views were later taken up by many within the Christian tradition. Indeed, Dorothy Yamamoto notes that 'the Thomist view of animals and their role has exerted enormous influence on the Christian tradition' (1998: 80); and Andrew Linzey states that Aquinas' writings on the topic of animals (especially, though not limited to, human moral responsibility towards them) 'has become the dominant Western religious position ... since the thirteenth century' (1995: 15).

A significant expression of this influence is found in the Catholic catechism. This document, which acts as a central expression of the Catholic Church's teachings for its many believers, shares a number of the points noted above. For instance animals 'are by nature destined for the common good of past, present, and future humanity' (2415), and any limitation to human dominion over animals is 'limited by concern for the quality of life of his neighbor, including generations to come' (2415). Moral duties towards animals, then, are not directed towards animals, but focused instead upon humanity. Though there is a recognition that creation is not as it should be, due to the sin of humanity – 'Harmony with creation is broken: visible creation has become alien and hostile to man' (400) – there is minimal discussion regarding the redemption of animals. Though the catechism speaks of a renewal 'which will transform humanity and the world' (1043), there is no mention of what this entails, and no means of understanding it to refer to the redemption of each and every creature that God has created. Indeed, on the section of heaven (1023–9) there is no mention of any non-human aspect of creation. Such ambiguity and/or silence regarding the presence of animals within the redeemed state is also found in the writings of a number of theologians writing on heaven/the new earth.[3] It is this ambiguity, or worse, this silence, regarding the presence of animals in a redeemed state which I call into question by utilizing modern biblical scholarship on a range of verses which include animal redemption in three different ways. In doing so I will both build up a substantial basis for the placement of animals within discussions regarding their presence in a redeemed creation, but also suggest why understandings of redemption should entail a universal scope, entailing each and every created animal.

Genesis

The first eschatological image which shows humans and animals living together in peace can be found in Genesis 1–2. Though it may seem strange to think of the beginning as eschatological, it is from the peaceful state of the Garden of Eden that later eschatological images such as Isaiah 11 and Revelation drew their inspiration (Watts 1985: 357; Wenham 1987: 33–34; Hamilton 1990: 140). What is presented within the Garden of Eden is the whole of creation living in peace with one another, to the extent that predation and the eating of meat is not permitted, as seen in Genesis 1.29-30:

> God said, 'See, I have given you every plant yielding seed that is upon the face of all the earth, and every tree with seed in its fruit; you shall have them for food. And to every beast of the earth, and to every bird of the air, and to everything that creeps on the earth, everything that has the breath of life, I have given every green plant for food.' And it was so.[4]

There is peace throughout, and it is the entire creation that God declares to be 'very good' in verse 31. Wenham (1987: 34) describes how the whole completed and perfected creation more adequately express the character of God than any of the individual parts can. While not every biblical scholar discusses these verses in particular,[5] for those that do there is a nearly unanimous view that Genesis 1.29-30 is descriptive of a cosmic peace between all creatures (Hamilton 1990: 140; von Rad 1970: 59; Davidson 1973: 26; Gowan 1988: 30; Westermann 2004: 11). One notable opposition to this view is Kidner (1967: 52) who suggests that the assigning of green plants for food does not mean that all things were vegetarian, but that ultimately all things depend on vegetation for life. Such a view, however, seems to be a convoluted and complicated reading which seeks to get around the fact that not all creatures are herbivores now, rather than expressing what the text is actually stating. Thus what is presented in Genesis 1.29-30 is an eschatological picture of an ideal state of existence, and crucially, it is one in which both humans and animals are present, each in their own right.

Isaiah

The next set of eschatological verses comes from Isaiah 11.6-9. The verses read:

> The wolf shall live with the lamb, the leopard shall lie down with the kid, the calf and the lion and the fatling together, and a little child shall lead them. The cow and the bear shall graze, their young shall lie down together; and the lion shall eat straw like the ox. The nursing child shall play over the hole of the asp, and the weaned child shall put its hand on the adder's den. They will not hurt or destroy on all my holy mountain; for the earth will be full of the knowledge of the Lord as the waters cover the sea.

These verses describe a creation at peace, where everyone is happily vegetarian. There is no more harm or destruction anywhere to be found. Later in Isaiah 65.25 the text makes this clear: 'The wolf and the lamb shall feed together, the lion shall eat straw like the ox; but the serpent – its food shall be dust! They shall not hurt or destroy on all my holy mountain, says the Lord.' John Oswalt (1986: 283) notes three ways of interpreting these verses: spiritualistic, figurative and literal. The spiritualistic interpretation views the animals as representing various aspects of the human, while the figurative suggests such images are descriptive of a larger narrative involving the removal of danger and the presence of peace. Finally, the literal interpretation views the description of the lion eating straw as a literal reality which will come about. Of these three, it is the literal interpretation (itself part of a larger figurative narrative) which is descriptive of the whole of creation at peace that many modern exegetes support (Brueggemann 1998: 101–3; Webb 1997: 75; Motyer 1993: 124–5; Watts 1987: 173–5; Smith 2007: 274; and Blenkinsopp 2000: 263). Again, this is an eschatological picture showing the future of what will be, and it is a future which includes animals. Indeed, it contains all manner of animals, including not only the pleasant ones and those that were farmed, but also the dangerous ones that threatened people. Isaiah's eschatological image is one of peace throughout creation, a creation which includes humans and non-humans alike, and a peace between all creatures.

Revelation

The third set of eschatological verses comes from Revelation 5.11-13. The text reads:

> Then I looked, and I heard the voice of many angels surrounding the throne and the living creatures and the elders; they numbered myriads of myriads and thousands of thousands, singing with full voice, 'Worthy is the Lamb that was slaughtered to receive power and wealth and wisdom and might and honour and glory and blessing!' Then I heard every creature in heaven and on earth and under the earth and in the sea, and all that is in them, singing, 'To the one seated on the throne and to the Lamb be blessing and honour and glory and might for ever and ever!'

A rather large gathering is described, and all of the members are singing about how wonderful God is. What is of key importance in this context is the substantial presence of animals within. To begin with, in both Revelation 5.3 and 5.13 the author has described the cosmic order ('in heaven, on earth, under the earth') as a means of expressing the scope of the whole of the created reality (Blount 2009: 120; Osborne 2002: 264). The voices of praise come from each realm of the cosmic order: heaven, earth and sea (Blount 2009: 120). Yet Rev. 5 is more detailed than simply saying there are a couple of representatives from each realm (though that would be significant enough). Grant Osborne notes (2002: 264) how the Greek term translated 'all creatures' or 'all creation' (πᾶν κτίσμα) denotes not just intelligent creatures such as humans and angels, but the entire animal kingdom. Likewise, the added 'and all that is in them' (καὶ τὰ ἐν αὐτοῖς πάντα) stresses that every single creature in the cosmos is participating in this worship (Osborne 2002: 264–5; Mounce 1998: 138). In addition to Osborne, the same idea of a cosmic worship involving the whole of creation is also noted by Denis Edwards (2009: 81),

G. K. Beale (1999: 365), Robert Mounce (1998: 138), Leon Morris (2002: 99) and Eugene Boring (2011: 111–12). Here, as in Genesis and Isaiah, there is a general scholarly consensus that such eschatological images are ones which show both human and animal together in the eschatological future, and the scope is one which includes every single living creature.[6]

This first section has revealed how humans and animals are repeatedly shown together in eschatological images. Contrary to the theology of Aquinas and those he has influenced, animals are frequently present in biblical descriptions of the next age. In addition to such eschatological images described above, the Bible also describes just how broad the redemptive purposes of God can be understood. The second part of this chapter is now going to examine the idea that God's redemptive concerns and actions are directed towards not only humanity, but all creation; and not simply the broad category of 'creation', as though God intends to save each type of creature, but rather that God's redemptive purposes are for each and every individual creature. To do so I will look at three New Testament texts which present the idea that God's restorative actions are for the whole of creation.

Romans

The first text to be examined is Romans 8.18-23 which reads as follows:

> I consider that the sufferings of this present time are not worth comparing with the glory about to be revealed to us. For the creation waits with eager longing for the revealing of the children of God; for the creation was subjected to futility, not of its own will but by the will of the one who subjected it, in hope that the creation itself will be set free from its bondage to decay and will obtain the freedom of the glory of the children of God. We know that the whole creation has been groaning in labour pains until now; and not only the creation, but we ourselves, who have the first fruits of the Spirit, groan inwardly while we wait for adoption, the redemption of our bodies.

These verses describe the sufferings that are currently being experienced by not only the church, but also by creation, sufferings from which both will be set free. Such a hope of salvation is based on the redemptive works of Christ, and the crucial point, for our purposes at least, is that Paul's expression of our hope necessarily includes the rest of the created order, for it is the whole of creation which suffers and is to be redeemed (Cobb 1998: 175). The key word on which such an interpretation stands is the Greek ἡ κτίσις, or 'creation'. C. E. B. Cranfield (1975: 411) notes that there have been a wide range of interpretations on the meaning of the word as Paul understood it here, ranging from (1) all humanity and angels, (2) unbelievers alone, (3) angels alone, (4) non-human creation and angels, (5) non-human and human and (6) non-human alone. Of these, (1) and (2) are unlikely given verse 20 which states that creation was subjected to futility not of its own will, and (3) and (4) would equally require an unlikely use of ἡ κτίσις with regard to angels (Cranfield 1975: 411). It is the fifth option which many modern commentators have chosen, where 'creation' indicates the whole of the non-human earthly realm (Moo 1996: 514; Cranfield 1975: 411–12; Hendriksen 1982: 266–7; Grabe 2005: 292). As E. Schweitzer (1961: 3) notes, 'Paul is not mainly interested in the individual's salvation, but in the redemption of the cosmos including all creatures.' Thus in these verses we see the idea that the whole of the animal creation shall be redeemed by God. Such an idea of the cosmic focus of God's creative concerns is also found in other letters of Paul, including both Colossians and Ephesians.

Colossians

The second of the texts I will examine is Colossians 1.15-20.

> He is the image of the invisible God, the firstborn of all creation; for in him all things in heaven and on earth were created, things visible and invisible, whether thrones or dominions or rulers or powers – all things have been created through him and for him. He himself is before all things, and in him all things hold together. He is the head of the body, the church; he is the beginning, the firstborn from the dead, so that he might come to have first place in everything. For in him all the fullness of God was pleased to dwell, and through him God was pleased to reconcile to himself all things, whether on earth or in heaven, by making peace through the blood of his cross.

These few verses present a cosmic Christ, one in whom all things are created (v. 16), all things are sustained (v. 17) and all things are redeemed (v. 20). Like the author of Revelation, though with different terms, the author describes the whole of the created realms ('in heaven and on earth') to show the full scope of God's redemptive concerns (Sumney 2008: 66). Francis Foulkes (1963: 53) writes: 'The phrase *all things* … is qualified by *both which are in heaven and which are on earth*. Paul has in view the whole creation, spiritual and material.' What concerns us most in this chapter is verse 20 which speaks of God reconciling 'to himself all things, whether on earth or in heaven, by making peace through the blood of his cross'. The Greek term translated 'all things' is τὰ πάντα, and Peter O'Brien (1982: 54–6) notes six different ways in which τὰ πάντα has been understood (e.g. as all humans, all angels or cosmic powers), yet ultimately only supports the interpretation which understands τὰ πάντα as 'all things'. In this he is not alone, for many exegetes (Bruce 1984: 74; Dunn 1996: 104; Grabe 2005: 290–3; Foulkes 1963: 53; Wright 1986: 76–80) and theologians (Edwards 2006: 111; Moltmann 1990: 194, 255; Southgate 2008: 78) share the same view. The reasoning is simple enough: the extent of Christ's creative, sustaining and redeeming interests, as well as the extent of his authority (since he is 'firstborn of creation' and 'before all things') is based on the same group entailing all things; if Christ did not reconcile all things to himself, then neither is he before all things. Jürgen Moltmann (1990: 255) expands on this idea and suggests that

> through Christ everything will be reconciled 'whether on earth or in heaven, making peace by the blood of his cross, through himself' (1.20). According to what is said here, Christ did not only die vicariously the death of suffering men and women, and 'the death of the sinner', so as to bring peace into the world of human beings. He also died 'the death of all the living' so as to reconcile everything in heaven and on earth, which means the angels and the beasts too, and to bring peace to the whole creation.

Thus, what is present in these verses from Colossians, is the idea that just as Christ created all that exists, so too does Christ's work on the cross have redemptive value for all that he has made; 'all things' really does mean, 'all things'. Indeed, part of the identity which the author has for God in this passage is based around God's creative, sustaining and redemptive concerns for the whole of the cosmos.

Ephesians

The final text that I will examine comes from Ephesians 1.8-10, which reads: 'With all wisdom and insight he has made known to us the mystery of his will, according to his good pleasure that he set forth in Christ as a plan for the fullness of time, to gather up all things in him, things in heaven and things on earth.' Here the author writes about the grace of God which will ultimately draw all things together in Christ. Again, the Greek term τὰ πάντα is used; and just as in the case of Colossians 1.20, biblical scholars are clear as to the universal scope of the meaning of the word. Larry Kreitzer (1997: 61) suggests that everything that has been made finds its purpose in Christ, while Edwards (2006: 112) goes into more detail: 'All things, absolutely everything in the universe, will be gathered up and transformed in the risen Christ' (Eph. 1.9-10, 20-23). Just as the scope of the meaning is spelt out in Colossians 1.20 by including the realms of heaven and earth, so too in this passage the terms heaven and earth are included to show the extent of the redemption. Andrew Lincoln (1990: 33–4) states, 'The elaboration "things on earth or in heaven" (τὰ ἐπὶ τοῖς οὐρανοῖς καὶ τὰ ἐπὶ τῆς γῆς) indicates that we are right to take τὰ πάντα in its widest sense of all things and all beings, that is, the cosmos as a whole and not just humanity.' Thus, here again the scope of God's redemptive concern and actions is seen to be inclusive of not just humanity, but also animals and the rest of creation. John Gibbs (1971: 142) states that 'it is the lordship of Christ over both creation and redemption which determines that there can be no creatureless redemption (Rom. 8:18ff., etc.) and ultimately no redemptionless creation (Eph. 1:10; Col. 1:20; etc.)'. John Cobb (1998: 179) likewise suggests that the logic of such verses clearly suggest that all animals must be included in such redemptive claims. What each of these authors, and the biblical verses which they are discussing, make abundantly clear is the inclusion of animals within God's redemptive plans;

God intends to save not just humans, but all manner of creatures. Once more, this reality is a different alternative to that of the tradition built upon the work of Aquinas, in which the place of animals in God's redemption is generally absent. Given that God is determined to save all creatures, the question still remains as to how, if at all, we can conceive of what such a future may entail for them. This question has been answered in a number of ways.

Animal Redemption

Given the various eschatological biblical images of animals and humans living at peace, and the New Testament examples which describe the cosmic extent of God's redemptive purposes, what does it mean to speak of animal redemption and restoration? There are two broad ways in which this is answered. The first of these has the creature exist eternally due to its having an objective impact within existence and there are a couple of ways in which this has been proposed. Alfred North Whitehead suggested that animals participate in eternal life through their impact on God; each creature is received into the divine life and exists forever as a result because essentially, they make an impact on God (1978: 347–51). In a related manner, there is also the idea that in addition to being inscribed into the memory of God, all creatures also exist within the dimensions of time and space (Edwards 2006: 116). Thus each creature that ever exists is inscribed, by the very essence of being, into the dimensions of time and space as well as in the mind of God. Despite the ease with which one can conceive of God remembering all the creatures and so giving them immortality, the fact that the subjective experience of each creature does not continue to exist, leads others to propose different ways of understanding animal redemption.

The second way of understanding this idea is subjective redemption, whereby the creature continues to exist and experience as an individual self or subject (Southgate 2008: 86; Edwards 2006: 116; McDaniel 1989: 169). Again, there are a couple of ways in which this has been understood. Jay McDaniel, who generally supports the first interpretation, does hope for a subjective state for redeemed animals. However for him, such a state of existence would be more temporary, whereby the creature could achieve a fulfilment they failed to find in their earthly life, after which they could peacefully die and be inscribed into the mind of God (1989: 47). For McDaniel, death is not a problem, rather it is being unfulfilled (1989: 46). Despite the clever joining of subjective and objective redemption here, such a position fails to address the biblical passages mentioned above which speak of humans and animals bodily sharing existence together in a renewed state.[7] Others have turned to another way of viewing a subjective renewed state which proposes that there will be a literal awakening and resurrection for every creature that ever existed. This is a common thought shared by a number of theologians. Moltmann (1990: 303) states: 'To put it simply: God forgets nothing that he has created. Nothing is lost to him. He will restore it all.'[8] John Wesley, in his sermon 'The Great Deliverance' (1811: 198) suggests that the whole of the non-human creation will be restored. Finally David Clough (2012: 151) states that we can hope that 'just as God has been gracious to non-human creatures in their creation and reconciliation, so God will be faithful to them in redemption'. What is pictured, is that not only will all the cute, fuzzy and 'loveable' animals be redeemed, but also all the ones many humans think they could rather do without. Every single creature and all living beings will exist in a state of peace. However, it is exactly this peaceful state of subjective experience that leads some to question what such an existence would mean for animals, especially those who are predators by nature.

There are two main concerns which have been raised with regard to the state of animals within a universal animal resurrection. The first of these was perhaps most famously made by C. S. Lewis in his book, *The Problem of Pain*. Within it, Lewis briefly discusses the possibility of animal thinking and consciousness with regard to animal immortality. He claims that though animals can feel pleasure and pain, the life of animals is likely just 'a succession of sensations' with no real 'self' that recognizes itself as experiencing such sensations (1998: 113). Given this case, there is little reason to resurrect such a creature to compensate it for earthly sufferings as it is not a self that could recognize and experience such things (1998: 113–14). Instead, Lewis (1998: 115) suggests that some animals may be redeemed through their association to humans – 'it seems to me possible that certain animals may have an immortality, not in themselves, but in the immortality of their masters'. Such a position however, assumes that animals can relate to God only through humans; this is a questionable claim given the numerous biblical texts which describe not only God covenanting with animals (Gen. 9.8-17; Hos. 2.18) and God commanding animals (1 Kgs 17.4; Jon. 2.11; Rev. 19.17), but also animals calling out to God or praising Him (Ps. 66; 98; 104, 148; Isa. 43.20). In addition, as Clough notes (2012: 146), if the basis for the redemption is not primarily compensation for suffering experienced but rather that God wills it to exist in the new creation just as God did in the old creation, then the thrust of Lewis's position loses its force.

The second issue that is raised with a universal resurrection to a peaceful coexistence is that those animals that currently live by predation will not be enabled to 'be themselves' if they are not able to hunt and kill. This is a point which Christopher Southgate (2008: 86) takes up and he comments: 'It is very hard to see how the leopardness of leopards could be fulfilled in eschatological coexistence with kids.' Such critiques are not damaging to objective immortality models, where the animal exists in the memory of God, for each creature exists as a memory and does not interact with others. However, Southgate (2008: 89) proposes a restored resurrected creation where the lion could hunt the lamb, but since there will not be pain or death, the lamb will not mind terribly. Others question whether it would be appropriate for some animals to be resurrected at all into such a state (e.g. dinosaurs) and in such a case these would be inscribed into the divine memory, while other creatures (such as dogs) would be bodily resurrected (Edwards 2006: 119). Such positions are generally held due to rejecting the theological idea of a Fall which has affected the whole of creation, as well as an idea of an ideal state of peace within creation; if there is no Fall, then all creatures are currently precisely as God intended them, predation included.[9] Andrew Linzey (1995: 82–3) argues against such a position stating that the Isaiah passages show

> not that animality will be destroyed by divine love but rather that animal nature is in bondage to violence and predation. The vision of Isaiah is directly relevant here: It invites us to the imaginative recognition that God's transforming love is not determined even by what we think we know of evolutionary biology.

This same position is taken up by Clough (2012: 168–72), who highlights that just as a human might live their life self-identifying as a warrior, such actions will not be enabled in the eschatological future. Rather, just as God's grace and mercy can change the ways in which humans interact with one another, so too can God's grace enable all creatures to live at peace while still retaining their individual natures. Wesley (1811: 198) discusses not only a resurrection for animals, but a restoration to new and improved states; where they will be free from not only 'irregular appetites' and 'thirst for blood', but also, somewhat amusingly, 'all the horridness of their appearance'. Regardless of Wesley's dislike of certain visual aspects of some animals, what each of these scholars are describing is a way in which through the grace of God, all creatures can indeed be true to their nature and live in peace, in following with the eschatological images found in Genesis, Isaiah and Revelation.

In conclusion, this chapter demonstrates how the concept of animal redemption has a place within the Bible, both through examples of eschatological images which show humans and animals living together, as well as texts describing the cosmic extent of God's redemptive purposes. Contrary to the lasting influence of Aquinas, which suggests that animals had no part in a redeemed creation, or leaves the topic undiscussed, this chapter has suggested the very opposite. In addition, a variety of ways that this redemption might look like have been examined, as well as potential concerns. With this evidence I suggest that the idea of a universal resurrection is the most convincing. It must be noted, however, that even among those proposing various positions, there is a general acceptance that we simply cannot know the final state of non-human creatures; these are more theologically based hopes, rather than assured things. The Bible, however, seems clear that animals will have a place within the future order, but what such a place will look like for the varying animals is less clear. Petroc and Eldred Willey (1998: 198) put it well: '*That* animals will be redeemed is certain. … *How* that redemption is to be conceived … is a matter on which scripture and tradition give us no definitive answer.'

Chapter 14

TEACHING PRACTICAL THEOLOGY FOR FLOURISHING

Katja Stuerzenhofecker

Introducing the Classroom for Flourishing

Education is fundamentally premised on processes of change which include, but are not limited to progression of learning, increase of knowledge and understanding, development of practical wisdom and personal identity. Holding education against the notion of salvation brings into focus how the educator might envisage the change process, whether in fact change is the most appropriate way of conceptualizing the educational intervention. This chapter addresses those educational spaces where change is not only conceived as the advancing of learning in the classroom, but also as advocacy of social change. This offers exciting opportunities for the design of learning and teaching which I want to begin to explore by recalling a recent conversation I had with a feminist activist and anthropologist. She was seeking my advice about her application for her first teaching job in higher education. She had been asked to present her teaching strategy in the job interview and she was unsure what was expected of the successful candidate. What else was there apart from lectures and seminars, essay and exam, she asked me with exasperation. Did I have any suggestions? Although she employs a sophisticated social justice agenda in her research and activism, she has not made the connection between practice, epistemology and pedagogy.[1] Yet, here is an exciting opportunity to realize the potential of the advocacy classroom as a space for 'prefiguring' (Maeckelbergh 2011) the social change she is aiming for by putting it into practice in the classroom itself. It needs to be acknowledged though that mainstream doctoral programmes do not encourage early career academics to develop sophisticated knowledge of a range of approaches to learning and teaching. In fact, the academic can still travel through her entire career without any study of pedagogy.

In this chapter I want to consider the classroom as a space for prefiguring emancipatory social change, which I understand through the lens of Grace Jantzen's concept of flourishing as a place of realized incarnational eschatology. I adopt Jantzen's horticultural metaphor in my consideration of the classroom as a 'walled garden', an artificially created habitat of specimens found in the wider environment, a microcosm tended by the educator as 'gardener'. While this consideration arises from my particular classroom in practical theology, I aim to offer a reflection which can be transferred and adapted to other learning contexts which have a broadly speaking liberation and conscientization agenda. Jantzen's work speaks directly to my classroom at the University of Manchester where students of all faiths and none come together to study the theme of gender issues in contemporary religious communities. It is Jantzen's pantheistic perspective which helps me to reconcile my urge as an educator for prefiguring my vision of social change while meeting students with respect and integrity in the diverse positions and ideologies that they hold.

My starting point is the assumption that there needs to be coherence of paradigms between academic discipline and pedagogy. The first of two reasons for this is that this coherence is required for the effectiveness of learning and teaching. What researchers would readily accept and expect of coherence between research content and research process, also applies to learning and teaching. Secondly, coherence of paradigms lends the educator's practice integrity and offers the opportunity to model in the classroom what she is aiming to promote in wider society. Elisabeth Schüssler Fiorenza (2009) has contributed a substantive proposal of this kind for her discipline entitled *Democratizing Biblical Studies: Toward an Emancipatory Educational Space* which gives me an incentive to aim for a corresponding project in my discipline of practical theology. As academics we do well to take our teaching role as seriously as our research,[2] and interrogate the politics of our pedagogical practices.

In the following then, I want to extend pastoral theologian Bonnie Miller-McLemore's (2012: 186) contention that 'if you want to understand practical theology ... look at what we do as we teach, not (just) what we say', and use Jantzen's concept of flourishing proactively to push my pedagogical strategy to a higher level of coherence with the 'espoused theology' (Cameron et al. 2010: 52–6) that I am articulating in my advocacy. I focus on three interlinked aspects which are significant in my practical theology classroom, namely the study of lived religion (Ganzevoort 2009), including students' reflection on their own experiences[3] as part of the living human web (Miller-McLemore 1996). This leads me to use the concept of flourishing as an alternative to salvation in my theological response to the following three questions: Why start teaching with anecdotal evidence and material conditions, why draw students' own experience into the learning process and how to respond to the multi-religious/secular pluralism present in the classroom. I will then indicate briefly in what ways Jantzen's political theology helps me to engage critically with the secular 'salvation' agendas of 'sustainability', 'social responsibility' and 'active citizenship' in current higher education in the UK. My concluding thoughts capture three ways in which flourishing challenges me to be vigilant in my practice as an educator.

Salvation, Transformation or Flourishing in Theological Anthropology and Pedagogy

Why seek another label for teaching and learning practices that might be described with existing theories of transformative pedagogy[4]? What is to be gained by exploring flourishing instead of transformation as an alternative to the Christian concept of salvation? The key differences between what Jantzen sees as the Christian model of exclusive and other-worldly salvation and her alternative political theology of flourishing can only be outlined very briefly before I apply the latter to pedagogy.

My main contention is that both transformation and salvation have a pejorative view of the human condition as in need of more or less urgent change or rescue. As Jantzen (1995: 85) argues, '"Salvation" ... is a term which denotes rescue. One is saved *from* something: from drowning, from calamity, from loss. These have negative connotations: it would be an odd turn of phrase to say that one had been saved from something desirable.' Flourishing offers a different assessment of a person's timeline of before and after a salvific intervention or transformation, since it does not judge the human condition as deficient by default. This is not to say that all persons find themselves in satisfactory situations which do not require improvement. What Jantzen focuses on here is not the psychological or social dimension – more on her thoughts on this later – but the anthropological foundation: 'If we think in terms of salvation, then the human condition must be conceptualized as a problematic state, a state in which human beings need urgent rescue' (1995: 87). Instead, the concept of flourishing shifts the emphasis towards the immediate future which is to be one of growth, increasing strength and vigour in continuity with the present and past. Consequently, the place for flourishing is in the here and now: in life before death. Instead, the traditional Christian salvation model is accused by Jantzen of supporting the oppressive *status quo* by its focus on the afterlife (Jantzen 1995: 96). It is hence considered to be a privatized, depoliticized religion (1995: 93).

Against this, Jantzen sets up her model of flourishing which prompts action for love of the world. It is said to achieve this through 'the promotion of values of life, creativity, diversity and justice' which goes beyond the human to include also 'non-human animals, the environment and the planet as a whole' (Graham 2009: 9). Jantzen's vision for the relationship of the immanent and the transcendent is radically incarnational: 'divinity – that which is most to be respected and valued – *means* mutuality, bodiliness, diversity and materiality' (Jantzen 1997: 274). 'Transcendence is not the opposite of immanence: indeed, immanence is the necessary condition of transcendence, since no one can achieve intelligence or creativity without the requisite physical complexity' (Jantzen 1997: 276). Hence, what is considered to be of the highest value and embodiment is inseparable. It follows from the interdependence between the transcendent and immanent that the basis of all moral reasoning is inductive and experiential (Graham 2009: 12). Jantzen's (1997: 282) consideration of embodiment further leads her to conclude that individuality and uniqueness – and hence diversities – arise from identities grounded in specific physical entities and their unique experiences.

Regarding the source of development, she says that 'flourishing occurs from an inner dynamic of growth' (Jantzen 1995: 85) nurtured by 'the divine source and ground' (Jantzen 1995: 87). Life is set 'within a nexus of relationships that we develop into personhood, learning to laugh and play and speak and think. At the most basic physical and psychological levels, human flourishing requires interconnection, not isolation. ... The model of flourishing is one which assumes the interconnectedness of people, and indeed of the ecosystem: flourishing is impossible by oneself alone' (Jantzen 1995: 91–2). In contrast, Jantzen recognizes the Christian emphasis on the saviour-figure 'who intervenes from outside the calamitous situation' (Jantzen 1995: 87) but who is essential because 'the people who need to be saved cannot normally save themselves' (Jantzen 1995: 85). 'Although ... flourishing of course draws upon external sources as a plant draws on the nutrients of earth and air and water, this sort of continuing interdependence within the natural order is of an utterly different kind than the desperate need of someone in crisis for an external saviour or rescuer' (ibid.).

Towards a Pedagogy of Flourishing in Practical Theology

Several points raised by Jantzen's concept of flourishing in contrast to salvation are particularly significant for emancipatory educational practice. In the following I want to explore three aspects of flourishing in the walled garden of my classroom where the educator acts as the gardener who aims to promote collective flourishing through her decisions about design and maintenance. I focus on three interlinked aspects which are significant in my context, namely the study of lived religion including students' reflection on their own experiences as part of the living human[5] web in all its diversities and interdependencies.

1. The Analysis of Anecdotal Evidence of Material and Social Conditions

When we proceed from an inductive and experiential basis of all moral reasoning as Jantzen urges, then the analysis of anecdotal evidence of material and social conditions is the starting point of good teaching for flourishing. It could be argued that this demand might have been more significant in Jantzen's discipline of philosophy of religion at the time of her writing than it is in contemporary practical theology where variations of the 'pastoral cycle', which begins analysis in the specific life situation, have been widely used for decades. However, the inductive method is not universally embraced by all practical theologians, especially not in their teaching, when it is rooted in an understanding of their discipline as applied theology. This school of practical theology takes as its starting point the insights of scripture and systematic theology in order to make use of them in concrete situations. Yet even those of us who hold to the 'pastoral cycle' model in some form in our research might not all apply it consistently in our teaching. Hence, Jantzen reminds us of the need for self-reflexivity: Do we choose as initial learning triggers theoretical texts or do we begin with real-life case studies and generative themes[6]?

Jantzen's incarnational political theology of justice and protest makes certain demands on the kinds of case studies and generative themes which are particularly useful as triggers in an advocacy classroom for flourishing. They need to encourage learners to confront 'social and economic issues not as marginal theological interests but as central to theological thought' (Jantzen 1995: 100). Since flourishing is rooted in bodily well-being, including physical and psychological health, and adequate material provision (Jantzen 1995: 95), the chosen triggers for learning should allow the exploration of what facilitates flourishing and what prevents it. Following on from this, the model of flourishing requires systems-thinking because it approaches life in its interconnectedness which provides the right conditions for healthy development. Consequently, case-study material should be explored holistically so as to make immediate and broader interconnections apparent, and to enable a thorough contextual analysis at multiple levels.

2. Students' own Experience

In the context of education, flourishing aligns well with student-centred learning which acknowledges the richness of students' prior knowledge and experiences. It is the task of education to build on prior knowledge and experiences, and to extend them. Jantzen's anthropological foundation, which posits flourishing to draw on existing inner resources within a healthy ecosystem of interdependencies, encourages me to envisage the learner to be on an ongoing journey of development rather than as a fallen creature in need of rescue.[7] This model of continuity is not in line with a 'salvation' vision of learning as transformation which brings about a rupture from outside the situation, and which is to be passively received by the learner. The model of flourishing offers an understanding of organic growth which does not vilify the *status prior* as deficient but organically builds on its existing resources.

In any case, not all students need to experience transformation understood as radical change because they might already be on the 'right' path – whatever that path might be in terms of intended learning outcomes – but they should all be supported to experience growth. To give an example, some of my students are already very knowledgeable of critical gender perspectives when they enter my gender advocacy classroom. They are not in need of transformation. In their case, my task is to provide a conducive environment for their continuing development, maybe with a step-change in their emerging understanding and commitment to a certain course of action.

Does the same apply to those students who enter the advocacy classroom with hostility to the studied vision of social justice, possibly because they are members of the privileged group?[8] Should they not be considered to be 'deficient' and in need of transformation? The temptation to respond in the affirmative highlights the dilemma of the advocacy classroom in my context of secular higher education. My institutional role does not allow me to indoctrinate students into a particular vision of social justice, yet I would not be teaching what I teach if I did not have my own convictions on the matter. Here, Jantzen's insistence on this-worldly flourishing in the immediate future together with her organic model of continuity sharpens my focus on the learning that can grow out of all students' biographies, whatever they might be. The educator is challenged to meet these biographies with integrity and to unlock their resources for active learning to take place.

Secondly, the logical extension of Jantzen's insistence on the study of the material and social conditions as the basis of all moral reasoning leads us even further than that to the inclusion of students' own life worlds as a subject of learning. The action orientation of the model of flourishing encourages students to see the relevance of their lives, aspirations and careers to their studies and *vice versa*. What Graham (2009: 12) notes of Jantzen's commentary on her own discipline of philosophy of religion also applies to practical theology: 'It is not about academic debate in some way abstracted from the concerns of everyday living, but knowledge generated in order to equip us for lives of virtue and wisdom.' So the circle of inductive inquiry is closed by establishing a movement from student's own experiences via study to its outworking in their lives. The method of theological reflection as an assessment task in the form of learning journals can serve here as a valuable pedagogical tool: it is 'about nurturing the habits of a guided and intentional life which seeks to shape itself towards the good and all that promotes human flourishing' (Graham 2011: 335–6).

Such reflection draws students in as seekers of meaning as well as knowledge constructors. When designed as the critical interrogation of subjectivity as embedded in networks of symbolic, material and social realities it serves to counter the construction of identity as an isolated agent. Further, it encourages the development of a reflexive disposition which works against an apolitical attitude of TINA – Margaret Thatcher's slogan, 'There is no alternative.' This slogan seems to be alive and well among a generation of undergraduates who were born after the end of Thatcher's premiership; I hear it literally all too often in our classroom discussions and I read it in students' learning journals that 'feminists have gone too far with their demands, but things are never going to change anyway'. As Graham (2009: 4) has observed in her evaluation of Jantzen's career, the power to 'think differently'[9] in order to act differently is crucial for the overcoming of injustice and oppression. Assessment tools such as carefully framed learning journals offer the opportunity to establish patterns of thinking differently which live on beyond the classroom and thus allow the prefiguring of an alternative social vision which includes students' own flourishing.

3. Pluralism in the Classroom for Flourishing

In a diverse classroom such as mine, Jantzen's model of universal flourishing challenges the way we deal with these diversities: clearly 'no salvation outside the church' can only be practised as the hegemonic model (see Jantzen 1995: 96–7) with a paternalistic pattern of hospitality[10] which sets the Christian narrative of salvation over all others. In the context of education, the educator would take on the role of the host who extends a hegemonic welcome to those deserving guests who buy into what is offered. This runs counter to Jantzen's understanding of interdependencies between diverse and unique individualities which all make a vital contribution to flourishing of the whole ecosystem. It follows from the previous section, that those students who are averse to the content of the advocacy classroom are of particular significance. Following Jantzen, they might be seen as representatives of those elements which hinder the flourishing of the whole ecosystem. In the rare event that those students have enrolled at all, their presence in the advocacy classroom poses healthy challenges to a hegemonic discourse, in all ways ranging from the analysis of the current situation and the naming of perceived problems to the development of responses.

Which leads me to another aspect of flourishing which is significant in the classroom, namely that of community. Jantzen urges us to resist the individualizing tendency of salvation and to hold fast to a vision of flourishing which highlights our interdependence on other humans and beyond. From a pedagogical perspective, this turns the focus on the development of a learning community where all are willing and able to offer their ideas and understanding, and participate in constructive critique of all offered views and actions in order to come to the best understanding we can achieve together. I am in agreement here with Higton (2012: 230) when he insists that the need for widening participation arises from the realization that 'if we do not widen participation [in higher education], none of us is learning as we might': 'The drive to include other voices, particularly those voices that have normally been ignored in conversations about the goods of our society, is a drive built in to the kind of learning we are called to do.' Graham (2011: 337) echoes this in her development of Jantzen when she considers the question of well-being: 'So once again, we encounter the very corporate and collective nature of the search for meaning, or the good life well-lived, taking place within "an ecology of virtue".' In my experience, this is the greatest challenge in facilitating an effective classroom and one where the educator's skill and perseverance in the face of student preferences for self-sufficiency are tested the most. Here indeed is the walled garden of the classroom, a microcosmic reflection of wider social contexts where the educator's agenda for prefiguring a mutually supportive and collaborative collective for the common good has to stand the test against divisive individualizing practices and ideologies, where indeed the definition of 'the common good' itself is open to negotiation.

4. *The Higher Education 'Salvation' Agenda*

This brings me to the wider ecology of learning within which we find ourselves and which is beyond our individual control. Educators who are employed in formal education are affected by numerous institutional policies which might or might not align with their own agenda. When it comes to higher education policies which can be described as secular aspirations to make a positive contribution to the common good, a 'salvation' agenda of sorts, there are three main policies which are currently in operation in the UK, namely sustainability, active citizenship and social responsibility. While it is not my purpose here to offer a full description and critique of these policies, I want to indicate with a number of questions the ways in which Jantzen's political theology of flourishing offers a framework for critique and counter-discourse. Where the educator's aim is to make a contribution to flourishing in diversity and mutuality, then narrow definitions of a HE 'salvation' agenda have to be rejected as merely remedies to ensure the smooth continuation of the *status quo*. The challenge is then to carve out an educational space for prefiguring an alternative vision within a hostile institutional environment.

First, Jantzen's thought reminds us to interrogate who gets to define 'sustainability' and how, and who benefits from this definition.[11] From her position in philosophy of religion, she calls us to examine the symbolic foundations of processes of exploitation and oppression. Do current higher education policies address this and if not, what has theology got to offer to fill this gap?[12] Jantzen's accusation that the Western cultural imagination is dominated by necrophilia and violence which she considers to be related to the Christian model of salvation (Graham 2009: 2) is of high relevance here. Do definitions of 'sustainability' break out of this deadly symbolic of violence and move us towards cosmic flourishing or do they work to uphold the *status quo* as much as possible for the benefit of the few?

Second and related to the issue of the 'sustainability' agenda, Jantzen's work urges us to question the aims of promoting in our graduates 'active citizenship' with its action orientation towards current social and environmental issues and challenges. Fundamentally, we are called to examine critically whether 'active citizenship' is shorthand for the socialization of willing agents of dominant interests[13] or whether it promotes a vision of inclusion in diversity and mutuality where definitions of well-being and strategies for its realization are sought cooperatively.

Finally, from the understanding of flourishing as located in a complex ecosystem of interdependencies we should question the adequacy of the top-down flow of knowledge as it is envisaged in current 'social responsibility' policies understood as the accessible dissemination of research findings to the wider population.[14] What should be the flows of communication which take advantage of the insights and experiences held in the whole ecosystem and allow all voices to contribute? What kinds of research methods are conducive to the democratic production of knowledge? What are the epistemological foundations of such research methods in contrast to the current top-down agenda of 'social responsibility'?

Challenges in the Classroom for Flourishing

If I am to name the challenges arising from a theology of flourishing for educational practice, three key issues present themselves in my classroom, which hinder the embodiment of alternatives to the *status quo*. It is first the challenge of how to inculcate in students a positive attitude towards peer learning and team work, the concrete classroom instantiations of diversity and mutuality. In my experience, students are inclined to focus on the attainment of their own degree as if life was just an accidental contemporaneity of isolated agents rather than a complex web of interdependencies. It is impossible to undo in one semester the workings of an educational system which offers individuals short-term rewards for compliance. But the walled garden of the classroom for flourishing is a good place for disrupting this socialization process by making our interdependencies apparent and to employ them proactively and reward them in collaborative assessment tasks which point beyond the narrow horizon of assessment criteria. This might stretch the educator's perseverance in the face of student dissatisfaction, it certainly requires careful design which guides students' reflection towards an appreciation for collaboration even in the face of free-riders and other obstacles to perceived 'success'.

The second challenge is how to prevent the establishment of a hegemonic discourse in the classroom which silences other voices. Not everybody who enrols on my module is a wholehearted feminist who embraces my own advocacy position, and why should they be? Whatever the perceived fault lines are for a particular module, students are programmed to seek out what they think the educator wants to hear. Where critical reflective learning has not yet become embedded in students' formal learning practice then the educator's own preferences can become hegemonic by students' readiness to afford it that place. Alternatively, vocal fractions of students can set the tone of what is perceived to be acceptable and reasonable, in my case it is often anti-religious perspectives which lay claims to being hegemonic. Regardless of whether the default position is perceived to be the educator's or other students', this dynamic might lead to some students' withholding differing perspectives. It is hard to affirm diversities which are not disclosed, but it is the educator's role to keep the classroom accessible through careful design of assessment tasks and attentive discussion management which seeks out the missing voices.

Finally, Jantzen's thought urges me not to lose sight of my own flourishing in this classroom. This is important in relation to students' expectations of the educator and the danger of hegemonic discourse which I have just mentioned: How can I retain the integrity of my advocacy vision in practice in the face of student resistance and when I have to be the inclusive host to many voices? My own reflective practice must consider not only my professional effectiveness in a narrow sense, but interrogate holistically whether the way my vision takes shape in the classroom is life-giving for myself and invigorates other areas of my being. This is especially so for the female educator who – *qua* female – is likely to have been socialized into a practice of self-denial for the sake of others. When Jantzen (1995: 92) interrogates the ecosystem within which flourishing is to take place, she is mindful of the danger of exploitation: '*Who* flourishes, and at whose expense?' I need to give myself the space to be thus reflective in order for my practice for flourishing to approximate my vision without burning myself out. A feminist reflective practice for flourishing cannot do without self-care.

Chapter 15

A MUSLIM CONFLICT OVER UNIVERSAL SALVATION

Jon Hoover

The dominant Sunnī Muslim theology of salvation is based on the principle of retribution. Believers in one God will be rewarded with everlasting Paradise while unbelievers will suffer eternally in Hell-Fire for their failure to believe. Believers may first have to endure time in the Fire to expiate their sins before entering Paradise, but no such hope may be entertained for unbelievers. Many Sunnīs support the eternal damnation of unbelievers with Qur'ānic verses such as 'Truly God has cursed the unbelievers and prepared for them a flaming fire, abiding therein forever' (Q. 33:64-5), but further support for this doctrine has also been found in an appeal to consensus (*ijmā'*) as in the words of medieval theologian al-Ījī (d. 1355): 'The Muslims have reached a consensus that the unbelievers will abide in the Fire forever; their chastisement will not be cut off' (1997: 3:397). In the traditional Sunnī doctrine of consensus, what Muslims have come to agree upon is binding and no longer subject to debate.

However, not everyone has always agreed. The doctrine of eternal damnation of unbelievers in the Fire received one of its most forceful critiques in the theology of fourteenth-century Damascene theologian Ibn Taymiyya (d. 1328) and his foremost disciple Ibn Qayyim al-Jawziyya (d. 1350). Ibn Taymiyya was a prolific and insightful thinker who has inspired a wide range of reform-minded Muslims in the modern period, and he is most famous as a key source of authority for Islamic militants such as Osama bin Laden (d. 2011). Ibn Taymiyya's student Ibn al-Qayyim was equally prolific, and his books are popular in Salafi circles throughout the world today. These two figures are not usually known for their moderation or their tolerance. So, it often comes as a surprise that they set forth arguments on both Qur'ānic and theological grounds that chastisement of unbelievers in Hell-Fire would come to an end, arguments that, as we will see later on, continue to attract some Muslim scholars today.

What follows is the story of how Ibn Taymiyya and Ibn Qayyim al-Jawziyya bypass the alleged consensus on eternal damnation of unbelievers in the Fire in order to give precedence to a reformist and therapeutic rationale for chastisement leading to universal salvation, and then how the Damascene jurist Taqī al-Dīn al-Subkī (d. 1355), by all appearances, forced Ibn al-Qayyim to back down on his views with a refutation of Ibn Taymiyya. This account draws together into a single narrative findings published earlier in two studies on Ibn Taymiyya and Ibn Qayyim al-Jawziyya's texts and argumentation (Hoover 2009; Hoover 2013; see also Khalil 2012: 80–102).

Ibn Taymiyya's Case for Universal Salvation

Ibn Taymiyya's case for universal salvation was known to several medieval writers, but modern scholars were unable to locate it in his own writings until his treatise on the topic was published in Saudi Arabia in 1995. The treatise is called *Al-Radd 'alā man qāla bi-fanā' al-janna wa al-nār* (The Response to Whoever Says that the Garden and the Fire Will Pass Away) or *Fanā' al-nār* (The Passing Away of the Fire) for short. *Fanā' al-nār* is the very last work that Ibn Taymiyya wrote before his death in 1328, which explains why no reflection on the subject has been found elsewhere in his corpus. His disciple Ibn Qayyim al-Jawziyya had asked him earlier about the duration of chastisement for unbelievers, but Ibn Taymiyya could only reply that it was a great question. He apparently did not know what to think. A while later, Ibn al-Qayyim presented Ibn Taymiyya a saying attributed to the Prophet Muḥammad's Companion 'Umar b. al-Khattāb that he had found in a ninth-century Qur'ān commentary. The statement from 'Umar reads: 'Even if the People of the Fire stayed in the Fire like the amount of sand of 'Ālij, they would have, despite that, a day in which they would come out.' The amount of sand of 'Ālij, a sandy expanse on the way to Mecca, was presumably very great, and the duration of punishment for people in the Fire will be similarly very long. Nonetheless, 'Umar's saying indicates that there will come a time when everyone in the Fire will leave it. This affirmation of universal salvation contradicted the mainstream Sunnī view of Ibn Taymiyya's day, and it bothered Ibn al-Qayyim enough to ask his teacher what it meant (Hoover 2009: 182–5).

The central arguments of Ibn Taymiyya's response in *Fanā' al-nār* are worth reviewing in some detail. A key section of the treatise presents textual support for the limited duration of chastisement in the Fire. Ibn Taymiyya begins with 'Umar's report just noted, 'Even if the People of the Fire stayed in the Fire like the amount of sand of 'Ālij, they would have, despite that, a day in which they would come out.' According to Ibn Taymiyya, this report interprets the Qur'ānic witness that those in Hell will be 'staying in it for long stretches of time (*lābithīna fīhā aḥqāban*)' (Q. 78:23). 'Umar's report clarifies that the 'long stretches of time' in this verse do come to an end. Medieval Sunnī theologians like Fakhr al-Dīn al-Rāzī (d. 1209) interpreted this verse to apply only to believing sinners in order to reconcile it to mainstream Sunnī doctrine: monotheistic sinners will be the ones suffering in the Fire for 'long stretches of time' before entering Paradise. However, Ibn Taymiyya rejects this interpretation and maintains that the verse applies to unbelievers as well.

Ibn Taymiyya also supports his case with the Qur'ānic verse claiming that the residents of the Fire will be 'abiding in the Fire, as long as the Heavens and the Earth endure, except as your Lord wills' (Q. 11:107). To interpret this, Ibn Taymiyya turns to a report from the Prophet's Companion Ibn 'Abbās, which reads, 'It is not necessary for anyone to judge God with respect to His creatures or to assign them to a garden or a fire.' In Ibn Taymiyya's view, this report means that the time spent in the Fire need not last forever in an absolute sense. Instead, it is contingent upon God's will and the continuing existence of this world (Ibn Taymiyya 1995: 52–70; Hoover 2009: 186).

The next section of Ibn Taymiyya's *Fanā' al-nār* refutes arguments for the perpetuity of the Fire, and two of these are pivotal. According to the first argument, the Qur'ān demonstrates the Fire's perpetuity with verses such as Q. 33:64-5 quoted above indicating that unbelievers will abide in the Fire forever. Despite such verses, Ibn Taymiyya counters that the Qur'ān does not say that the Fire will never pass away. Rather, those in Hell-Fire will 'abide therein forever' only for the duration of the chastisement. The terms 'abide' and 'forever' need not mean that chastisement will continue without end.

The second argument is that the Muslim community has come to consensus on perpetual chastisement of unbelievers in the Fire and that there was no disagreement over this matter among the Salaf, that is, the first two or three generations of Muslims following the Prophet Muḥammad. Ibn Taymiyya denies that the Salaf had arrived at a consensus on the everlasting chastisement of unbelievers in the Fire. He asserts instead that none of the Prophet's Companions ever said that the Fire would last forever in an absolute sense. Moreover, the Successors, the generation following the Companions, had divergent opinions on the matter. For Ibn Taymiyya a consensus of the Salaf is the only authoritative kind of consensus, and such a consensus does not exist on this question. He rejects the dominant Sunnī understanding of his day that the Muslim community may come to a binding consensus after the era of the Salaf. Such a consensus, Ibn Taymiyya believes, would simply be too difficult to verify given the size and spread of the community, and it would be susceptible to correction should a stronger proof emerge. This Salafi approach to religious authority is the fundamental difference dividing Ibn Taymiyya from traditionalist Sunnism (Ibn Taymiyya 1995: 71–9; Hoover 2009: 186–7; al-Matroudi 2006: 57–9, 186–7).

In *Fanā' al-nār* Ibn Taymiyya also provides theological arguments based on God's attributes, beginning from God's mercy. God's mercy (*raḥma*) and God's forgiveness necessarily entail that the blessing of Paradise last forever without end. However, none of God's names or attributes necessarily entails the perpetuity of chastisement. Moreover, God's mercy is overwhelming and all-encompassing in accord with the Qur'ān – '[God] has written mercy for Himself' (Q. 6:12) – and with hadith reports from the Prophet: 'My mercy precedes my anger' and 'My mercy overcomes my anger.' In view of God's overpowering mercy, Ibn Taymiyya reasons, there can be no everlasting chastisement. In a further argument, Ibn

Taymiyya appeals to God's attribute of wisdom, God's wise purpose (*ḥikma*), in everything that God creates. Given that God's wise purpose in chastisement is cleansing and purifying souls from sin, there could be no imaginable wise purpose in God creating everlasting chastisement (Ibn Taymiyya 1995: 80–3; Hoover 2009: 188–9).

Not only does Ibn Taymiyya's Salafi approach to consensus and religious authority clash with Sunnī traditionalism, but his optimistic appeal to God's wise purposes in all that God creates conflicts with the dominant Ashʿarī theological view that God's acts without purpose or reason. For strict Ashʿarīs, there is no explanation for what God does apart from God's sheer will. Ibn Taymiyya spends considerable energy refuting this Ashʿarī voluntarism in other works, and he affirms that God creates all things for wise purposes such that this is the best of all possible worlds. God creates even evils for wise purposes that contribute to the greater good of educating and purifying human beings and spurring them on to worship God alone. The rebellion of Pharaoh and his destruction teach all later generations a lesson concerning what to avoid. Illness and falling into sin foster humility, and suffering expiates sins. Ibn Taymiyya's rejection of the Sunnī traditionalist notion of consensus and reports like those noted above from ʿUmar and Ibn ʿAbbās open the door to rethinking the mainstream doctrine of eternal chastisement. Then it was probably Ibn Taymiyya's theology of God's wise purposes that, above all else, impelled him to argue for limited chastisement. Punishment of unbelievers in everlasting Fire does not fit with Ibn Taymiyya's view of a God who creates all human beings for wise purposes and draws them to worship God alone. Ibn Taymiyya never states absolutely in *Fanā' al-nār* that salvation will be universal, but that is clearly the upshot of his argument (Hoover 2009: 189–190; Hoover 2007).

Ibn al-Qayyim's Arguments for Universal Salvation

Ibn Taymiyya's *Fanā' al-nār*, written just before his death in 1328, seems not to have aroused much interest until his student Ibn Qayyim al-Jawziyya copied portions of it into his book on eschatology *Hādi al-arwāḥ ilā bilād al-afrāḥ* (Spurring Souls on to the Realms of Joys). To the best of our knowledge, this book dates to 1345, some seventeen years after Ibn Taymiyya's death. As we will see below, this is also when Ibn al-Qayyim begins having difficulties with the Shāfiʿī chief judge in Damascus Taqī al-Dīn al-Subkī. In *Hādī* Ibn al-Qayyim follows the order of presentation in Ibn Taymiyya's *Fanā' al-nār* closely and examines the relevant texts from the Qur'ān and reports from ʿUmar, Ibn ʿAbbās and others in support of limited chastisement. He also greatly elaborates the theological arguments for limited chastisement in the Fire in a strongly therapeutic direction. God's wise purpose in the Fire is cleansing, not vengeance, therapy, not retribution. Ibn al-Qayyim writes in *Hādī*, 'Trial and punishment are the remedies appointed to remove maladies. They are not removed by any other means. And the Fire is the Great Remedy' (Ibn Qayyim al-Jawziyya n.d.: 332; trans. Hoover 2009: 189). He explains elsewhere in *Ḥādī*, 'The wise purpose [of God] – Glory be to Him – required that He make a remedy (*dawā*') appropriate to each malady (*dā*') and that the remedy for the malady be among the most toilsome of remedies. The Compassionate Physician cauterizes one who is ill with the Fire, cauterization after cauterization, to remove the vile matter besmirching the upright nature' (Ibn Qayyim al-Jawziyya n.d.: 326; trans. Hoover 2009: 190).

Ibn al-Qayyim also appeals to considerations of benefit and God's attributes. He argues that eternal chastisement does not benefit anyone. God is above needing any benefit that might be derived from it, and God's beloved do not gain any blessing from it either. With respect to God's attributes, Ibn al-Qayyim argues that God's mercy and good pleasure are essential attributes that will overcome God's non-essential attributes of wrath and anger thus implying that the Fire will end. Moreover, God's wise purpose precludes the evil of eternal Hell-Fire: 'It is not in the divine wise purpose that evils remain perpetually without end and without interruption forever such that [evils] and goods would be equivalent in this' (Ibn Qayyim al-Jawziyya n.d.: 341; trans. Hoover 2009: 190).

These arguments might lead us to think that Ibn Qayyim al-Jawziyya unequivocally affirms limited chastisement in the Fire. At the very end of his discussion, however, he quotes the Qur'ān, 'Surely your Lord does whatever He wills' (Q. 11:107), and notes that this final appeal to God's will was the view of 'Alī b. Abī Ṭālib, cousin and son-in-law of the Prophet. It thus appears that Ibn al-Qayyim backs away from his arguments and simply withholds judgement on the duration of the Fire. Ibn al-Qayyim makes this agnostic position much clearer in his later work *Shifā' al-ʿalīl* (The Healing of the Sick) where he quotes several more sayings of the Salaf leaving the duration of the Fire to God's will beyond that of 'Alī b. Abī Ṭālib (Hoover 2009: 190–3).

In *Shifā'* Ibn al-Qayyim expands Ibn Taymiyya's theodicy of optimism in which God creates all things for wise purposes, and he raises and responds to numerous questions about evil, one of which is, 'What pleasure or good ensues from severe chastisement that does not break off or abate?' (Ibn Qayyim al-Jawziyya 1994a: 540; trans. Hoover 2009: 191). The answer in short is none; there is no good reason for everlasting chastisement. Ibn al-Qayyim elaborates his arguments for limited duration of chastisement in the Fire much as he does in *Ḥādī*, but he encounters a somewhat more difficult theological dilemma. In *Ḥādī* Ibn al-Qayyim argues that God's attributes of mercy and good pleasure are essential but anger and wrath are not, which allows him to say that the chastisement that flows from God's anger and wrath need not be eternal. In *Shifā'* Ibn al-Qayyim locates the source of chastisement instead in God's essential attributes of justice, might and wise purpose. This has the advantage of bringing chastisement under the apparently more rational regime of God's justice and wisdom – God's attribute of anger may imply volatility and capriciousness – but it would also seem to imply that chastisement must be eternal by virtue of the eternality of these attributes. Ibn al-Qayyim denies that this is so. Rather, God's attributes of justice, might and wise purpose indicate when chastisement should end as these attributes come under the rule of mercy and forgiveness. Ibn al-Qayyim explains:

> If it is said, 'Chastisement emanates from His might, His wise purpose and His justice. These are beautiful names and attributes of perfection. What emanates from them is perpetual by virtue of their perpetuity,' it is said, 'By God, chastisement indeed emanates from might, wise purpose and justice. The end [of chastisement], when what is intended is obtained, emanates from might, wise purpose and justice. Chastisement and its interruption do not fall outside the sphere of His might, His wise purpose and His justice. However, when it ends, might is conjoined with mercy, and mercy is conjoined with liberality, beneficence, pardon and forgiveness. Might and wise purpose do not cease and do not decrease. On the contrary, everything that He created, that He creates, that He commanded and that He commands emanates from His might and His wise purpose.' (Ibn Qayyim al-Jawziyya 1994a: 562; trans. Hoover 2009: 192)

As already noted above, Ibn al-Qayyim ends his discussion of chastisement in *Shifā'* by making his agnosticism more explicit than he did in *Hādī*. He also notes that there is no textual support for the perpetuity of the Fire. However, he himself is left with textual support in the Qur'ān and in traditions such as those of 'Umar and Ibn 'Abbās for two different positions: the passing away of the Fire and agnosticism as to its duration. In *Hādi* and *Shifā'* he takes the safer course of favouring the agnostic texts, but in a third work he gives freer rein to the arguments for limited duration of the Fire (Hoover 2009: 192–3).

This third work is Ibn al-Qayyim's *Al-Ṣawā'iq al-mursala* (The Thunderbolts Sent Out), an extensive work of theology written soon after *Hādī* and *Shifā'*. As the second half of *Al-Sawā'iq al-mursala*, in which Ibn al-Qayyim discusses the duration of the Fire, is not known to be extant, we must rely on the abridgement *Mukhtaṣar al-ṣawā'iq al-mursala* by Ibn al-Qayyim's contemporary Muḥammad b. al-Mawṣili (d. 1372). The abridgement is reliable so far as we can tell, and for the sake of simplicity I will speak of *Mukhtaṣar al-ṣawā'iq* as Ibn al-Qayyim's work and refer to it henceforth simply as *Ṣawā'iq*.

As in *Hādī* and *Shifā'*, Ibn al-Qayyim in *Ṣawā'iq* undermines the claim of consensus for eternal punishment of unbelievers, interprets the relevant texts from the Qur'ān and the Salaf and argues that God's mercy will overcome all else. He also calls the Fire God's whip 'to lead His servants to His mercy and His Garden' (Ibn Qayyim al-Jawziyya 2004: 664; trans. Hoover 2009: 195), and he marshals a new argument against eternal chastisement: God's justice and blessing preclude chastising someone forever for associationism and unbelief that is only of limited length in this life. Moreover, Ibn al-Qayyim leaves aside his earlier agnosticism on the duration of the Fire and urges his readers to recognize that considerations of benefit, the character of God's names and attributes, the texts of revelation and the witness of the Salaf all lead to the conclusion that chastisement must come to an end. Agnosticism as to the duration of chastisement is an option only for those who cannot grasp all of this. In Ibn al-Qayyim's own words,

> Those who say that the chastisement of unbelievers is a benefit to them and a mercy to them circle around this sense and do not penetrate its depth. But what benefit to them is there in chastisement that does not end, that is perpetual by virtue of the perpetuity of the Lord – Most High is He?! Ponder this point very thoroughly, and give it its due reflection. Join that with the senses of His names and His attributes, with what His word and the word of His Messenger indicate, and with what the Companions and those after them said. Do not rush to speak without knowledge or to condemn. If the dawn of what is correct shines on you, [that is good]. If not, then ascribe the judgment to what God ascribes it in His statement, 'Surely your Lord does whatever He wills' (Q. 11:107), and hold firm to the statement of 'Alī b. Abī Ṭālib – May God be pleased with him. He mentioned that the People of the Garden enter the Garden and the People of the Fire enter the Fire. He described their state. Then he said, 'After that, God does what He wills.' (Ibn Qayyim al-Jawziyya 2004: 663; trans. Hoover 2009: 196)

Ibn al-Qayyim here overcomes his earlier misgivings about the duration of the Fire. His therapeutic rationality completely eclipses the retributive logic of mainstream Sunnī eschatology, and this, supported by the relevant textual indicants, leads him on to unreserved affirmation of universal salvation.

Al-Subkī's Opposition to Ibn Qayyim al-Jawziyya

There is very little for the historian to go on to ascertain how Ibn Qayyim al-Jawziyya's arguments for the limited duration of Hell-Fire were received. Ibn al-Qayyim does not tell us anything about his audience and their responses, nor do there appear to be reports about this controversy in contemporary chronicles. However, we do know that in 1348 the powerful Shāfiʿī chief judge in Damascus Taqī al-Dīn al-Subkī intervened with a treatise called *Al-Iʿtibār bi-baqā' al-janna wa al-nār* (The Consideration of the Perdurance of Paradise and the Fire) to shut down Ibn Qayyim al-Jawziyya's argumentation for limited duration of the Fire, and, as we will see below, it appears to have worked. This intervention was part of a wider conflict between al-Subkī on the one hand and Ibn Taymiyya and Ibn al-Qayyim on the other. Al-Subkī had written against Ibn Taymiyya on divorce and other legal matters while the latter was still alive. The first sign of trouble between al-Subkī and Ibn al-Qayyim appeared in 1341 when al-Subkī tried to prevent the release of Ibn Taymiyya's books that had been locked up in the Citadel of Damascus from the time of his death. Al-Subkī suffered the humiliation of having his efforts thwarted, and the books were turned over to Ibn al-Qayyim and one of Ibn Taymiyya's brothers. Then, in 1345, al-Subkī confronted Ibn al-Qayyim over legalities concerning the correct conduct of horse races, and Ibn al-Qayyim had to back down. Later, in

1348 or 1349 and soon after completing *I'tibār*, al-Subkī wrote a long refutation of
Ibn al-Qayyim's anti-Ash'arī theological poem *Al-Kāfiya al-shāfiya* (The Sufficient
Healing [Poem]). Al-Subkī is explicit in stating that one specific follower of Ibn
Taymiyya – obviously Ibn al-Qayyim – is insidiously spreading Ibn Taymiyya's
beliefs. Apparently, Ibn al-Qayyim's poem and his Taymiyya doctrines had become
sufficiently popular that al-Subkī saw the need to refute them. Finally, in 1349 the
two scholars also disagreed on divorce law and had to be reconciled in public (Bori
and Holtzman 2010: 22–6: Hoover 2013: 397–9).

Al-Subkī's 1348 *I'tibār* is a direct refutation of Ibn Taymiyya's *Fanā' al-nār*.
Al-Subkī does not refer to Ibn Qayyim al-Jawziyya, and he does not quote or
discuss any text from Ibn al-Qayyim's books not already found in Ibn Taymiyya's
treatise. Nonetheless, the target of al-Subkī's ire in historical context is clearly Ibn
al-Qayyim. By 1348, Ibn al-Qayyim's extensive argumentation for limited duration
of the Fire in *Hādī*, *Shifā'* and probably *Ṣawā'iq* had seeped out into the public
domain enough to threaten the orthodoxy of the day, much as had Ibn al-Qayyim's
anti-Ash'arī polemic in his *Al-Kāfiya al-shāfiya*, and it called for al-Subkī's response
(Hoover 2009: 200n. 21; Hoover 2013: 399).

Al-Subkī's refutation neither engages Ibn Taymiyya's reformist rationale based
on God's mercy and wise purpose nor elaborates the retributive basis of his own
views with any sophistication. Rather, he spends much of *I'tibār* quoting Qur'ānic
verses traditionally understood to support the eternal damnation of unbelievers
in the Fire, and he invokes the authority of consensus at the very beginning of the
treatise: 'The doctrine of the Muslims is that the Garden and the Fire will not pass
away. Abū Muḥammad b. Ḥazm has transmitted that this is held by consensus and
that whoever opposes it is an unbeliever by consensus' (Al-Subkī 1987: 32; trans.
Hoover 2009: 187). Expressing any doubt about the Fire's eternity is to break with
the consensus of the Muslim community and fall into unbelief.

The full import of al-Subkī's appeal to consensus becomes clear in his response
to Ibn Taymiyya's charge that there was no consensus among the Salaf. According
to al-Subkī, reports from the Salaf like those invoked by Ibn Taymiyya to support
the limited duration of the Fire should not be understood literally. They should
be subjected to reinterpretation (*ta'wīl*) to correspond with the consensus, and
statements of the Salaf that appear to challenge a consensus should be interpreted
so as 'to give a favorable opinion of them [that is, the Salaf]' (Al-Subkī 1987: 79,
trans. Hoover 2009: 187). Al-Subkī thus asserts the superior authority of a later
consensus within the Muslim community over the earlier testimony of the Salaf.
He leaves no room for Ibn Taymiyya and Ibn Qayyim al-Jawziyya's reformative
appeal to the Salaf. The consensus on eternal damnation of unbelievers is inviolable
(Hoover 2009: 187–8).

Ibn Qayyim's Affirmation of Eternal Chastisement for Unbelievers

It appears that Ibn Qayyim al-Jawziyya bowed to al-Subkī's pressure to stop
arguing for the limited duration of the Fire just as he yielded to al-Subkī in their

conflicts over horse racing legalities and divorce procedures. There is no evidence dating Ibn al-Qayyim's latest lengthy deliberation on the duration of Hell-Fire – that found in *Ṣawā'iq* – to after al-Subkī's 1348 *I'tibār*, and it most likely came before. Additionally, Ibn al-Qayyim briefly affirms the eternity of Hell-Fire in three books. One of these, *Zād al-ma'ād* (The Provision for the Afterlife), is the last work that he wrote before his death in 1350 and thus definitely dates to after al-Subkī's refutation. The other two works, *Al-Wābil al-ṣayyib* (The Heavy Shower) and *Ṭarīq al-hijratayn* (The Road of the Two Migrations), may also be late, but they cannot be dated precisely.

The discussions in all three of these works draw a contrast between people who are fair (*ṭayyib*) and foul (*khabīth*) and explain that the fair and the foul are mixed in this world while only Paradise is fitting for the fair and Hell-Fire for the foul in the hereafter. In *Al-Wābil al-ṣayyib* Ibn al-Qayyim sets out the traditional Sunnī view that the disobedient in whom the foul and the fair are mixed will eventually leave Hell for Paradise, the abode of pure fairness. However, the abode of pure foulness will remain forever. In *Ṭarīq al-hijratayn* Ibn al-Qayyim simply affirms that the abode of Paradise and the abode of Hell both serve God's wise purpose and are permanent. This work also includes an extensive review of eighteen levels of humans and jinn in Paradise and the Fire in the hereafter. Throughout these discussions, the question of an end to the chastisement of foul unbelievers is never entertained (Hoover 2013: 392–4).

Ibn al-Qayyim's last work *Zād al-ma'ād* is a wide-ranging collection of hadith reports from the Prophet. The introduction to this multivolume tome explains how following the Prophet leads to happiness in this world and in the hereafter, and Ibn al-Qayyim includes observations on how God in his power and wise purpose choses some things over others and how he creates some creatures to be fair and others foul. This leads him to consider the ultimate destiny of the fair and the foul, and he proceeds to exclude the completely foul from any possibility of reform: 'When an associator (*mushrik*) is foul in constitution and foul in essence, the Fire does not cleanse his foulness. On the contrary, if he were to come out of it, he would return as foul as he was [before], like a dog when it enters the sea and then comes out of it. Therefore, God – Most High is He – forbade the Garden to the associator' (Ibn Qayyim al-Jawziyya 1994b: 1:68; trans. Hoover 2013: 391).

It has been argued that Ibn al-Qayyim says nothing in this passage that opposes his earlier arguments for universal salvation. Ibn al-Qayyim never formally retracted his belief, and he is simply exercising prudence here in view of Taqī al-Dīn al-Subkī's wrath while in fact affirming nothing more than that the purification of associators will take an extremely long time (Khalil 2012: 100–1). It is very well possible that Ibn al-Qayyim continued to harbour belief in universal salvation in his heart, especially as he does not explicitly renounce it. However, the statement from *Zād al-ma'ād* just quoted clearly states that an associator can never attain Paradise, and there is no sign in the surrounding discussion of Ibn al-Qayyim's earlier therapeutic concern to show that God's wise purpose in chastisement is cleansing foul unbelievers to render them fair. Ibn al-Qayyim's final testament, at least outwardly, is thus to everlasting punishment of the foul in Hell-Fire, and it is apparent that al-Subkī succeeded in preventing Ibn al-Qayyim from writing in any way that might betray belief to the contrary (Hoover 2013: 391–2, 396–9).

Epilogue

Ibn Taymiyya and Ibn Qayyim al-Jawziyya present a powerful challenge to the dominant Sunnī doctrine that condemns unbelievers to everlasting chastisement in Hell-Fire. Their Salafī rejection of traditionalist Sunnī consensus undermines the structure of religious authority in which the doctrine of eternal damnation is rooted, and their theological vision of God's mercy and wise purpose using Hell-Fire as a therapeutic instrument leading even unbelievers to eventual salvation overwhelms the retributive rationality giving it sense. Al-Subkī's rejoinder misses this theological aspect entirely, and he devotes his efforts to restoring mainstream Sunnī doctrine primarily through Qur'ānic quotation and appeal to consensus. In the end, al-Subkī succeeded in squelching Ibn al-Qayyim's voice for universal salvation in the late 1340s more by virtue of his influence as a leading scholar in the dominant Shāfi'ī legal school than by force of argument.

Many other opponents through the centuries and to the present have condemned Ibn Taymiyya and Ibn al-Qayyim for denying the eternity of Hell-Fire. The charge has obviously stung as some defenders of the two fourteenth-century theologians have tried to absolve them of holding such a purported error. In a prime example 'Alī al-Ḥarbī, a scholar working in Saudi Arabia, argued in 1990 that Ibn Taymiyya upheld the Fire's eternity. Despite very modest evidence to the contrary—this was before the publication of *Fanā' al-nār* in 1995—al-Ḥarbī could not imagine that so great an Islamic reformer as Ibn Taymiyya could believe in the limited duration of Hell-Fire. Al-Ḥarbī also side-stepped important clues for the dating of Ibn al-Qayyim's works in order to portray his undeniable arguments for universal salvation in *Ḥādī*, *Shifā'* and *Ṣawā'iq* as little more than youthful exuberance before he settled down to correct belief in his mature years (Hoover 2013). Despite such valiant efforts to advance the orthodoxy of the Fire's eternity, even for Ibn Taymiyya and Ibn al-Qayyim themselves, the Muslim community has not been able to thwart the allure of a therapeutic vision of Hell-Fire, and other scholars have expressed deep admiration for Ibn Taymiyya and Ibn Qayyim al-Jawziyya's universalist argumentation. The early twentieth-century reformer in Egypt Rashīd Riḍā (d. 1935) cited and praised Ibn al-Qayyim's arguments for universal salvation in *Ḥādī* to challenge exclusivist attitudes and commend God's great mercy. Riḍā's views provoked considerable opposition, and in response he moderated his enthusiasm for universalism by clarifying that both he and Ibn al-Qayyim ultimately left the duration of Hell-Fire to God's will. A generation later, the rector of al-Azhar University in Cairo Mahmūd Shaltūt (d. 1963) wrote favourably of Ibn al-Qayyim's arguments, and much more recently, in 2002 and

2003, the widely influential Qatarī-based revivalist Yūsuf al-Qaraḍāwī (b. 1926) affirmed Ibn al-Qayyim's universalist argumentation as well (Khalil 2012: 101–6, 126–32). Given the powerful precedents for both sides of the argument, there is little doubt that Muslim deliberation over universal salvation will continue well into the future. At stake is whether retribution or therapy is the fundamental purpose of God's chastisement of wayward and unbelieving human beings. Both rationales for punishment are deeply embedded in the Islamic religious tradition and in human experience more generally.

Chapter 16

SIGNS OF SALVATION: INSECURITY, RISK AND THE END OF THE WORLD IN LATE MODERNITY

Steve Knowles

Events of the early twenty-first century – the terrorist atrocities of 9/11 and 7/7, and more recently, the Charlie Hebdo murders in Paris; the 2008 global financial crash; the Fukushima Daiichi nuclear disaster in 2011 and innumerable environmental disasters – have brought into sharp focus the paradoxical nature of modernity. They are events that highlight both the triumphs of modernity as well as the Promethean ignominy that is part of the detritus of the late modern landscape. Modernity's craving for order through the rationalization and routinization of life and the scientific enterprise was thought to lead to an end to chaos and disorder and to the elimination of ambiguity and contingency. Instead it has served to accentuate and underline both order and chaos. Not only has the idea of order functioned to emphasize chaos, ironically it has been party to creating it. As Zygmunt Bauman notes, 'Order and chaos are *modern twins*' (1991: 4).

Living at a time when the triumphs of modernity seem to undermine security has led to an increased awareness of risk and risk-taking. Since the end of the Second World War, the subject of risk has become an increasingly important sociological factor when considering the course of modernity in the second half of the twentieth century and in the early twenty-first century. Mary Douglas (1980), Anthony Giddens (1991) and Ulrich Beck (1992; 2009) have all contributed to debate concerning the nature of risk. In particular, it is the work of Beck, who has written extensively on contemporary risk and the idea that we inhabit a 'world risk society', which will provide the conceptual framework for this discussion.

Late modernity has also spawned other shifts in the sociological landscape. Partridge notes that the 'late modern West has witnessed the spread of [the] "luxuriant undergrowth" of religiosity' (2004: 58). But that is not all. As well as a fervent capacity to produce new religion making-characteristics (Lyon 1999; Carrette and King 2005), an unintended consequence of late modernity has been the steady rise of fundamentalisms, both secular and religious (Marsden 1991; Riesebrodt 1993; Hoover and Kaneva 2009; Marty and Appleby 1991). Indeed, some religious fundamentalist groups reason that the existence of insecurity caused by global catastrophes correlates with what they perceive to be 'signs of the end times'. Such catastrophic events are a sign that the end of the world as we know it is imminent.

The effects of modernity – or more specifically late modernity within the framework of world risk society[1] – on representations of Christian fundamentalism online is a crucial aspect of this analysis. The contention is that it is the external influences brought about by living in a culture of risk – a world risk society – and the existential threats that accompany this that cause believers to link these threats and catastrophes directly with their own apocalyptic beliefs. Moreover, making such connections between biblical prophecy and global risk affirms two things. First, it provides ongoing affirmation of faith in the face of widespread anxiety; thus re-asserting ontological security found in the sanctuary that is salvation through faith in Christ. Second, such signs act as evidence for those who do not yet believe in Christ. Bible prophecy teachers interpret catastrophic events and technological advances as proof that the end of the world is close at hand and Christ will soon return to rapture believers. Therefore, the signs serve evangelistically to encourage non-believers to put their faith in Christ – to receive salvation – before it is too late. Salvation is affirmed and found in such events and developments.

The chapter is divided into three parts. First, an outline of Ulrich Beck's world risk society thesis will provide an important part of the sociological context within which fundamentalism has flourished, particularly in the last fifty years. Second, an introduction to one specific aspect of Christian fundamentalism – namely 'rapture culture' (Frykholm 2004) provides the theological context for the discussion. Third, examples of contemporary 'rapture culture' are examined which demonstrates the influence of risk and the concomitant insecurity that serves such a theological perspective. Within this culture signs of the end of the world provide succour and point to the possibility that salvation is close at hand.

World Risk Society

From mundane questions of whether it is safe to use a mobile phone or a microwave oven, to the more menacing and altogether foreboding apocalyptic questions regarding nuclear power/weapons, we all, to varying degrees assess risk in our daily lives. However, it seems that there is a raised awareness of it today. That is not to say that existential insecurity is a new phenomenon; on the contrary, it has always accompanied human existence (Beck 2009: 4). Since the early twentieth century, advances in technology have resulted in the Promethean myth of the Enlightenment being turned on its head. Indeed, what lies at the very heart of contemporary Western society is the opportunity to choose between grades of risk that suit our context given the likely events of the future (Denney 2005: 10–11). The management of risk guides our lives in an extensive range of decision-making: from issues regarding public health to the recommended alcoholic units we can consume; from planting corn to marketing and selling cereals (Bernstein 1998: 2).

Advances in science and cutting-edge technologies have brought hope as well as despair and fear (Furedi 2006), and the triumphs of modernity have given way to risky consequences. Radicalization of the processes of modernization has resulted in decisions being taken the consequences of which are unknown. As Denney notes, 'Despite the reliance on a logic based upon technology, uncertainty now forms the basis of a post-traditional society' (2005: 29).

In 1986 Ulrich Beck's *Risk Society* was published[2] and met with critical acclaim. Here, as well as in other works, including most notably *World at Risk* (2009), Beck outlined what he saw as the transition from industrial society to risk society. Although risks have always been prevalent throughout human history, contemporary risk is qualitatively different to that which previously existed. Risk in pre-industrial society 'assaulted the nose or the eyes and were thus perceptible to the senses, while the risks of civilization today typically *escape perception*' (Beck 1992: 21). Beck argues that as a consequence of the global reaches of risk the political stakes are heightened and all areas of society are affected. We are 'all members of a global community of threat' (2009: 8). Government policy legitimates the restriction of freedoms whilst at the same time trying to protect them.

Jim McGuigan sums up Beck's position by noting that his central idea is that industrial society threatens its own existence (2006: 138). For Beck, there are serious side effects to industrial society's progress. Modernization has spawned a multitude of humanly manufactured risks. Beck remarks that 'the key difference between classical and modern risk lies at another level. The risks generated by industrial and large-scale technologies are the result of conscious decisions' (2009: 25): they are the unintended consequences of such advances. We now inhabit a world risk society (2009). That is, a world in which the advances of technological progress have brought about and led to uncertainty, doubt and fear. We have moved from industrial society to risk society (Beck 1992: 10–11). This has led to late modernity (risk society) becoming reflexive which in turn leads to radicalized individualization (Beck 2009). ' "Individualization" ... means, first, the disembedding and, second, the re-embedding of industrial society ways of life by new ones, ones in which the individuals must produce, stage and cobble together their biographies themselves' (Beck 1994: 13).

Decision-making in a post-traditional society means that the onus which was once at the societal level is now very much in the hands of the individual. Members of society have to make decisions that would normally be shaped and made *for* them. Traditional services provided through the welfare state, education, the trade union movement, the institution of marriage and other support mechanisms that have been so heavily relied upon within modernity have seen their influence wane. Moreover, the challenge of the degendering of employment and the 'crisis of the patriarchal family' sends a seismic shudder through the foundations of personal security (Castells 2010: 420). Simon Clarke notes that, 'Gender roles [and] notions of class are called into question, people now make their own decisions about their lives and futures as traditional ways of thinking and doing disintegrate' (2006: 172). As a result responsibility increasingly lies with the individual. The implications of this are that individuals are exposed more than ever to making their own decisions, and as a consequence, take greater risks. Rather than this being a liberating and emancipatory process it flings individuals into the turbulence of risk society. A corollary of this is that existential insecurity and uncertainty become an important force in the lives of individuals.

In *World at Risk* (2009), Beck develops this further by 'make[ing] a distinction between three "logics" of global risks ... namely, environmental crises, global financial risks and terrorist threats' (13). These are significant distinctions because, as we shall see, they also reflect the typology of 'signs' identified by many within 'rapture culture' that pertain to the end of the world.

One of the unintended consequences of living in a world risk society is the rise of fundamentalisms. In terms of the discussion here, Giddens usefully describes fundamentalism as 'beleaguered tradition' (2002: 49). It is tradition that remains, even retreats within its own set of boundaries, and as a reaction to modernization and globalization defends life lived and understood within the precincts of traditionally accepted norms. In a sense, it is acontextual. What matters most is not how beliefs, philosophies or morals etc. are understood in the contemporary context; rather, it is how they are defended, promoted and maintained in a manner that solidifies, even promotes the tradition. Nancy Ammerman describes it as a retrieval of the past (1991: 8). However, it is more than this. It is a vigorous resistance to any threat to the essential truths of the tradition. Fundamentalisms are flights from the anxieties of a turbulent world to a position of (apparent) security: a re-alignment with an ontological position of surety that is earnestly undertaken in an often reactionary way. Manuel Castells writes that a key feature among the cultural communities of fundamentalists is that 'they appear as a reaction to prevailing social trends, which are resisted on behalf of autonomous sources of meaning. They are, at the onset, defensive identities that function as refuge and solidarity, to protect against a hostile, outside world' (2010: 68). In other words they are 'communities of resistance' (Castells 2010: 68).

Giddens argues that 'fundamentalism gives new vitality and importance to the guardians of tradition' (2002: 48). These guardians, often those in authority, are in a position to interpret sacred texts, preserve truths and teach and pass on the tradition. In recognition of the destabilizing influences of modernity on taken-for-granted traditions the guardians of them often instigate vigorous defensive mechanisms that serve to embed, retrench and re-enforce them.

Rapture Culture

The rapture in the context of Christian fundamentalism is the belief that prior to his second coming, Christ will first return to take believers both alive and dead up into the air with him. As in many fundamentalist groups it is a literal rendering of the Bible which takes centre-stage. The text which is cited as evidence for this is

1 Thessalonians 4:17: 'Then we who are alive, who are left, will be caught up in the clouds together with them to meet the Lord in the air; and so will be with the Lord forever.'[3] Believers will be raptured into the air with Christ and avoid the period of tribulation that follows. This pretribulation understanding is associated with dispensational theology and more specifically with the theology of John Nelson Derby (1800–82), the Church of Ireland priest who was pivotal in developing the doctrine sometimes known as the secret rapture. Dispensationalism is the belief that history is split into a series of set administrations in which God deals with humanity.[4]

Although not what Derby originally intended, the temptation with many subsequent interpreters of premillennial, pretribulation dispensationalist beliefs has been to examine the 'signs of the times' – catastrophes such as turmoil in the Middle East, financial meltdown, famine, nuclear disaster, acts of terrorism etc. – and link them directly to biblical prophecy.[5] It is no surprise that in times of great geopolitical unrest this speculation is at its most intense. Since the end of the Second World War the connection of Bible prophecy with contemporary events has increased dramatically. The Bible prophecy teacher probably most responsible for bringing this form of biblical prophecy into mainstream Western popular culture is Hal Lindsey. His book, *The Late Great Planet Earth* (1970)[6] systematically 'turned the Bible into a manual of atomic-age combat' (Boyer 1992: 127). In the style of a Hollywood blockbuster, Lindsey brought together examples of what he saw happening in the world at the time with Bible verses he thought foreshadowed a nuclear holocaust.

One of the central events, for Lindsey, that indicated to him that the world was in the last days was the founding of the modern state of Israel in 1948. In his view what we now have is the clearest indicator that the rapture can happen imminently because this was the fulfilment of Jesus' promise found in Matthew 24:33-34. The founding of the state of Israel interpreted through the words of Jesus means that the rapture can occur within a generation. In Lindsey's estimate, a generation was approximately forty years which means that the rapture could occur by 1988.[7] Although the time came and went, Lindsey has still continued to promote his version of biblical prophecy in print, online and through his weekly programme *The Hal Lindsey Report*.[8] Central to Lindsey's contribution to Bible prophecy teaching is that he believed that time was short given the events taking place in the world before Christ returned. For him, it was important to communicate the nearness of the end so that more people would believe in Christ and be saved. Moreover, Lindsey's interpretation of prophecy also acted to reinforce, confirm and embed the beliefs of those who adhered to such a view.

Although there are many examples of what can be termed 'ticking clock' dispensationalism,[9] perhaps the best way to illustrate and summarize this is to quote Lindsey himself from his follow up to *The Late Great Planet Earth – There's a New World Coming* (1973): 'To the sceptic who says that Christ is not coming soon, I would ask him to put the book of Revelation in one hand and the daily newspaper in the other, and then sincerely ask God to show him where we are on his prophetic time-clock' (306).

Although it can be argued that Lindsey was probably the most influential premillennial Bible prophecy teacher after the Second World War, he is not the most successful in terms of sales. That honour goes to Tim LaHaye, who along with Jerry Jenkins authored the commercially successful Left Behind series.[10] As Matthew Sutton notes, 'The Left Behind books explain American premillennial eschatology from beginning to end through fiction' (2014: 364). Set in a post-rapture world, they draw on a premillennial approach to biblical prophecy interpretation, and develop a narrative that brings together the typical symbols of what they perceive to be end-time indicators: for example, advances in technology, turmoil in the Middle East, anti-Semitism and global financial meltdown.

What these novels do, along with Lindsey's work and others is, as Crawford Gribben rightly notes, 'offer a complex analysis of the dangers and the opportunities of modernity, together with a hesitating apologia for isolation from it' (2009: x). More specifically, they represent a reaction to the products and technological advances of late modernity because both the potential of and the actual occurrence of what might be deemed to be the catastrophic bring insecurity and anxiety. In these catastrophic events can be found signs of salvation through the piecing together of their prophetic jigsaw. Ironically, it is only through their adoption and interaction with technology that they are able to offer such interpretations.

Having briefly looked at two of the biggest post-Second World War influences on contemporary rapture culture we shall now turn to a current example of it in digital media.

Prophecy in the News

Prophecy in the News is a multimedia Christian ministry based in Oklahoma City, Oklahoma, USA. It holds the view that the Bible should be understood literally. Their theology is dispensational and the pretribulation rapture is a central doctrine. It was founded and developed by J. R. Church (d. 2011), a Baptist minister, in the early 1980s. The current face of *Prophecy in the News* is Dr Kevin Clarkson, who has been the host of the television programme/online website since September 2014.[11] Clarkson provides analysis on current global affairs in relation to Bible prophecy as well as interviewing numerous preachers, teachers and authors on the subject.

Although originating as a weekly television programme, and still available in this format, the principal platform utilized to communicate their beliefs is the internet.[12] The website[13] incorporates the television programme and the magazine, and has many of the usual features found on similar sites: the organization's history; details of publications and new products; television programme scheduling; links to their television programmes including an archive; contacts; FAQs; and details of how to donate. There are also links to *Prophecy in the News*' social media outlets: Facebook and their own YouTube channel, as well as their television programmes being available as podcasts on iTunes. The television programmes are uploaded on to the YouTube channel and are available on the website. These include not only 'daily'[14] updates on world events but also interviews with Bible prophecy authors who uphold a rapture view and belief that we are in the end times. *Prophecy in the News* also sponsors major prophecy conferences.[15]

As far as the subject matter of the television/online broadcasts is concerned, it can be noted that a wide variety of subject areas are covered relating to Bible prophecy and the end times. They include: Iran's nuclear programme; the emergence of new technology; the future of Islam; genetic Armageddon; updates on the so-called Islamic State (ISIS); relations between USA and Israel; and the dismissal of climate change to name but a few. Two interviews, one from 'The Daily Updates' and another from the general television schedule are examined which provide evidence of how significant events and interpretations of them form the basis of why they believe we live in the end times. Both interviews incorporate analysis of events and developments that have not only become typical within rapture culture but also reflect living in a world risk society.

The Daily Update broadcast online on 11 December 2014 is an interview conducted by Dr Kevin Clarkson with well-known Bible prophecy teacher Bill Salus.[16] The focus is on Salus' new book entitled *Nuclear Showdown in Iran* (2014). Salus talks about the danger of Iran developing nuclear missiles. He claims that the recent breakdown in negotiations between, on the one hand, the United States and its European allies and, on the other hand, Iran regarding the development of nuclear power (Dec 2014) points to the possibility that Iran will continue to stall in the negotiations until they have developed their own nuclear weapons. Salus argues this by providing what he believes is prophetic evidence found in Jeremiah 49:34-49, which he claims, indicates Iran's attempt to destroy Israel. Indeed, for both Salus and Clarkson, Iran is dedicated to the destruction of Israel and is working towards this goal. As a consequence, Salus contends, this will in turn bring about nuclear disaster for Iran which the text in Jeremiah points to. Salus also talks of a further danger that is found in the capability of Iran's Inter-Continental-Ballistic-Missile (ICBM) programme which is capable of striking not only Israel but also the East Coast of the United States with nuclear warheads. He claims that Iran makes the terrorist organization Islamic State (ISIS) seem like 'boy scouts'. For Salus, Iran is a ruthless, oppressive, sovereign country that represses its own citizens; it is probably the most cruel and brutal regime in the Middle East.

Another important aspect that Clarkson and Salus consider is that Iran, with a predominantly Shiite Muslim population, has an eschatology of its own which motivates it to provoke war which will in turn usher in the return of the Islamic messiah (Mahdi). Together, these observations provide signs that we are in the last days which could mean the rapture at any moment.

The second example from *Prophecy in the News* is Clarkson's two-part interview with Pastor Billy Crome,[17] first broadcast on 2 December 2014.[18] Entitled 'The Final Countdown',[19] the discussions cover a wide range of topics that pertain to the 'end times' and link to Bible prophecy. Specifically, Clarkson places the conversation in the context of what has become known as the 'Little Apocalypse': the Olivet discourse in Matthew 24–25 where Jesus speaks about the end times. Their wide-ranging conversation includes some of the following: the fate of Israel; the building of the third temple in Jerusalem; the current state of US/Israel relations; the global rise of anti-Semitism; the correlation between technology and the image of the AntiChrist; the Russia/Ukraine conflict; and what is referred to rather ambiguously as 'world upheavals'. It is this last category which will be the focus here as it encapsulates a number of different sub-topics over the two programmes.

The subject of world upheavals includes: weather patterns; wars and rumours of wars; new technology, with a focus on the military; pestilence which includes a discussion on Ebola; and issues of morality in society. In the discussion about wars and rumours of wars Crome identifies Russia as having a pivotal role in destroying Israel by both arming Islamic nations to destroy Israel and as a key nation that can be identified in the Old Testament prophecies in Ezekiel 38–39. In a feat of hermeneutical gymnastics, Crome then goes onto argue that other passages can be linked to the broad category of wars and rumours of wars. Specifically, he cites Rev. 6 (v. 8) as an important passage that can be understood this way. This passage refers to the destruction of one-quarter of the earth by sword, famine, pestilence and wild beasts; however, for Crome, the wild beasts can also be linked to the emergence of modern technology for which wars are a catalyst. He cites the work of the Defence Advanced Research Project Agency (DARPA)[20] who are working on developing robotic animals. In particular, it is the development of a robotic cheetah that for Crome is most disturbing. He claims that DARPA are planning to arm the robotic cheetah and that it will be used to attack humans. He does add the disclaimer that the text he uses to support this (Rev. 6) might be referring to normal wild animals; however, for him, because we live in such times of technological advancement with wars and rumours of wars serving as the backdrop, such developments are more likely to point to the end times.

In the second part of the interview with Billy Crome,[21] Clarkson sets the scene by talking about the decay in the moral climate in the United States which for him is epitomized in the decline and redefining of marriage. Clarkson claims this is due to the influence of a socialist agenda which pervades the United States as well as having a massive influence globally. Crome agrees and calls this the 'eclipse point'; that is the point at which we see the decline of the Judeo-Christian ethic. Instead what exists now is the increasing influence of the secular and atheist agendas which have led to the church, understood as the traditional bulwark against such changes, becoming weakened. For Crome, the moral climate of the times has changed and the traditional moral standards of society are crumbling.

This view of Western society resonates with the notion of individualization that has emerged as part of the late modern mindset; except there are fundamental differences in causal explanations. For Crome and Clarkson, they are simply signs of the times; they are examples of Bible prophecy coming to pass and they concern what Guyer describes as an evacuation of the 'near future' (Guyer 2007: 409). That is to say, what concerns Bible prophecy teachers is 'the now' and its consequences for eternity. This is brought about by the sheer intensity and immediacy with which information is received and consequently can be disseminated through the lens of premillennial Bible prophecy in a networked[22] world risk society.

These topics will be familiar to those well-versed in Bible prophecy over the last forty years and broadly line up with what Lindsey has been publicizing since the late 1960s. As Susan Harding notes regarding the premillennial predisposition towards such issues, 'History ... is centered in the Middle East and narrated as a relentless road toward fulfilment of biblical prophecies in which reemergent biblical empires plunge into war' (Harding 2000: 238).

The point of bringing these examples together from within what I am naming rapture culture is twofold. First, it should be clear why world risk society is an appropriate framework within which to consider this. The direct correlation of Bible prophecy and emerging technologies, terrorist attacks and the dangers of nuclear weapons constitute some of the main risk typologies that Beck outlines. Moreover, concern for what is understood to be the moral decline in (Western) society is directly related to the rise of individualization: another important element of world risk society. By placing these Bible prophecy claims and narratives within the broad framework of world risk society more sense can be made of them in terms of the impact of 'world risk society'. Glynis Breakwell has noted elsewhere, 'It seems that we are genuinely seeing the impact of beliefs per se upon risk perception' (2007: 62). However, we are also seeing the other side of this: the influence of risk on the way some religious beliefs are interpreted.

The innovative way in which prophecy is linked to contemporary events and catastrophes is due to the context as much as beliefs. Although there is a history of premillennial Christians looking for 'signs of the times' in relation to prophecy, the accelerated way in which information is received and processed within world risk society exerts a pressure through its sheer immediacy and force. Crome, in his interview, talks about his inability to keep up with technological advances being made and their connection to prophecy. Without multimedia communication systems within societies that are networked, much of the information would be unavailable. Moreover, many such movements would not exist. Thus, the claim that 'fundamentalisms cannot be fully understood without reference to the *media*' (Hoover and Kaneva 2009: 3) is particularly relevant to this analysis.

Second, salvation is found in the 'signs of the times', both in terms of verification of existing salvation and in salvation itself. That is to say, the existential insecurity brought about by the kinds of developments noted are related directly to Bible prophecy and provide ongoing confirmation and the immanence of it. As Daniel Wojcik argues in terms of the psychological impact, 'Rapture beliefs may serve as a defence mechanism or compensatory fantasy, reducing individual fears and responsibility concerning nuclear apocalypse and transforming anxiety about predicted catastrophes into passive acceptance of these foreordained events' (1997: 57).

Furthermore, the purpose of the broadcasts is not only to keep regular viewers up to date with how prophecy in their view relates to current global affairs but to inform those who do not believe in Christ that salvation is possible and available: they are an evangelistic tool. The signs are there to see if, in the words of Clarkson, 'you have eyes to see'.[23] In other words, for any unbeliever watching the programme, the signs of the last days are a clarion call to those who have yet to put their faith in Christ. Clarkson closes the Crome interview with a plea to non-believers to put their faith in Christ and to keep looking up for his return.

In conclusion, the notion of world risk society has permeated contemporary society which, in light of technological advances, has introduced greater dangers than previously thought imaginable. An unintended consequence is the rise of fundamentalisms which have emerged as a result of insecurity, existential angst and the erosion of 'traditional values'. 'Rapture culture' is one example that has grown in late modernity. The psychological force of this leads to possible catastrophes, risks and dangers being interpreted through a premillennial Bible prophecy lens. This has meant that many now find evidence in the Bible for claiming that we are living in the end times. Through this, ontological security and certainty is reiterated and restated in the salvific work of Christ; and existential angst is allayed by reassurance in this narrative by those who will be raptured when Christ returns: the signs point to this. Moreover, such signs are utilized as evangelistic tools that can demonstrate to the non-believer that to be saved from the impending fate they must put their faith in Christ before it is too late. Thus, signs of salvation can be found in the everyday events of contemporary society.

Notes

Chapter 1

1 We would like to thank Ralph W. Hood Jr. and John R. Shook for helpful feedback on earlier versions of this chapter.
2 We would like to thank Barbara Keller, Constantin Klein and Christopher F. Silver for their contribution to the fruitful and ongoing cross-cultural collaboration investigating 'spirituality' led by Heinz Streib and Ralph Hood. These researchers graciously allowed us to utilize narrative segments for the chapter presented here. Further appreciation is due to Silver for also allowing us access to his qualitative data for 'Joey's' narrative. The Bielefeld University Center for the interdisciplinary Research on Religion and Society (CIRRuS) can be accessed online at: http://www.uni-bielefeld. de/theologie/forschung/religionsforschung/.
3 Mk 16.16 [online]. Available at: http://biblehub.com/mark/16-16.htm [Accessed 17 November 2014].
4 This statement holds true, as far as we can tell, for anything except, for example 'child birth', which obviously requires a specific biological capacity that males simply do not have. Thus, unless one is prepared to argue that theists are biologically unique from non-theists, any experience that can be had can be had by anyone. This, however, does not deny individual differences in the capacity to experience various phenomena.

Chapter 2

1 Alcoholics Anonymous World Services [1939] 2001: 276.
2 The Recovery Movement is well established in the United States and is the subject of attention of cultural historians such as Trysh Travis (2009) and William White (2014). In the UK the Movement has been establishing an identity and gaining momentum through the work of organizations such as the UK Recovery Federation and UK Recovery Walks Charity.
3 In the Twelve-Step model, it is common to hear members describe themselves as suffering from a disease for which there is no known cure. Thus 'active' refers to the state of drinking/using. The terms 'addict' or 'alcoholic' are used by Twelve-Step practitioners about themselves. See discussion on page 42.
4 Known within the fellowships as 'Bill W.' and 'Dr Bob'.
5 The word 'alcoholic' is used here because this is how Wilson and Smith describe themselves.
6 (1) We admitted we were powerless over alcohol [drugs] – that our lives had become unmanageable. (2) Came to believe that a power greater than ourselves could restore us to sanity. (3) Made a decision to turn our will and our lives over to the care of God as we understood Him. (4) Made a searching and fearless moral

inventory of ourselves. (5) Admitted to God, to ourselves, and to another human being the exact nature of our wrongs. (6) Were entirely ready to have God remove all these defects of character. (7) Humbly asked Him to remove our shortcomings. (8) Made a list of all persons we had harmed, and became willing to make amends to them all. (9) Made direct amends to such people wherever possible, except when to do so would injure them or others. (10) Continued to take personal inventory, and when we were wrong, promptly admitted it. (11) Sought through prayer and meditation to improve our conscious contact with God as we understood Him, praying only for knowledge of His will for us and the power to carry that out. (12) Having had a spiritual awakening as the result of these steps, we tried to carry this message to alcoholics, and to practice these principles in all our affairs (reproduced with permission from the General Service Board UK of Alcoholics Anonymous).

7   The nickname, in wide circulation to this day, for the volume *Alcoholics Anonymous*, from which the fellowship took its name (Alcoholics Anonymous World Services [1939] 2001).

8   The meeting in Akron, Dr Bob's home town, conserved the link with the Oxford Group, unlike the early meetings in New York (Pittman 1993).

9   Fellowship members are usually identified by first name only for reasons of anonymity.

10 The Preamble:

Alcoholics Anonymous is a fellowship of men and women who share their experience, strength and hope with each other that they may solve their common problem and help others to recover from alcoholism. The only requirement for membership is a desire to stop drinking. There are no dues or fees for AA membership; we are self-supporting through our own contributions. AA is not allied with any sect, denomination, politics, organization or institution; does not wish to engage in any controversy; neither endorses nor opposes any causes. Our primary purpose is to stay sober and help other alcoholics to achieve sobriety. (© 1947 by the AA Grapevine, Inc).

11 It also centres on the notion that harmful use of alcohol is 'but a symptom' of a 'spiritual malady' (Alcoholics Anonymous 1939, 2001: 64).

12 Steps Six and Seven.

13 This is a controversy of dimensions too large to address in detail here. Some of it constellates around questions of free will and determinism, see, for example, Cook (2006) and Messer (2015), and is related to the many forms of the 'disease model' of addiction.

14 Participants in the study (n.100) are six months or more abstinent. The median length of 'clean-time' in the cohort was fifteen years. The longest length of continuous abstinence was forty-eight years. For more information, see www.chester.ac.uk/higherpowerproject.

15 Participants chose how they wish to be named in the research. Some chose their own names, others chose pseudonyms or nicknames. The practice of using a first name and an initial is commonplace in fellowships.

16 For example – the preface to the Fourth Edition of *Alcoholics Anonymous* (the 'Big Book') states that 'there exists strong sentiment against any radical changes being made in it' (ix).

17 'The rooms' is a frequently used shorthand for meetings of Twelve-Step fellowships.

Chapter 4

1 My intention here is not to essentialize the classical tradition. Even the ascetic theologies of early Christians cannot be seen as straightforwardly hostile towards women, body and nature since most Christian ascetics contended that what was good for the body was also good for the soul (Ruether 1987: 229; Miles 1981). However, the tendency to establish the body as a *vehicle* for the soul or to suggest that the soul gathers energy at the *expense* of the body is nevertheless a danger within early Christian and subsequent theology, and similar dangers resurface in this weight loss group as women seek escape from their 'fat'.

2 The organization's 'Woman of the Year' award exposes the organization's target audience as female. Mark observes this gender bias when he tells me, 'I can't remember ever seeing a man on the front cover of the *organization's* magazine. I think ... there probably isn't a male consultant or if there is, there are not many. So it is very female orientated.'

3 Members use the language of 'target' to refer to the ideal weight they are aiming towards. Members set their own target weight or 'Personal Achievement Target' (PAT) as it is named by the organization.

4 'Target member' refers to those members who have attained their PAT.

5 The language of 'Syn' is used by this organization to refer to foods like crisps, chocolate, ice cream, cake and alcohol that are high in saturated fats and sugar. For more on this, see Bacon (2013) and Bacon (2015).

6 I am using 'fat' to signify a fluid construct. Although members seldom speak about 'fat', they use terms such as 'overweight' to depict not only physical size but also their own subjective perception of size. Often members feel or see themselves as fat even if others do not.

7 It is interesting that the language of 'synergy' used within Eastern theology to depict the process of *theosis* reappears also in this weight loss group. 'Synergy', according to the organization, expresses the idea that by accurately combining 'Free Foods', 'Healthy Extras' and 'Syn' members optimize their weight loss. Although very different to the meaning ascribed within Orthodox thought, the term retains the sense that growth towards 'perfection' is dependent on a person's effort and intentional activity. 'Syn' is presented as a derivative of 'Synergy', although Syn too retains many of the features of classical Christian thought. For more, see Bacon (2013, 2015).

Chapter 5

1 I use these labels interchangeably throughout the chapter.

2 There is no space for an extensive consideration of the term 'alternative' to describe non-traditional forms of salvation. However, it is worth noting that the concept of 'alternative' has connotations associated with the marginal or peripheral, less important and even 'the other' which is somewhat problematic for a non-judgemental consideration of people's experiences.

3 It is notable that Islam, on the other hand, is on the increase in the UK according to the most recent census, while reporting 'no religion' is equally on the rise reaching a quarter of the population (Office for National Statistics 2012).

4   In some senses, these accounts have some resonance with what Wilson (1996) terms the 'before-and-after' narrative. This narrative construction hinges upon the contrast between the negative, traumatic or lesser circumstances of the 'before' versus the positive, glowing or transformed situation of the 'glorious hereafter' (7). Nonetheless, as is evident in the more detailed analysis, this rhetorical and linguistic pattern does not appear in exactly this form; often the 'before' context remains an implicit construction (see Castro 2009: 228–35 where I discuss this further).

5   I interviewed thirty people, in various locations in York, Bristol and London. I recruited participants via an advert with the following wording: 'Have you ever had an experience where you: – lost a sense of space and time? – felt at one with the universe, nature or something "higher"? – felt profoundly moved or deeply affected?' which was placed at the University of York and at several locations in the town centre. Additionally, several of the participants were recruited via 'snowballing' or word of mouth (for more information, see Castro 2009).

6   *Elsewhere* he reports improvements in his life as being a direct result of his experience. For example, his marriage breaks down, he recalls being very low and he experiences reassurance from the female manifestation. Subsequently, he meets his future wife.

7   Spirit photographs are photographic anomalies that have been interpreted by some (traditionally Spiritualists, but more recently by popular paranormal sites e.g. http://www.paranormal360.co.uk/) as depicting the dead or spirits either in the form of ectoplasm (the alleged material manifestation of spirit commonly seen in photographs from the Victorian period), as a 'ghostly' face supposedly identifiable as a deceased individual, as a cloudy substance on the photo and more recently orbs as 'spirits' or 'angels' (e.g. http://www.dianacooper.com/orbs/index.php). However, there are many potentially ordinary explanations for such phenomena including double exposure, faulty equipment, dust on the lens and orbs as a natural by-product related to particles of light and the depth of field in digital camera lenses (for more on the latter theory, see Townsend 2007).

8   There is some difference in the participants she engages with, however, as they all have an explicit interest in, and are regular practitioners of, spiritual matters, whereas many of my participants are not – at least, not before their TEs.

9   'Everyday spirituality' captures the way in which MacKian's (2012) participants seek out a connection with spirit as part of their daily lives and spiritual practice.

Chapter 7

1   I owe thanks to Pauline Worley (Bielefeld) for proofreading.

2   Stolz (2006: 18f.) also discusses the English translation of the terms that are essential for Weber's sociology of religion: '*Heilsgut*' ('salvation good'), '*Heilsziele*' ('salvation goals'), '*Heilsmittel*' ('salvation means') and '*Verheißungen der Religionen*' ('promises of the religions').

3   This stimulus is taken from the research project on secularity in East Germany (see e.g. Wohlrab-Sahr, Karstein and Schaumburg 2005).

Chapter 8

1 Acts 16:30.
2 These reflect early studies, for example, Breysig (1905).
3 See, for example, Sutcliffe and Bowman (2000).
4 See Heelas (1996).
5 For example, Woodhead and Heelas (2000: 431–75).
6 See Alles (1986: 288).
7 See Davies and Powell (2015).
8 Out of personal, if not historical, interest, the examiners of that doctoral thesis were Godfrey Lienhardt (working within the field of anthropology) and Trevor Ling (working within the History of Religions).
9 See James (1902).
10 Cf. Davies (1984: 71 and 2011: 195).
11 From Douglas J. Davies, unpublished paper 'The New Secularization' given at historian Huw McLeod's retirement Seminar, Birmingham University 2010.

Chapter 9

1 Postcolonial critique is a critical perspective emerging from those of colonized heritage with regard to the era of modern European colonialism from the fifteenth to the twentieth centuries, but which is also alert to continuing neocolonial structures and processes in the contemporary world. In this perspective, colonial Christianity is subject to critique insofar as it acted as a vehicle for the European colonial project – and a strong theme of colonial subjugation emerges in biblical criticism of both Old and New Testament texts.
2 While European colonialism took place over five centuries, by the mid-nineteenth century American Protestant missionaries were as influential as Europeans in the modern missionary movement that accompanied European colonialism, and American as well as European writers advocated the benefits of colonial expansion. From this time, the term Euro-American has some purchase, particularly from postcolonial perspectives of those of colonized heritage in the continents of Latin America, Africa and Asia.
3 The impact of the European modern colonial project on contemporary Euro-American Christian theology is reflected here. As I aim to show in this chapter, the Eurocentric generic habit is as essential to understanding the contemporary Christian debate on salvation as the received tradition (Orthodox, Catholic and Protestant) concerning the doctrine of salvation. Postcolonial criticism is sensitive to the imposition of these generic categories, while Eurocentric discourse is usually unaware of the colonizing impetus driving inclusivism.
4 These disciplines have been named as 'history of religions', 'comparative religion', 'world religions' and 'religious studies'.
5 For examples of a chorus of Western scholars who detect continuing colonialism and 'monism' in the pluralist move, see: Jinkins 2004: 14, 4 and 58; Eddy 2002: 185; Heim 1995: 23, 31–42; Tanner 1993.
6 This is not to suggest that all Christian theology is accounted for through these three focal points. Rather my discussion brings to the fore significant forms of

contemporary theology where universalist notions of salvation are re-presented; my contention is that local Euro-American cultural concerns are reflected here.

7 The collection is an evangelical debate with Thomas Talbott's 'dogmatic universalism', where most contributors uphold the view that the concept of 'evangelical universalism' is an oxymoron (Hillborn and Horrocks 2003: 239): by this logic, to speak of universalism is necessarily to lose the 'evangelical' designation.

8 A notable example is *The Evangelical Universalist* (MacDonald 2006), which takes issue with the evangelical universalist oxymoron by arguing for the availability of grace in hell: for MacDonald, the doors of both hell and heaven are always open.

9 Inclusion of Kim's text here demonstrates the privileged position of white Euro-American feminist theologians in being invited to dialogue with feminist theologians of postcolonial, colonized heritage. Kim's Asian American perspective facilitates an exchange within world Christianity.

Chapter 10

1 17 September 2001. For footage, see https://www.youtube.com/watch?v=7TRVcnX8Vsw [accessed 21 March 2015].

2 Words attributed to a companion of the Prophet, recounted by Makhul (d. 731), quoted in Affsaruddin 2014: 48.

3 For example, 'The Islamic Ruling on the Permissibility of Martyrdom Operations'. http://www.religioscope.com/pdf/martyrdom.pdf [accessed 22 March 2015].

4 For a comparative analysis, see Middleton 2011.

5 For discussion, see: van Henten 2012; Pattemore 2004: 68–116.

6 Some interpret Colossians 1:24 as Paul's contribution to the 'Messianic woes' that must be completed before the end comes (see Wilson 2005: 168–72).

7 See Middleton 2014 for a discussion of the meaning of μάρτυς.

8 For example, Rom. 3.2; Eph. 3.1; Trall. 5.2.

9 Translation Holmes 2007.

10 Similar comparisons are made between the martyrs and Christ throughout early Christian martyrologies. For examples, see Middleton 2006: 82–4.

11 See also *Mart. Justin* (recencion C), 1:1.

12 Translation Greer 1979.

13 *Mart. Poly.* 17:3–18:3 may reflect an attempt to counter excessive cultic devotion to the martyrs. For a discussion, see Hartog 2013: 320–4.

Chapter 13

1 The reason for choosing these particular texts is that they present the clearest case for both the presence of animals in eschatological images and the redemptive effects of Christ. Excluding the wide range of verses that describe the care God has for animals (e.g. Jon. 4.11, Ps. 145.8-9, Mt. 6.25-26), there are also other verses that describe animals eschatologically (Mk 1.12-13), as of redemptive concern to God (Ps. 36.6) and as worshipping God eternally (Ps. 145.21). Given the space constraints, I have chosen those verses that are both clearest and least contested regarding their meanings for the topics discussed.

2 For work on this, see Berkman 2009: 21–40; Yamamoto 1998: 80–9; Barad 1998: 102–11.

3 There are a number of authors who simply leave the topic of the non-human creation out of their discussions of the redeemed state. See, for example, Morse (2010), McGrath (2007: 482–5), Stacey (1990: 182–207) and Grudem (1994: 1158–67). In such cases where the 'new earth' is mentioned, (e.g. Grudem 1994: 1160–1) the focus is entirely upon the physical earth, with no mention of animals.

4 This and all subsequent biblical quotations are taken from the NRSV translation.

5 For example, there is no discussion of verses 1.29-30 by Reno (2010), Towner (2001), Amos (2004) or Waltke (2001).

6 One example of an exegete of Revelation who does not note this is George Eldon Ladd. In his commentary (1972: 93), he fails to mention animals with regard to these verses, but does claim that such verses are descriptive of how 'God will restore order and peace to his fallen universe'.

7 This is a critique McDaniel (1989: 11) accepts, as he finds such passages as Isaiah 11 'difficult to imagine' due to the predator–prey relationships found within. This position is based on not accepting a cosmic Fall, and is addressed in more detail below.

8 For Moltmann's views supporting this position, see 1990: 273–307.

9 Such a rejection of a theological conception of the Fall can be found in Southgate 2008: 28–35.

Chapter 14

1 A discipline-relevant example of this lack of extensive pedagogical literacy can be found in the recent publication of Mike Higton's *A Theology of Higher Education* (2012). Although Higton has a highly developed social and educational vision, he too only recognizes the assessment tools of exam and essay (see Higton 2012, Index: assessment). Higton's understanding of learning as discipleship (ibid.: 195f.) is a classic instance of *ex cathedra* master – disciple teaching (Fiorenza 2009: 133–6), and hence the traditional essay and exam format are coherent with Higton's vision. However, other elements of his vision, namely sociality in the university and the shared search for the common good, suggest that his strategy would benefit from a serious consideration of other pedagogical tools such as peer learning which he mentions only briefly (Higton 2012: 187).

2 Miller-McLemore (2012: 187) notes a lack of attention to pedagogy in practical theology in her US context; O'Loughlin (2008) records the same for theology as a whole in Britain.

3 The amount of practical theological literature on this aspect is too vast to offer a definitive source. Paulo Freire is a key religious voice on experiential learning for action by insiders of a given context, and his work continues to be significant in theological education.

4 The key voice is Jack Mezirow who has contributed numerous publications on the subject of transformative learning beginning with *Transformative Dimensions of Adult Learning* (1991).

5 It is worth acknowledging with reference to Jantzen's holistic eco-feminist vision that Miller-McLemore's web is limited to humans. This is sufficient in my current

discussion of the classroom interactions among humans. Yet, a more holistic investigation which also includes the physical aspects of the classroom as a built environment and their impact on flourishing within would be of great interest not least to disabled participants like myself.

6   Thomas Groome (2011: 286–9) credits Paulo Freire with the development of the model of generative themes as the starting point of empowering learning. See further Fiorenza's (2009: 153–60) combination of Freire and psychoanalyst Ruth Cohn's theme-centred interaction model to arrive at a radically democratic pedagogy with a global dimension.

7   For this view, see Higton (2012: 158): 'Human learning is incomplete because human beings are sinful, and so see in distorted, deluded ways – hence the need for crucifixion on the way to truth.'

8   For a discipline-relevant investigation of social justice education with the 'privileged', see, for example, Turpin (2008). She refers to the classic conversation with Freirean pedagogy from the perspective of privilege in Evans et al. (1986).

9   This is developed at length by Jantzen in chapter three of *Becoming Divine: Towards a Feminist Philosophy of Religion* (1998).

10 My understanding of the traditional Christian model of hospitality as paternalistic draws on Letty Russell's (2009) critique and her counterproposal of 'just hospitality' which celebrates difference and otherness as God's gift to safeguard against domination through homogenizing hegemony.

11 The Higher Education Funding Council for England (HEFCE) is a key source for policy development in 'sustainability' in my institutional context. See, for example, HEFCE (2005), *Sustainable Development in Higher Education: Consultation on a Support Strategy and Action Plan*, Bristol: HEFCE.

12 For a discussion of theology's marginalization in the sustainability discourse in higher education in spite of its significant relevant resources, see Stuerzenhofecker et al. (2010).

13 It is telling that this is often linked to 'employability', see, for example, the University of Manchester's 2020 Agenda, pp. 12–13.

14 For example, the University of Manchester's 2020 Agenda, p. 16 limits 'social responsibility' to public engagement activities.

Chapter 16

1   Although I refer to this period as 'late modernity', Ulrich Beck employs both 'second modernity' and 'risk society' to describe the current milieu.

2   The English edition was published in 1992.

3   Bible references are taken from the New Revised Standard Version.

4   The seven dispensations are Innocence, conscience, government, promise, law, grace and millennial kingdom. For a brief overview, see G. Shuck, 'Christian Dispensationalism', in C. Wessinger (ed.), *The Oxford Handbook of Millennialism* (Oxford: Oxford University Press, 2011).

5   It was never Derby's intention to link prophecy to contemporary events. See S. Knowles, 'Risk or Rapture: Signs of the End or Symptoms of World Risk Society', *Culture and Religion* 15, 4 (2014): 419–35.

6 *The Late Great Planet Earth* has sold in access of 20 million copies since its publication in 1970.

7 This was re-iterated in Lindsey's *The 1980s: Countdown to Armageddon* (New York: Bantam, 1980).

8 See www.hallindsey.com.

9 For example, Whisenant 1988; LaHaye and Jenkins 1995–2007; Hunt 1990; Walvoord 1974; Dyer 1991.

10 To date, at least 65 million copies of the 16 book series have been sold (1995–2007).

11 Prior to this, Clarkson co-hosted the show with Gary Stearman who has since gone on to develop his own Bible prophecy ministry called *Prophecy Watchers* (www. prophecywatchers.com).

12 A print version of the magazine – *Prophecy in the News* – is also still offered and available by subscription.

13 www.prophecyinthenews.com [accessed 17 February 2015].

14 Although there is a link to 'daily updates' on the website, an examination of the archives makes it clear that 'daily' bulletins are not recorded. Indeed, there seems to be no pattern to the release of such items.

15 At the time of writing, *Prophecy in the News* was sponsoring the Orlando Prophecy Summit, 5–7 March 2015.

16 http://www.prophecyinthenews.com/category/daily-update/ [accessed 26 January 2015].

17 Crome is pastor of a church in Las Vegas and specializes in teaching Bible prophecy. Although split in two parts, it is essentially one interview.

18 The interview can be accessed at http://www.prophecyinthenews.com/the-final-countdown-part-1/ [accessed 17 February 2015].

19 'The Final Countdown' is the title of Crome's teaching on Bible prophecy available on DVD.

20 Details about DARPA can be found at http://www.darpa.mil/default.aspx [accessed 17 February 2015].

21 This interview can be accessed at http://www.prophecyinthenews.com/the-final-countdown-part-2/ [accessed 17 February 2015].

22 'Network Society' is Manuel Castells' phrase.

23 This is a common phrase used among evangelical fundamentalists that God will provide answers to the questions of those who are willing to look up to Him. See, for example, Mt. 13:15; Mt. 8:18.

REFERENCES

AA Agnostica, http://aaagnostica.org/ [accessed 9 November 2014].

AA Grapevine, Inc, ed. (2014), *Sober & Out: Lesbian, Gay, Bisexual and Transgender AA Members Share their Experience, Strength and Hope,* New York: AA Grapevine, Inc.

Abbink, J. (2005), 'Being Young in Africa: The politics of despair and renewal', in J. Abbink and V. I. Kessel (eds), *Vanguards or Vandals: Youth, Politics and Youth in Africa,* 1–36, Leiden: Brill Academic Publishers.

Adar, K. G. and Munyae, I. M. (2001), 'Human Rights Abuse in Kenya Under Daniel Arap Moi, 1978-2001', *African Studies Quarterly,* 5 (1): 1.

Affsaruddin, A. (2014), 'Martyrdom in Islamic Though and Praxis: A Historical Perspective', in D. Janes and A. Houen (eds), *Martyrdom and Terrorism: Pre-Modern to Contemporary Perspectives,* 40–58, Oxford: Oxford University Press.

Alcoholics Anonymous World Services (1939, 4th edition 2001), *Alcoholics Anonymous. The Story of How Many Thousands of Men and Women have Recovered from Alcoholism,* New York: Alcoholics Anonymous World Services.

Alcoholics Anonymous World Services (1957), *Alcoholics Anonymous Comes of Age: A Brief History of A. A,* New York: Alcoholics Anonymous World Services Inc.

Aldo, B. (2013), *AA Cults I Have Known.* http://www.thefix.com/content/cult-aa-Atlantic-Group-Clancy-Pacific-Group-London-Joys2092 [accessed 8 November 2014].

Al-Ījī, 'Aḍud al-Dīn (1997), *Kitāb al-Mawāqif* (with the commentary of al-Jurjānī), 3 vols, Beirut: Dār al-Jīl.

Alles, G. D. (1986), 'Semantic Functionalism and the Paradigm of Meaning', *History of Religions,* 25 (3): 288–90.

Al-Matroudi, A. I. (2006), *The Ḥanbalī School of Law and Ibn Taymiyyah: Conflict or Conciliation,* London: Routledge.

Al-Subkī, Taqī al-Dīn (1987), *Al-I'tibār bi-baqā' al-janna wa al-nār,* ed. Ṭaha al-Dusūqī Ḥubayshī, Cairo: Maṭba'at al-fajr al-jadīd.

Ammerman, N. (1991), 'North American Protestant Fundamentalism', in M. Marty and R. S. Appleby (eds), *Fundamentalisms Observed: The Fundamentalist Project,* vol. 1, 1–65, Chicago: Chicago University Press.

Ammerman, N. T., ed. (2007), *Everyday Religion: Observing Modern Religious Lives,* Oxford; New York: Oxford University Press.

Amos, C. (2004), *The Book of Genesis,* Peterborough: Epworth Press.

Anttonen, V. (2000), 'Sacred', in W. Braun and R. T. McCutheon (eds), *Guide to the Study of Religion,* 271–82, London: Cassell.

Aquinas, T. and Clark, M. T. (2000), *An Aquinas Reader,* New York: Fordham University Press.

Aquinas, T. (2006), *Summa Theologiae,* Volume 16, Purpose and Happiness (Ia2æ.1-5), trans. T. Gilby, Cambridge; New York: Cambridge University Press.

Aristarkhova, I. (2012), 'Hospitality and the Maternal', *Hypatia,* 27 (1): 163–81.

Arnal, W. E. and McCutcheon, Russell T. (2013), *The Sacred is the Profane: The Political Nature of 'Religion'*, Oxford: Oxford University Press.

Arrowood, R. B. and Pope, J. B. (2014), 'Terror Management Theory: A Theoretical Perspective on Origination, Maintenance, and Research', *Modern Psychological Studies*, 20 (1): 87–95.

Astley, J. (2002), *Ordinary Theology. Looking, Listening and Learning in Theology*, Aldershot: Ashgate.

Astley, J. (2010), *Christian Doctrine*, London: SCM.

Augustine (1991), *Sermons, III (51-94) on the New Testament*, trans. E. Hill, ed. J. Rotelle, New York: New City Press.

Augustine (1993), *Sermons III/7 (230-272B) on the Liturgical Seasons*, trans. E. Hill, ed. J. Rotelle, New York: New City Press.

Augustine (1995), *Sermons III/10 (341-400) on Various Subjects*, trans. E. Hill, ed. J. Rotelle, New York: New City Press.

Augustine (2011), *The Soliloquies of St Augustine*, CreateSpace Independent Publishing Platform.

Augustine (n.d.), *On Christian Doctrine*, Grand Rapids, MI: Christian Classics Ethereal Library.

Ayallo, I. (2004), *Highlight of Sex Related Practices in Luo Related to Canaanite Rites: Their Impact on the Empowerment of Women*. Bachelor of Divinity Research Paper, St. Pauls University (unpublished).

Ayallo, I. (2012), *Public Policy Dialogue for Socially-Inclusive Public Policy Making Processes in Kenya: The Role of the Anglican Church*. Doctor of Philosophy, Auckland University of Technology (unpublished).

B., Dick. (1992), *The Oxford Group & Alcoholics Anonymous*, Maui, HI: Paradise Research Publications Inc.

Back, K. and Bourque, L. (1970), 'Can Feelings be Enumerated?' *Behavioral Science*, 15: 487–96.

Bacon, H. (2013), 'Sin or Slim? Christian morality and the politics of personal choice in a secular commercial weight loss setting', *Fieldwork in Religion*, 8 (1): 92–109.

Bacon, H. (2015), 'Fat, Syn and Disordered Eating: The Dangers and Powers of Excess', *Fat Studies. An Interdisciplinary Journal of Body Weight and Society*, 4 (2): 92–111.

Bailey, E. (1999), *Implicit Religion: An Introduction*, London: Middlesex University Press.

Barad, J. (1998), 'Aquinas' Inconsistency on the Nature and the Treatment of Animals', *Between the Species*, 4 (2): 102–11.

Barrett, J. and Lanman, J. (2008), 'The Science of Religious Beliefs', *Religion*, 38 (2): 109–24.

Basil (1962), 'The Long Rules', in R. J. Deferrari (ed.), *The Fathers of the Church. A New Translation*, vol. 9, trans. Sister M. Monica Wagner, 223–338, Washington, DC: The Catholic University of America Press.

Bauckham, R. (1999), 'Eschatology in "The Coming of God"', in R. Bauckham (ed.), *God will be All in All: The Eschatology of Jürgen Moltmann*, Edinburgh: T&T Clark.

Bauman, Z. (1991), *Modernity and Ambivalence*, New York: Cornell University Press.

Baumeister, R. (1991), *The Meanings of Life*, New York, New York: Guilford Press.

Beale, G. (1999), *The Book of Revelation*, Grand Rapids: William B. Eerdmans.

Beck, U. (1992), *Risk Society: Toward a New Modernity*, London: Sage.

Beck, U. (2009), *World at Risk*, London: Polity Press.

Beck, U., Giddens, A. and Lash, S. (1994), *Reflexive Modernisation: Politics, Tradition and Aesthetics in the Modern Social Order*, London: Polity Press.

Becker, K., Morali, I., D'Costa, G. and Borrmans, M., eds (2010), *Catholic Engagement with World Religions: A Comprehensive Study*, Maryknoll; New York: Orbis.

Bell, K. and McNaughton, D. (2007), 'Feminism and the Invisible Fat Man', *Body & Society*, 13 (1): 107–31.

Benotsch, E. G., Stevenson, L. Y., Sitzler, C. A., Kelly, J. A., Makhaye, G., Mathey, E. D., Somlai, A. M., Brown, K. D., Amirkhanian, Y., Fernandez, M. I. and Opgenorth, K. M. (2004), 'HIV prevention in Africa: programs and populations served by non-governmental organizations', *Journal of Community Health*, 29: 319–36.

Berger, P. (1967), *The Sacred Canopy*, Garden City, NY: Doubleday.

Berkman, J. (2009), 'Towards a Thomistic Theology of Animals', in Celia Deane-Drummond and David Clough (eds), *Creaturely Theology*, 21–40, London: SCM Press.

Bernstein, P. L. (1998), *Against the Gods: The Remarkable Story of Risk*, New York: John Wiley and Sons.

Bhabha, H. K. (2004), *The Location of Culture*, London: Routledge.

Blenkinsopp, J. (2000), *Isaiah 1-39*, London: Yale University Press.

Bloch, M. (1992), *Prey into Hunter*, Cambridge: Cambridge University Press.

Bloom, M. (2005), *Dying to Kill: The Allure of Suicide Terror*, New York: Columbia University Press.

Blount, B. K. (2005), *Can I get a Witness? Reading Revelation through African American Culture*, Louisville: Westminster John Knox.

Blount, B. (2009), *Revelation: A Commentary*, Louisville: Westminster John Knox Press.

Boeve, L. (2007), *God Interrupts History: Theology in a Time of Upheaval*, London: Continuum.

Boff, L. (1992), *Introducing Liberation Theology*, Kent: Burns and Oates.

Bohnsack, R. (2010), 'Documentary Method and Group Discussions', in R. Bohnsack, N. Pfaff and W. Weller (eds), *Qualitative Analysis and Documentary Method in International Educational Research*, 99–124, Opladen, Farmington Hills: Budrich.

Boon, M. (2002), *The Road of Excess: A History of Writers on Drugs*, Cambridge, MA: Harvard University Press.

Bordo, S. (1993), *Unbearable Weight: Feminism, Western Culture, and the Body*, Berkeley, Los Angeles and London: University of California Press.

Bori, C. and Holtzman, L. (2010), 'Introduction', in C. Bori and L. Holtzman (eds), *A Scholar in the Shadow: Essays in the Legal and Theological Thought of Ibn Qayyim al-Ǧawziyyah*, 13–44, Rome: Istituto per l'Oriente C. A. Nallino.

Boring, M. E. (2011), *Revelation*, Louisville: Westminster John Knox Press.

Bowman, M. and Valk, U. (2012), *Vernacular Religion in Everyday Life: Expressions of Belief*, London: Routledge.

Boyer, P. (1992), *When Time Shall Be No More*, Cambridge, MA: Harvard University Press.

Boyer, P. (2003), 'Religious Thought and Behaviour as By-Products of Brain Function', *Trends in Cognitive Sciences*, 7 (3): 119–24.

Braidotti, R. (1994), *Nomadic Subjects. Embodiment and Sexual Difference in Contemporary Feminist Theory*, New York; Chichester; West Sussex: Columbia University Press.

Brandon, S. G. F. (1963), *Man and His Destiny in the World Religions*, Manchester: Manchester University Press.

Breakwell, G. (2007), *The Psychology of Risk*, Oxford: Oxford University Press.

Bredin, M. (2003), *Jesus, Revolutionary of Peace: A Non-Violent Christology in the Book of Revelation*, Paternoster Biblical Monographs, Milton Keynes: Paternoster.

Breysig, K. (1905), *Die Entstehung des Gottesgedankens und der Heilbringer*, Berlin: Bondi.

Brierley, P. (2006), *Pulling out of the Nosedive: A Contemporary Picture of Churchgoing*, London: Christian Research.

Brierley, P. (2008), *UK Christian Handbook religious trends 7 – 2007/2008: British Religion in the 21st Century What the Statistics Indicate*, Swindon: Christian Research.

Brock, R. N. and Parker, R. A. (2008), *Saving Paradise: How Christianity Traded Love of This World for Crucifixion and Empire*, Boston: Beacon Press.

Brown, P. (1980), *The Cult of the Saints: Its Rise and Function in Latin Christianity*, Chicago: Chicago University Press.

Broyles, L. M., Binswanger, I. A., Jenkins, J. A., Finnell, D. S., Faseru, B., Cavaiola, A. and Gordon, A. J. (2014), 'Confronting Inadvertent Stigma and Pejorative Language in Addiction Scholarship: A Recognition and Response', *Substance Abuse*, 35 (3): 217–21.

Bruce, F. F. (1984), *The Epistles to the Colossians, to Philemon, and to the Ephesians*, Grand Rapids: William B. Eerdmans.

Bruce, S. (2002), *God is Dead: Secularisation in the West*, Oxford: Blackwell.

Brueggemann, W. (1998), *Isaiah 1-39*, Louisville: Westminster John Knox Press.

Buck, P. L. (2012), 'Voluntary Martyrdom Revisited', *JTS* (ns), 63: 125–35.

Bucke, R. M. (1905), *Cosmic Consciousness: A Study in the Evolution of the Human Mind*, Philadelphia: Innes & Sons. Available from http://djm.cc/library/Cosmic_Consciousness_edited02.pdf [accessed 16 August 2013].

Bunt, G. R. (2003), *Islam in the Digital Age: E-Jihad, Online Fatwas and Cyber Islamic Environments*, London: Pluto Press.

Burgess, T. (2005), 'Introduction to Youth and Citizenship in East Africa', *Africa Today*, 51 (3): vii–xxvi.

Cameron, H., Bhatti, D., Duce, C., Sweeney, J. and Watkins, C. (2010), *Talking about God in Practice: Theological Action Research and Practical Theology*, London: SCM Press.

Campbell, C. (2007), *The Easternization of the West: A Thematic Account of Cultural Change in the Modern Era*, Boulder: Paradigm.

Carrette, J. and King, R. (2005), *Selling Spirituality: The Silent Takeover of Religion*, London: Routledge.

Cartledge, M. (2010), *Testimony in the Spirit. Rescripting Ordinary Pentecostal Theology*, Farnham: Ashgate.

Cassidy, J. P. and Davies, D. J. (2003), 'Cultural and Spiritual Aspects of Palliative Medicine', in D. Doyle, G. Hanks, N. Cherny and Kenneth Calman (eds), *Oxford Textbook of Palliative Medicine*, 951–7, Oxford: Oxford University Press.

Castelli, E. A. (2004), *Martyrdom and Memory: Early Christian Culture Making*, New York: Columbia University Press.

Castells, M. (2010), *The Power of Identity*, 2nd edn, Oxford: Blackwell.

Castillo, J. M. (2004), 'Utopia Set Aside', in L. C. Susin, J. Sobrino and F. Wilfred (eds), *A Different World Possible*, 35–41, London: SCM.

Castles, S. and Miller, M. J. (2003), *The Age of Migration: International Population Movements in the Modern World*, 3rd edn, Basingstoke: Palgrave.

Castro, M. (2009), *Talking of Transcendence: A Discursive Exploration into How People Make Sense of their Extraordinary Experiences*, Unpublished thesis: University of York.

Chapple, E. and Coon, C. S. (1947), *Principles of Anthropology*, London: Cape.

Christ, C. P. (1987), 'Finitude, Death, and Reverence for Life', *Semeia*, 40: 93–108.

Christ, C. P. (2003), *She Who Changes: Re-Imagining the Divine in the World*, New York: Palgrave Macmillan.

Christ, C. P. (2011), 'The Last Dualism: Life and death in goddess feminist theology', *Journal of Feminist Studies in Religion*, 27 (1): 129–45.

Chrysostom, J. (1889), 'Homilies on Philippians', in P. Schaff (ed.), *Nicene and Post-Nicene Fathers*, First Series, vol. 13, Buffalo, New York: Christian Literature Publishing Co., http://www.newadvent.org/fathers/230213.htm [accessed 19 March 2015].

Clarke, S. (2006), *From Enlightenment to Risk: Social Theory and Contemporary Society*, London: Palgrave.

Clough, D. (2012), *On Animals: Systematic Theology Vol. 1*, London: T&T Clark.

Cobb, J. B., Jr. (1998), 'All Things in Christ?', in A. Linzey and D. Yamamoto (eds), *Animals on the Agenda*, 173–80, London: SCM Press.

Cobb, M., Puchalski, C. M. and Rumbold, B., eds (2012), *Oxford Textbook of Spirituality in Healthcare*, Oxford: Oxford University Press.

Coleman, T. J. III, and Hood, R. W. Jr. (2015), 'Reconsidering Everything: From Folk Categories to Existential Theory of Mind', [Peer commentary on the paper 'From Weird Experiences to Revelatory Events' by A. Taves], *Religion and Society: Advances in Research*, 6 (1): 18–22.

Coleman, T. J. III, Silver, C. F. and Hood, R. W. Jr. (in press), '"… if the universe is beautiful, we're part of that beauty."– A "Neither Religious nor Spiritual" Biography as Horizontal Transcendence', in H. Streib and R. Hood (eds), *The Semantics and Psychology of Spirituality*, Dordrecht, NL: Springer. DOI 10.1007/978-3-319-21245-6_22.

Comte-Sponville, A. (2008), *The Book of Atheist Spirituality: An Elegant Argument for Spirituality Without God*, London: Bantam Books.

Conradie, E. M. (2005), *Hope for the Earth: Vistas on a New Century*, Oregon: Wipf and Stock Publishers.

Cook, C. (2006), *Alcohol, Addiction and Christian Ethics*, Cambridge, UK; New York: Cambridge University Press.

Cook, D. (2007), *Martyrdom in Islam*, Cambridge: Cambridge University Press.

Core, J. (2013), *To Thine Own Self be True | AA Agnostica*. http://aaagnostica. org/2013/03/31/to-thine-own-self-be-true/ [accessed 9 November 2014].

Cottingham, J. (2005), *The Spiritual Dimension: Religion, Philosophy and Human Value*, Cambridge: Cambridge University Press.

Cranfield, C. E. B. (1975), *Romans*, London: T&T Clark.

Daggers, J. (2013), *Postcolonial Theology of Religions: Particularity and Pluralism in World Christianity*, London: Routledge.

Daggers, J. (2014), 'In a Trinitarian Embrace: Reflections from a Local Eucharistic Community in a Global World', in G. J. Kim and J. Daggers (eds), *Reimagining with Christian Doctrines: Responding to Global Gender Injustices*, New York: Palgrave.

Datta, D. and Njuguna, J. (2009), 'Food security in HIV/AIDS response: Insights from Homa Bay, Kenya', *Journal of Social Aspects of HIV/AIDS Research Alliance*, SAHARA J, 6 (4): 170–78.

Davidson, R. (1973), *Genesis 1-11*, Cambridge: Cambridge University Press.

Davidson, Ivor J. and Rae, M. A. (2010), *God of Salvation Soteriology in Theological Perspective*, Surrey: Ashgate.

Davies, D. J. (1973), 'Aspects of Latter-day Saint Eschatology', in M. Hill (ed.), *The Sociological Yearbook of Religion*, 122–35, London: SCM.

Davies, D. J. (1978), 'The Notion of Salvation in the Comparative Study of Religions', *Religion*, 8: 85–100.

Davies, D. J. (1979), *The Notion of Meaning and Salvation in Religious Studies'*, PhD Thesis, University of Nottingham.

Davies, D. J. (1984), *Meaning and Salvation in Religious Studies*, Brill: Leiden.

Davies, D. J. (2000a), *Studies in Pastoral Theology and Social Anthropology*, 2nd edn, Birmingham: Institute for the Study of Worship and Religious Architecture.

Davies, D. J. (2000b), *The Mormon Culture of Salvation*, Farnham: Ashgate.

Davies, D. J. (2002), *Anthropoloy and Theology*, Oxford: Berg.

Davies, D. J. (2010), *Joseph Smith, Jesus, and Satanic Opposition: Atonement, Evil and the Mormon Vision*, Farnham: Ashgate.

Davies, D. J. (2011), *Emotion, Identity and Religion: Hope, Reciprocity and Otherness*, Oxford: Oxford University Press.

Davies, D. J. and Powell, A. (2015), *Sacred Selves, Sacred Settings: Reflecting Hans Mohl*, Farnham: Ashgate.

Davies, D. J. and Rumble, H. (2012), *Natural Burial: Traditional-Secular Spiritualities and Funeral Innovation*, London: Continuum.

Davis, L. J. (2013), 'The End of Identity Politics: On disability as an unstable category', in L. J. Davis (ed.), *The Disability Studies Reader*, 4th edn, 263–77, London; New York: Routledge.

Day, A. (2011), *Believing in Belonging. Belief & Social Identity in the Modern World*, Oxford; New York: Oxford University Press.

Day, A., Vincett, G. and Cotter, C., eds (2013), *Social Identities Between the Sacred and the Secular*, Farnham: Ashgate.

de Castella, T. (2013), 'Spiritual but not religious', *BBC News Online*, 3 January 2013. http://www.bbc.co.uk/news/magazine-20888141 [accessed 20 August 2013].

De la Rocha, Z. (2014), *Rage Against the Machine*, [online] Ratm.com. Available at: http://www.ratm.com/lyrics/battle/guerilla.html [accessed 17 November 2014].

de Morgan, A. (2008), *A Budget of Paradoxes*, vol. II, New York: Dover Publications, INC. Retrieved from http://www.pgdp.net.

Dehandschutter, B. (1982), 'Le Martyre de Polycarp et le development de la conception du martyre au deuxième siècle', in E. A. Livingstone (ed.), *Studia Patristica* 17, 659–68, Oxford: Pergamon Press.

Denney, D. (2005), *Risk and Society*, London: Sage.

Derrida, J. (1990), *Writing and Difference*, trans. Alan Bass, London: Routledge.

Determinist (pseudonym) (2000), 'Cosmic consciousness experience at age 16', in *The Archives of Scientist's Transcendent Experiences*. http://www.issc-taste.org/arc/dbo.cgi?set=expom&id=00067&ss=1 [accessed 20 August 2013].

Donne, J. (1839), *The Works of John Donne*, vol. I, ed. Henry Alford, London: John W. Parker.

Douglas, M. (1963), *The Lele of the Kasai*, Institute of African Affairs: Oxford University Press.

Douglas, M. (1966), *Purity and Danger: An Analysis of Concepts of Pollution and Taboo*, London: Routledge and Kegan Paul.

Douglas, M. and Wildavsky, A. (1980), *Risk and Culture: An Essay on the Selection of Technological and Environmental Dangers*, Berkeley: University of California Press.

Droge, A. J. (1988), '*Mori Lucrum*: Paul and Ancient Theories of Suicide', *NovT*, 30: 263–86.

Droge, A. J. (1989), 'Did Paul Commit Suicide?', *Bible Review*, 5: 14–21.

Droge, A. J. and Tabor, J. D. (1992), *A Noble Death: Suicide and Martyrdom among Christians and Jews in Antiquity*, San Francisco: HarperSanFrancisco.

Droogers, A. and van Harskamp, A., eds (2014), *Methods in the Study of Religious Change*, Sheffield: Equinox.

Dunn, J. D. G. (1996), *The Epistles to the Colossians and to Philemon*, Grand Rapids: William B Eerdmans.

Durkheim, E. ([1912] 1947), *The Elementary Forms of the Religious Life: A Study in Religious Sociology*, trans. J. W. Swain, London: The Free Press.

Durkheim, E. (1995), *The Elementary Forms of Religious Life*, New York: Free Press.

Dyer, C. (1991), *The Rise of Babylon*, Wheaton, IL: Tyndale.

Ebertz, M. (1992), 'Der geschenkte Himmel, oder: Vom Unglück zum Glück im Jenseits', in A. Bellebaum (ed.), *Glück und Zufriedenheit. Ein Symposion*, 164–200, Opladen: Westdeutscher Verlag.

Eddy, P. R. (2002), *John Hick's Pluralist Philosophy of World Religions*, Aldershot: Ashgate.

Edwards, D. (2006), 'Every Sparrow that Falls to the Ground', *Ecotheology*, 11: 103–23.

Edwards, D. (2009), 'The Redemption of Animals in an Incarnational Theology', in Celia Deane-Drummond and David Clough (eds), *Creaturely Theology*, 81–99, London: SCM Press.

Eliade, M. (1959), *The Sacred and the Profane*, New York: Harcourt, Brace.

Erasmus, J. C. (2005), 'Religion and social transformation: A case study from South Africa. Transformation', *An International Journal of Holistic Mission Studies*, 22: 139–48.

Evans, A. F., Evans, R. A. and Kennedy, W. B. (1986), *Pedagogies for the Non-poor*, Maryknoll, NY: Orbis Books.

Facebook page for *Agnostics and Atheists in AA*. https://www.facebook.com/pages/Agnostics-and-Atheists-in-AA/168374259840358?sk=info [accessed 9 November 2014].

Fazzino, L. (2014), 'Leaving the Church Behind: Applying a Deconversion Perspective to Evangelical Exit Narratives', *Journal of Contemporary Religion*, 29 (2): 249–66.

Feyerabend, P. (1999), *Conquest of Abundance*, Chicago: University of Chicago Press.

Feyerabend, P. (2011), *Tyranny of Science*, ed. E. Oberheim, Cambridge, UK: Polity Press.

Fiorenza, E. S. (1995), *Jesus: Miriam's Child, Sophia's Prophet: Critical Issues in Feminist Christology*, London: SCM.

Fiorenza, E. S. (2009), *Democratizing Biblical Studies. Toward an Emancipatory Educational Space*, Louisville, KY: Westminster John Knox Press.

Fitzgerald, T. (2000), *The Ideology of Religious Studies*, Oxford: Oxford University Press.

Fletcher, J. H. (2005), *Monopoly on Salvation? A Feminist Approach to Religious Pluralism*, London: Continuum.

Forrester, D. (2005), 'Theological and Secular Discourse in an Age of Terror', in E. Graham and A. Rowlands (eds), *Pathways to the Public Square: Practical theology in an Age of Pluralism*, 31–40, Munster: Lit Verlag.

Foulkes, F. (1963), *The Epistle of Paul to the Ephesians*, London: Tyndale Press.

Fox, M. P., Rosen, S., MacLeod, W. B., Wasunna, M., Bii, M., Foglia, G. and Simon, J. L. (2004), 'The impact of HIV/AIDS on labour productivity in Kenya', *Tropical Medicine & International Health*, 9: 318–24.

Francis, L. (2009), *Empirical Theology in Texts and Tables. Qualitative, Quantitative and Comparative Perspectives*, Leiden: Brill.

Frederiks, M. T. (2005), 'HIV and AIDS: Mapping Theological Responses in Africa', *Exchange*, 37 (1): 4–22.

Freire, P. (1970), *Pedagogy and the Oppressed*, New York: Herder and Herder.

Freud, S. (1962), *The Future of an Illusion*, New York; London: WW Norton.

Freud, S. (2005), *Civilization and its Discontents*, trans. James Strachey, New York: Norton.

Frey, J. and Schröter, J., eds (2005), *Deutungen des Todes Jesu im Neuen Testament*, Tübingen: Mohr Siebeck.

Frykholm, A. (2004), *Rapture Culture*, Oxford: Oxford University Press.

Furedi, F. (2006), *Culture of Fear Re-Visited*, London: Continuum.

Gambetta, D., ed. (2005), *Making Sense of Suicide Missions*, Oxford: Oxford University Press.

Gambetta, D. (2005a), 'Can we Make Sense of Suicide Missions?', in D. Gambetta (ed.), *Making Sense of Suicide Missions*, 255–99, Oxford: Oxford University Press.

Ganzevoort, R. R. (2009), 'Forks in the Road When Tracing the Sacred. Practical Theology as Hermeneutics of Lived Religion', presidential address International Academy of Practical Theology, Chicago, www.ruardganzevoort.nl/pdf/2009_Presidential.pdf [accessed 19 May 2014].

Gergen, K. (1999), *An Invitation to Social Construction*, London: Sage.

Gibbs, J. (1971), *Creation and Redemption*, Leiden: E.G. Brill.

Giddens, A. (1991), *The Consequences of Modernity*, London: Polity Press.

Giddens, A. (2002), *Runaway World: How Globalisation is Re-Shaping Our Lives*, London: Profile Books.

Gill, T. B. (2010), 'Modeling the Impact of HIV/AIDS upon Food Security of Diverse Rural Households in Western Kenya', *Agricultural Systems*, 103: 265–81.

Ginsberg, A. (1970), 'Introduction', in Timothy Leary (ed.), *Jail Notes*, 6–15, New York: Grove Press.

Goodenough, U. (1998), *The Sacred Depths of Nature*, New York: Oxford University Press.

Gowan, D. (1988), *Genesis 1-11*, Edinburgh: Handsel Press.

Grabe, P. (2005), 'Salvation in Colossians and Ephesians', in J. G. van der Watt (ed.), *Salvation in the New Testament: Perspectives on Soteriology*, 287–304, Leiden: Brill.

Graham, E. L. (2009), 'Redeeming the Present', in E. L. Graham (ed.), *Grace Jantzen. Redeeming the Present*, 1–20, Farnham: Ashgate.

Graham, E. L. (2011), 'Frailty and Flourishing: Good News for Humanity – Response to Alister McGrath', *Practical Theology*, 4 (3): 333–38.

Granberg, E. (2006), ' "Is That All There Is?" Possible Selves, Self-Change, and Weight Loss', *Social Psychology Quarterly*, 69 (2): 109–26.

Greeley, A. (1975), *The Sociology of the Paranormal: A Reconnaissance*, London: Sage.

Greenfield, R. (2006), *Timothy Leary: A Biography*, Orlando: Harcourt.

Greer, R. A., trans. (1979), *Origen, An Exhortation to Martyrdom, Prayer, and other Selected Work*, New Jersey: Paulist Press.

Greggs, T. (2010), 'Beyond the Binary: Forming Evangelical Eschatology', in T. Greggs (ed.), *New Perspectives for Evangelical Theology: Engaging with God, Scripture and the Word*, 153–67, London: Routledge.

Greggs, T. (2011), *Theology Against Religion: Constructive Dialogue with Bonhoeffer and Barth*, London: T&T Clark.

Griel, A. and Robbins, T. (1994), 'Introduction: Exploring the boundaries of the sacred', in D. Bromley (ed.), *Religion and the Social Order. Vol. 4, Research and Theory on Quasi-Religion*, 1–23, Grennwich, CT: JAI Press.

Griel, A. and Robbins, T., eds (1994), *Between Sacred and Secular: Research and Theory on Quasi-Religion*, Greenwich: JAI Press.

Gribben, C. (2009), *Writing the Rapture: Prophecy Fiction in Evangelical America*, Oxford: Oxford University Press.

Grof, S. (1972), 'Varieties of Transpersonal Experiences: Observations from LSD psychotherapy', *Journal of Transpersonal Psychology*, 4 (1): 45–80.

Groome, T. H. (2011), *Will there be Faith? A New Vision for Educating and Growing Disciples*, New York: HarperOne.

Grudem, W. (1994), *Systematic Theology: An Introduction to Biblical Doctrine*, Leicester: Inter-Varsity Press.

Guevara, C. (2000), *Che Guevara Talks to Young People*, ed. M. Waters, New York: Pathfinder.

Gutierrez, G. (1973), *A Theology of Liberation: History, Politics and Salvation*, trans. Sister C. Inda and J. Eagleson, Maryknoll; New York: Orbis.

Gutierrez, G. (1988), *A Theology of Liberation*, London: SCM.

Gutierrez, G. (1988), *A Theology of Liberation*, London: SCM.

Gutierrez, G. (1999), 'The Task and Content of Liberation', in C. Rowland (ed.), *The Cambridge Companion to Liberation Theology*, 534–42, Cambridge: Cambridge University Press.

Guyer, J. I. (2007). 'Prophecy and the Near Future: Thoughts on Macroeconomic, Evangelical, and Punctuated Time', *American Ethnologist*, 34 (3): 409–21.

Hagner, D. A. (1998), 'Gospel, Kingdom, and Resurrection in the Synoptic Gospels', in R. N. Longenecker (ed.), *Life in the Face of Death: The Resurrection Message of the New Testament*, 99–121, Michigan: William B. Eerdmans Publishing Co.

Hall, D. J. (2006), 'Preaching to People with Cancer: The eschatology of the body', *Journal for Preachers*, 29 (2): 29–36.

Hamilton, M. (2000), 'An Analysis of the Festival for Mind-Body-Spirit, London', in S. Sutcliffe and M. Bowman (eds), *Beyond New Age: Exploring Alternative Spirituality*, 188–200, Edinburgh: Edinburgh University Press.

Hamilton, V. (1990), *The Book of Genesis: Chapters 1-17*, Grand Rapids: William B. Eerdmans.

Hanegraaff, W. J. (1996), *New Age Religion and Western Culture: Esotericism in the Mirror of Secular Thought*, Leiden: Brill.

Haraway, D. J. (2000), 'A Cyborg Manifesto: Science, Technology and Socialist-Feminism in the Late Twentieth Century', in N. Badmington (ed.), *Posthumanism*, 69–84, Basingstoke: Palgrave.

Harding, S. (2000), *The Book of Jerry Falwell: Fundamentalist Language and Politics*, Princeton: Princeton University Press.

Harris, S. (2010), *The Moral Landscape*, New York: Free Press.

Hart, T. (1997), 'Redemption and Fall', in C. Gunton (ed.), *The Cambridge Companion to Christian Doctrine*, 189–206, Cambridge: Cambridge University Press.

Hartley, C. (2001), 'Letting Ourselves Go: Making Room for the Fat Body in Feminist Scholarship', in J. E. Braziel and K. LeBesco (eds), *Bodies Out of Bounds. Fatness and Transgression*, 60–73, Berkeley, Los Angeles and London: University of California Press.

Hartog, P. (2013), *Polycarp's Epistle to the Philippians and the Martyrdom of Polycarp: Introduction, Text, and Commentary*, Oxford Apostolic Fathers, Oxford: Oxford University Press.

Harvey, G. (2009), *Religions in Focus: New Approaches to Tradition and Contemporary Practices*, London: Equinox.

Harvey, G. (2013), *Food, Sex and Strangers: Understanding Religion as Everyday Life*, Abingdon: Routledge.

Hayles, N. K. (1999), *How We Became Posthuman: Virtual Bodies in Cybernetics, Literature, and Informatics*, London: University of Chicago Press.

Hedges, P. (2010), *Controversies in Interreligious Dialogue and the Theology of Religions*, London: SCM.

Heelas, P. (1996), *The New Age Movement: The Celebration of the Self and the Sacralization of Modernity*, Oxford: Blackwell.

Heelas, P. (2007), 'The Holistic Milieu and Spirituality: Reflections on Voas and Bruce', in K. Flanagan and P. C. Jupp (eds), *A Sociology of Spirituality*, 63–80, Aldershot: Ashgate.

Heelas, P. (2008), *Spiritualities of Life: New Age Romanticism and Consumptive Capitalism*, Oxford and Cambridge, MA: Blackwell.

Heelas, P. and Woodhead, L. (2005), *The Spiritual Revolution: Why Religion is Giving Way to Spirituality?* Malden, MA, USA, Oxford, UK, Victoria, Australia: Blackwell.

Heim, S. M. (1995), *Salvations*, Maryknoll; New York: Orbis.

Hendriksen, W. (1982), *Romans. Vol. 1 Chapters 1-8*, Edinburgh: The Banner of Truth Trust.

Hengel, M. (1981), *The Atonement: The Origins of the Doctrine in the New Testament*, Philadelphia, PA: Fortress Press.

Hessel-Robinson, T. (2010), 'Nurturing Hope in the Face of Ecocatastrophe@ Advent, Eschatology and the Future of Creation', *Liturgical Ministry*, 19: 9–20.

Heyes, C. (2006), 'Foucault Goes to Weight Watchers', *Hypatia*, 21 (2): 126–49.

Heyward, C. (2010), *The Redemption of God. A Theology of Mutual Relation*, Eugene, OR: Wipf & Stock.

Hick, J. (1996), 'A Pluralist View', in S. N. Gundry, D. L. Okholm and T. R. Phillips (eds), *Four Views on Salvation in a Pluralistic World*, 27–59, Grand Rapids, MI: Zondervan.

Hick, J. and Knitter, P. F., eds (1987), *The Myth of Christian Uniqueness*, London: SCM.

Higgs, J. (2006), *I Have America Surrounded: The Life of Timothy Leary*, London: Friday Project.

Higton, M. (2008), *Christian Doctrine*, London: SCM.

Higton, M. (2012), *A Theology of Higher Education*, Oxford: Oxford University Press.

Hilborn, D. and Horrocks, D. (2003), 'Universalistic Trends in the Evangelical Tradition: An historical perspective', in R. Parry and C. Partridge (eds), *Universal Salvation? The Current Debate*, 219–44, Carlisle: Paternoster.

Holmes, M. W. (2007), *The Apostolic Fathers: Greek Texts and English Translations*, 3rd edn, Grand Rapids: Baker Academic.

Holmes, P. R. (2007), 'Spirituality: Some disciplinary perspectives', in K. Flanagan and P. C. Jupp (eds), *A Sociology of Spirituality*, 23–42, Aldershot: Ashgate.

Hood Jr., R. W. (2012), 'Methodological Agnosticism for the Social Sciences? Lessons from So-rokin's and James's Allusions to Psychoanalysis, Mysticism, and Godly Love', in M. Lee and A. Young (eds), *The Science and Theology of Godly Love*, 121–40, Dekalb: Northern Illinois University Press.

Hood, R. and Morris, R. (1983), 'Toward a Theory of Death Transcendence', *Journal for the Scientific Study of Religion*, 22 (4): 353.

Hood, R. and Williamson, W. (2008), *Them That Believe*, Berkeley: University of California Press.

Hood, R., Hill, P. and Spilka, B. (2009), *The Psychology of Religion*, New York: Guilford Press.

Hoover, J. (2007), *Ibn Taymiyya's Theodicy of Perpetual Optimism*, Leiden, Brill.

Hoover, J. (2009), 'Islamic Universalism: Ibn Qayyim al-Jawziyya's Salafi Deliberations on the Duration of Hell-Fire', *The Muslim World*, 99: 181–201.

Hoover, J. (2013), 'Against Islamic Universalism: 'Alī al-Harbī's 1990 Attempt to Prove that Ibn Taymiyya and Ibn Qayyim al-Jawziyya Affirm the Eternity of Hell-Fire', in B. Krawietz and G. Tamer (eds), *Islamic Theology, Philosophy and Law: Debating Ibn Taymiyya and Ibn Qayyim Al-Jawziyya*, 377–99, Berlin: de Gruyter.

Hoover, S. M. and Kaneva, N. (2009), *Fundamentalisms and the Media*, London: Continuum.

Houtman, D. and Aupers, S. (2007), 'The Spiritual Turn and the Decline of Tradition: The spread of post-Christian spirituality in fourteen Western countries', *Journal for the Scientific Study of Religion*, 46 (3): 305–20.

http://www.dianacooper.com/orbs/index.php [accessed 20 August 2013].

http://www.paranormal360.co.uk/ [accessed 20 August 2013].

Hunt, D. (1990), *Global Peace and the Rise of the Anti-Christ*, Eugene, OR: Harvest House.

Hunt, V. (1996), 'The Place of Deaf People in the Church', in International Ecumenical Working Group (eds), *The Place of Deaf People in the Church*, 20–33, Northampton: Visible Communications.

Huntington, S. P. (1996), *The Clash of Civilizations and the Remaking of World Order*, New York: Simon and Schuster.

Huxley, A. (1959), *The Doors of Perception and Heaven and Hell*, Harmondsworth: Penguin.

Ibn Qayyim al-Jawziyya (1987), *Kitāb al-ṣawāʿiq al-mursala ʿalā al-Jahmiyya wa al-muʿaṭṭila*, 4 vols, ed. ʿAlī b. Muḥammad al-Dakhīl Allāh, Riyadh: Dār al-ʿĀṣima.

Ibn Qayyim al-Jawziyya (1991a), *Al-Wābil al-ṣayyib min al-kalim al-ṭayyib*, ed. Sayyid Ibrāhīm, Cairo: Dār al-Ḥadīth.

Ibn Qayyim al-Jawziyya (1991b), *Ṭarīq al-hijratayn wa bāb al-saʿādatayn*, ed. Abū Ḥafṣ Sayyid Ibrāhīm b. Ṣādiq b. ʿImrān, Cairo: Dār al-Ḥadīth.

Ibn Qayyim al-Jawziyya (1994a), *Shifāʾ al-ʿalīl fī masāʾil al-qaḍāʾ wa al-qadar wa al-ḥikma wa al-taʿlīl*, ed. Al-Sayyid Muḥammad al-Sayyid and Saʿīd Maḥmūd, Cairo: Dār al-Ḥadīth.

Ibn Qayyim al-Jawziyya (1994b), *Zād al-maʿād fī hudā khayr al-ʿibād*, 6 vols, ed. Shuʿayb al-Arnaʾūṭ and ʿAbd al-Qādir al-Arnaʾūṭ, Beirut: Muʾassasat al-risāla.

Ibn Qayyim al-Jawziyya (2004), *Mukhtaṣar al-ṣawāʿiq al-mursala ʿalā al-Jahmiyya wa al-muʿaṭṭila*, Muḥammad b. al-Mawṣilī (abridger), ed. al-Ḥasan b. ʿAbd al-Raḥmān al-ʿAlawī, Riyadh: Maktabat adwāʾ al-salaf.

Ibn Qayyim al-Jawziyya (n.d.), *Ḥādī al-arwāḥ ilā bilād al-afrāḥ*, ed. Ṭāha ʿAbd al-Raʾūf Saʿd, Cairo: Dār ihyāʾ al-kutub al-ʿarabiyya.

Ibn Taymiyya (1995), *Al-Radd ʿalā man qāla bi-fanāʾ al-janna wa al-nār*, ed. Muḥammad b. ʿAbd Allāh al-Samharī, Riyadh: Dār al-balansiyya.

Isasi-Díaz, A. M. (1996), *Mujerista Theology. A Theology for the Twenty First Century*, New York: Orbis.

Isherwood, L. (2007), *The Fat Jesus. Feminist Explorations in Boundaries and Transgressions*, London: Darton, Longman & Todd.

James, W. (1902), *The Varieties of Religious Experience*, London: Longmans Harvey.

James, W. (1985), *The Varieties of Religious Experience*, Cambridge, MA: Harvard University Press.

Janneh, A. (2009), *African Youth Report 2009: Expanding Opportunities for and with Young People in Africa*, Addis Ababa, Ethiopia. Retrieved from http://www.uneca.org/eca_programmes/acgd/publications/africanyouthreport_09.pdf.

Jantzen, G. M. (1984), 'Do We Need Immortality?', *Modern Theology*, 1 (1): 33–44.

Jantzen, G. M. (1995), 'Feminism and Flourishing', *Feminist Theology*, 4: 81–101.

Jantzen, G. M. (1997), 'Feminism and Pantheism', *Monist*, 80 (2): 266–85.

Jantzen, G. M. (1998), *Becoming Divine: Towards a Feminist Philosophy of Religion*, Manchester: Manchester University Press.

Jantzen, G. M. (2009), *Violence to Eternity: Death and the Displacement of Beauty, Volume 2*, London: Routledge.

Jensen, M. P. (2010), *Martyrdom and Identity: The Self on Trial*, London: T & T Clark.

Jinkins, M. (2004), *Christianity, Tolerance and Pluralism*, London: Routledge.

Johnson, E. (1995), *She Who Is: the Mystery of God in a Feminist Theological Discourse*, New York: Crossroad.

Jones, L. S. (2001), 'Hope Deferred: Theological reflections on reproductive loss (Infertility, Miscarriage, Stillbirth)', *Modern Theology*, 17 (2): 227–45.

Kagwanja, P. M. (2005a), 'Clash of Generations? Youth identity, violence and the politics of transition in Kenya, 1997-2002', in J. Abbink and V. I. Kessel (eds), *Vanguards or Vandals: Youth, Politics and Youth in Africa*, 81–109, Leiden: Brill Academic Publishers.

Kagwanja, P. M. (2005b), ' "Power to Uhuru": Youth Identity and Generational Politics in Kenya's 2002 Elections', *African Affairs*, 105: 51–75.

Kamberelis, G. and Dimitriadis, G. (2005), *On Qualitative Inquiry: Approaches to Language and Literacy Research*, New York: Teachers College Press.

Kärkkäinen, V. M. (2003), *An Introduction to the Theology of Religions: Biblical, Historical and Contemporary Perspectives*, Downers Grove: Inter-Varsity Press.

Kärkkäinen, V. M. (2004), *One with God. Salvation as Deification and Justification*, Collegeville, MN: Liturgical Press.

Keller, C. (1996), *Apocalypse Now and Then: A Feminist Guide to the End of the World*, Boston: Beacon Press.

Keller, C. (1997), 'Seeking and Sucking: On relation and essence in feminist theology', in R. S. Chopp and S. G. Devaney (eds), *Horizons in Feminist Theology: Identity, Tradition, and Norms*, Minnesota: Fortress Press.

Keller, C. (2003), 'Salvation Flows: Eschatology for a feminist wesleyanism', *Quarterly Review*, 23 (4): 412–24.

Kenya Central Bureau of Statistics (2009), 'Kenya Facts and Figures', available: http://www.knbs.or.ke/knbsinformation/pdf/Facts%20and%20Figures%202009.pdf [accessed June 2009].

Khalil, M. H. (2012), *Islam and the Fate of Others: The Salvation Question*, Oxford: Oxford University Press.

Kidner, D. (1967), *Genesis*, Downers Grove: Inter-Varsity Press.

Kim, G. J. (2002), *The Grace of Sophia: A Korean North American Women's Christology*, Cleveland: Pilgrim Press.

Kirui, S. K. (2009), *Promoting Social Inclusion of Youth in the MDGs*. Accessed www.uneca.org/.../Stephen%Kirui%20Promoting%20social%20inclusion%20of%20.

Klawiter, F. C. (1980), 'The Role of Martyrdom and Persecution in Developing the Priestly Authority of Women in Early Christianity: A Case Study in Montanism', *Church History*, 49: 251–61.

Knitter, P. (1985), *No Other Name? A Critical Survey of Christian Attitudes Towards the World Religions*, New York: Orbis Books.

Knitter, P. (2002), *Introducing Theologies of Religions*, Maryknoll, New York: Orbis.

Knott, K. (2005), *The Location of Religion: A Spatial Analysis*, London; New York: Routledge.

Knott, K. (2013), 'The Secular Sacred: In between or both/and?', in A. Day, G. Vincett and C. Cotter (eds), *Social Identities Between the Sacred and the Profane*, 145–60, Farnham: Ashgate.

Knowles, S. (2014). 'Risk or Rapture: Signs of the End or Symptoms of World Risk Society', *Culture and Religion*, 15 (4): 419–35.

Kobia, S. (2003), *The Courage to Hope: The Roots for a New Vision and the Calling of the Church in Africa*, Geneva: WCC Publications.

Kreitzer, L. (1997), *The Epistle to the Ephesians*, Epworth Commentaries, Peterborough: Epworth Press.

Kurtz, E. (1979), *Not-God: A History of Alcoholics Anonymous*, Center City, MN: Hazelden Educational Services.

Kurtz, P. and Wilson, E. (1973), *Humanist Manifesto II*, [online] American Humanist Association. Available at: http://americanhumanist.org/Humanism/Humanist_Manifesto_II [accessed 17 November 2014].

Kwok, P. (2005), *Postcolonial Imagination and Feminist Theology*, London: SCM.

Lacan, J. (2001), *Ecrits: A Selection*, trans. Alan Sheridan, London: Routledge.

Ladd, G. E. (1972), *A Commentary on the Revelation of John*, Grand Rapids: William B. Eerdmans.

Ladd, P. (2003), *Understanding Deaf Culture: In Search of Deafhood*, Clevedon: Multilingual Matters.

LaHaye, T. and Jenkins, J. (1995–2007), *Left Behind*, Carol Stream, IL: Tyndale House.

Laski, M. (1961), *Ecstasy: A Study of Some Secular and Religious Experiences*, London: The Cressett press.

Leary, T. (1970), *Jail Notes*, New York: Grove Press.

Leary, T. (1995), *High Priest*, 2nd edn, Berkeley: Ronin.

Leary, T. (1997), *Psychedelic Prayers and Other Meditations*, Berkeley: Ronin.

Leary, T. (1998), *The Politics of Ecstasy*, Berkeley: Ronin.

Leary, T. (n.d.), *Your Brain is God*, Berkeley: Ronin.

Leary, T. and Sirius, R. U. (1997), *Design for Dying*, London: Thorsons.

Leary, T., Metzner, R. and Alpert, R. (1995), *The Psychedelic Experience: A Manual Based on the Tibetan Book of the Dead*, New York: Citadel Press.

Lee, M. V. (1998), 'A Call to Martyrdom: Function as Method and Message in Revelation', *NovT*, 40: 164–94.

Lelwica, M. (1999), *Starving for Salvation. The Spiritual Dimensions of Eating Problems Among American Girls and Women*, New York, Oxford: Oxford University Press.

Lelwica, M. (2010), *The Religion of Thinness. Satisfying the Spiritual Hungers Behind Women's Obsession with Food and Weight*, Carlsbad, CA: Gürze Books.

Lelwica, M. with Hoglund, E. and McNallie, J. (2009), 'Spreading the Religion of Thinness from California to Calcutta', *Journal of Feminist Studies in Religion*, 25 (1): 19–41.

Lenson, D. (1995), *On Drugs*, Minneapolis: University of Minnesota Press.

Levin, J. and Steele, S, (2005) 'The Transcendent Experience: Conceptual, theoretical and epidemiologic perspectives', *Explore*, 1 (2): 89–101.

Lewis, C. S. (1998), *The Problem of Pain*, London: Fount Harper Collins.

Lim, K. Y. (2009), '*The Sufferings of Christ are Abundant in Us*': A Narrative Dynamics Investigation of Paul's Sufferings in 2 Corinthians*, LNTS 399, London: T & T Clark.

Lincoln, A. (1990), *Ephesians*, Word Biblical Commentary, vol. 42, Dallas: Word Books.

Lindbeck, G. (2009), *The Nature of Doctrine: Religion and Theology in a Postmodern Age*, 25th anniversary edn, Louisville: Westminster John Knox Press.

Lindsey, H. (1973), *There's a New World Coming: A Prophetic Odyssey*, Santa Ana, CA: Vision House.

Lindsey, H. and Carlson, C. (1970), *The Late Great Planet Earth*, Basingstoke: Marshall Pickering.

Linzey, A. (1995), *Animal Theology*, Chicago: University of Illinois Press.

Longhurst, R. (2012), 'Becoming Smaller: Autobiographical spaces of Weight Loss', *Antipode*, 44 (3): 871–88.

Lossky, V. (1976), *The Mystical Theology of the Eastern Church*, New York: St Vladimir's Seminary Press.

Luckmann, T. (1967), *The Invisible Religion*, New York: Macmillan.

Luckmann, T. (1985), 'Über die Funktion der Religion', in P. Koslowski (ed.), *Die Religiöse Dimension der Gesellschaft. Religion und ihre Theorien*, 26–41, Tübingen: Mohr.

Ludlow, M. (2000), *Universal Salvation: Eschatology in the Thought of Gregory of Nyssa and Karl Rahner*, Oxford: Oxford University Press.

Ludlow, M. (2003), 'Universalism in the History of Christianity', in R. Parry and C. Partridge (eds), *Universal Salvation? The Current Debate*, 191–218, Carlisle: Paternoster.

Lynch, G. (2007), *The New Spirituality: An Introduction to Progressive Belief in the Twenty-First Century*, London: IB Tauris.

Lynch, G. (2012), *On the Sacred*, Durham: Acumen.

Lyon, D. (1999), *Postmodernity*, Buckingham: Open University Press.

Lyon, D. (2000), *Jesus in Disneyland: Religion in Postmodern Times*, Oxford: Polity Press.

MacDonald, G. (2006), *The Evangelical Universalist*, Eugene, OR: Wipf & Stock.

MacKian, S. (2011), 'Crossing Spiritual Boundaries: Encountering, articulating and representing otherworlds', *Methodological Innovations Online*, 6 (3): 61–74.

MacKian, S. (2012), *Everyday Spirituality: Social and Spatial Worlds of Enchantment*, Basingstoke, UK: Palgrave Macmillan.

Maeckelbergh, M. (2011), 'Doing is Believing: Prefiguration as Strategic Practice in the Alterglobalization Movement', *Social Movement Studies*, 10 (1): 1–20.

Marlowe, M. (2005), 'What is Arminianism?', http://www.bible-researcher.com/arminianism.html [accessed 25 April 2014].

Marsden (1991), *Understanding Fundamentalism and Evangelicalism*, Grand Rapids, MI: Eerdmans.

Marshall, C. D. (2001), *Beyond Retribution: A New Testament Vision for Justice, Crime, and Punishment*, Grand Rapids, Michigan: William B. Eerdmans.

Marty, M. E. and Appleby, R. S., eds (1991), *Fundamentalisms Observed: The Fundamentalist Project*, vol. 1, Chicago: Chicago University Press.

Maruna, S. (2001), *Making Good: How Ex-convicts Reform and Rebuild Their Lives*, Washington, DC: American Psychological Association.

Marx, K. and Engels, F. (1999), *The German Ideology. Part One; with Selections from Parts Two and Three, Together with Marx's Introduction to a Critique of Political Economy*, trans C. J. Arthur, London: Lawrence & Wishart.

Maslow, A. ([1976] 1964), *Religions, Values and Peak Experiences*, Columbus, OH: Ohio State University Press.

McCauley, R. and Lawson, E. (2002), *Bringing Ritual to Mind*, Cambridge, UK: Cambridge University Press.

McCloughry, R. and Morris, W. (2002), *Making a World of Difference: Christian Reflections on Disability*, London: SPCK.

McCutcheon, R. T. (1997), *Manufacturing Religion: The Discourse on Sui Generis Religion and the Politics of Nostalgia*, Oxford and New York: Oxford University Press.

McDaniel, J. (1989), *Of God and Pelicans: A Theology of Reverence for Life*, Louisville: Westminster John Knox Press.

McDaniel, J. (1998), 'Can Animal Suffering be Reconciled with Belief in an All-Loving God?', in A. Linzey and D. Yamamoto (eds), *Animals on the Agenda*, 161–70, London: SCM Press.

McGrath, A. E. (2007), *Christian Theology: An Introduction*, 4th edn, Oxford: Blackwell Publishing.

McGuigan, J. (2006), *Modernity and Postmodern Culture*, 2nd edn, Maidenhead: Open University Press.

McGuire, M. B. (2008a), *Lived Religion: Faith and Practice in Everyday Life*, Oxford; New York: Oxford University Press.

McGuire, M. B. (2008b), 'Toward a Sociology of Spirituality: Individual Religion in Social/ Historical Context', in E. Barker (ed.), *The Centrality of Religion in Social Life: Essays in Honour of James A. Beckford*, 215–31, Hampshire: Ashgate.

McRuer, R. (2006), *Crip Theory: Cultural Signs of Queerness and Disability*, New York: New York University Press.

Mercadante, L. A. (1996), *Victims and Sinners: Spiritual Roots of Addiction and Recovery*, Louisville, KY: Westminster John Knox Press.

Messer, N. (2015), 'Determinism, Freedom and Sin: Reformed Theological Resources for a Conversation with Neuroscience and Philosophy', *Studies in Christian Ethics*, 28 (2): 163–74.

Mezirow, J. (1991), *Transformative Dimensions of Adult Learning*, San Francisco: Jossey-Bass.

Middleton, P. (2006), *Radical Martyrdom and Cosmic Conflict in Early Christianity*, London: T & T Clark.

Middleton, P. (2011), *Martyrdom: A Guide for the Perplexed*, London: T & T Clark.

Middleton, P. (2012), 'Enemies of the (Church and) State: Martyrdom as a Problem for Early Christianity', *Annali di Storia dell'Esegesi*, 29 (2): 161–81.

Middleton, P. (2013), 'Early Christian Voluntary Martyrdom: A Statement for the Defence', *JTS* (ns), 64: 556–73.

Middleton, P. (2014), 'What is Martyrdom?', *Mortality: Promoting the Study of Death and Dying*, 19: 117–33.

Middleton, P. (2015), 'Christology, Martyrdom, and Vindication in the Gospel of Mark and the Apocalypse: Two New Testament Views', in C. Keith and D. T. Roth (eds), *Mark, Manuscripts, and Monotheism: Essays in Honor of Larry W. Hurtado*, 219–37, LNTS 528, London: T & T Clark.

Miles, M. (1981), *Fullness of Life. Historical Foundations for a New Asceticism*, Eugene, Oregon: Wipf & Stock.

Miller-McLemore, B. J. (1994), *Also a Mother: Work and Family as Theological Dilemma*, Nashville: Abingdon Press.

Miller-McLemore, B. J. (1996), 'The Living Human Web: Pastoral Theology at the Turn of the Century', in J. Stevenson Moessner (ed.), *Through the Eyes of Women: Insights for Pastoral Care*, 9–26, Minneapolis: Fortress.

Miller-McLemore, B. J. (2012), *Christian Theology in Practice. Discovering a Discipline*, Grand Rapids, MI: William B. Eerdmans.

Moltmann, J. (1990), *The Way of Jesus Christ: Christology in Messianic Dimensions*, trans. Margaret Kohl, London: SCM Press.

Moltmann, J. (1997), *The Source of Life: The Holy Spirit and the Theology of Life*, London: SCM Press.

Moltmann, J. (2010), *Sun of Righteousness Arise! God's Future for Humanity and the Earth*, London: SCM Press.

Moo, D. (1996), *The Epistle to the Romans*, Grand Rapids: William B. Eerdmans.

Morris, L. (2002), *The Book of Revelation: An Introduction and Commentary*, Grand Rapids: William B. Eerdmans.

Morris, W. (2008), *Theology without Words: Theology in the Deaf Community*, Aldershot: Ashgate.

Morris, W. (2011), 'Transforming Tyrannies: Disability and Christian theologies of salvation', in H. Bacon, W. Morris and S. Knowles (eds), *Transforming Exclusion: Engaging Faith Perspectives*, 121–34, London: T&T Clark.

Morris, W. (2014), *Salvation as Praxis. A Practical Theology of Salvation for a Multi-Faith World*, London: Bloomsbury.

Morse, C. (2010), *The Difference Heaven Makes: Rehearing the Gospel As News*, London: T&T Clark.

Moss, C. R. (2010), *The Other Christs: Imitating Jesus in Ancient Christian Ideologies of Martyrdom*, Oxford: Oxford University Press.

Moss, C. R. (2012), 'The Discourse of Voluntary Martyrdom: Ancient and Modern', *Church History*, 81: 531–51.

Motyer, J. A. (1993), *The Prophecy of Isaiah*, Downers Grove: InterVarsity Press.

Mounce, R. (1998), *The Book of Revelation*, Grand Rapids: William B. Eerdsmans.

Mount Shoop, M. W. (2010), *Let the Bones Dance: Embodiment and the Body of Christ*, Kentucky: Westminster John Knox Press.

Mwaura, P. N. (2008), 'Stigmatization and Discrimination of HIV/AIDS Women in Kenya: A Violation of Human Rights and its Theological Implications', *Exchange*, 37 (1): 35–51.

National AIDS Control Council (2009), *Kenya National AIDS Strategic Plan 2009/10-2012/13*, Nairobi: National AIDS Control Council.

National AIDS Control Council (2010), *UNGASS 2010: United Nations General Assembly Special Session on HIV and AIDS*, Nairobi: National AIDS Control Council.

National Audit Office (2002), 'The 2001 Outbreak of Foot and Mouth Disease', *Environment, Energy and Sustainability*, http://www.nao.org.uk/report/the-2001-outbreak-of-foot-and-mouth-disease/ [accessed 16 August 2013].

Nelson, J. (1992), *Body Theology*, Louisville, KY: Westminster/John Knox Press.

Nietzsche, F. (1994), *Human, All Too Human*, trans. Stephen Lehmann, London: Penguin.

Nimmo, P. (2010), 'Election and Evangelical Thinking: Challenges to our ways of conceiving the Doctrine of God', in T. Greggs (ed.), *New Perspectives for Evangelical Theology: Engaging with God, Scripture and the Word*, 29–43, London: Routledge.

Njoroge, N. J. (2006), 'Let's Celebrate the Power of Naming', in I. A. Phiri and S. Nadar (eds), *African Women, Religion, and Health: Essays in Honor of Mercy Amba Ewudziwa Oduyoye*, 59–74, Maryknoll, New York: Orbis Books.

O'Brien, P. (1982), *Colossians, Ephesians*, Waco: Word Books.

O'Collins, G. (2008), *Salvation for All: God's Other Peoples*, Oxford: Oxford University Press.

O'Loughlin, R. (2008), 'Inquiry-based Learning in Theology and Religious Studies: An investigation and analysis', The Subject Centre for Philosophical and Religious Studies, http://www.basr.ac.uk/trs_resources/pubs_and_resources/documents/493.htm [accessed 19 May 2014].

O'Sullivan, S. (1996), *I Used to be Nice: Sexual Affairs*, London: Cassell.

Office for National Statistics (2012), 'Religion in England and Wales 2011', *Part of 2011 Census Key Statistics for Local Authorities in England and Wales Release*, 11 December 2012. http://www.ons.gov.uk/ons/rel/census/2011-census-key-statistics-for-local-authorities-in-england-and-wales/rpt-religion.html [accessed 20 August 2013].

Orvis, S. (2003), 'Kenyan Civil Society: Bridging the Urban-Rural Divide?', *The Journal of Modern African Studies*, 41 (2): 247–68.

Osborne, G. R. (2002), *Revelation*, Grand Rapids: Baker Academic.

Osmond, H. (1999), 'May Morning in Hollywood', in Aldous Huxley, *Moksha*, ed. Michael Horowitz and Cynthia Palmer, 32–9, Rochester: Park Street Press.

Oswalt, J. N. (1986), *The Book of Isaiah Chapters 1-39*, Grand Rapids: William B. Eerdmans.

Owen, S. (2011), 'The World Religions paradigm. Time for a change', *Arts and Humanities in Higher Education*, 10 (3): 253–68.

Paden, W. E. (1991), 'Before "the Sacred" Became Theological: Rereading the Durkheimian Legacy', *Method and Theory in the Study of Religion*, 3: 10–23.

Paden, W. E. (2011), 'Reappraising Durkheim for the Study and Teaching of Religion', in P. B. Clarke (ed.), *The Oxford Handbook of The Sociology of Religion*, 31–47, Oxford: Oxford University Press.

Palmer, G. and Braud, W. (2002), 'Exceptional Human Experiences, Disclosure, and a More Inclusive View of Physical, Psychological, and Spiritual Well-being, *Journal of Transpersonal Psychology*, 34 (1): 29–61.

Pape, R. (2003), 'The Strategic Logic of Suicide Terrorism', *American Political Science Review*, 97: 343–61.

Parry, R. and Partridge, C., eds (2003), *Universal Salvation? The Current Debate*, Carlisle: Paternoster.

Partridge, C. H. (2003), 'Sacred Chemicals: Psychedelic Drugs and Mystical Experience', in C. Partridge and T. Gabriel (eds), *Mysticisms East and West: Studies in Mystical Experience*, 96–131, Carlisle: Paternoster Press.

Partridge, C. H. (2004), *The Re-Enchantment of the West*, vol. 1, London: Continuum.

Pateman, C. (1970), *Participation and Democratic Theory*, Cambridge: Cambridge University Press.

Pattemore, S. (2004), *The People of God in the Apocalypse: Discourse, Structure, and Exegesis*, SNTSMS 128, Cambridge: Cambridge University Press.

Perkins, J. (1995), *The Suffering Self: Pain and Representations of Pain in Early Christianity*, London: Routledge.

Pervo, R. I. (2009), *Acts: A Commentary*, Heremenia, Minneapolis: Fortress Press.

Petrella, I. (2004), *The Future of Liberation Theology: An Argument and Manifesto*, Aldershot: Ashgate.

Pittman, B. (1993), *The Roots of Alcoholics Anonymous*, Center City, MN: Hazelden.

Primiano, L. (1995), 'Vernacular Religion and the Search for Method in Religious Folklife', *Western Folklore*, 54 (1): 37–56.

Przyborski, A. and Wohlrab-Sahr, M. (2008), *Qualitative Sozialforschung: Ein Arbeitsbuch*, München: Oldenbourg.

Putnam, R. D. (1995), 'The Prosperous Community: Social Capital and Public Life', in W. D. Burham (ed.), *The American Prospect Reader in American Politics*, Chatham, NJ: Chatham House, pp. 61–70.

Race, A. (1983), *Christians and Religious Pluralism: Patterns in the Christian Theology of Religions*, London: SCM Press.

Rambo, S. (2011), 'A "Wretched Choice"? Evangelical Women and the Word', in E. A. Holmes and W. Farley (eds), *Women, Writing, Theology: Transforming a Tradition of Exclusion*, 33–52, Texas: Baylor University Press.

Raphael, M. (1996), *Thealogy and Embodiment. The Post-Patriarchal Reconstruction of Female Sacrality*, Sheffield: Sheffield Academic Press.

Rau, B. (1994), 'Policy and HIV/AIDS prevention: lessons learned', *Aidscaptions*, 1: 30–2.

Rau, B. (1996), 'Influencing HIV/AIDS policy in Kenya: NGOs build consensus. Policy profile', *Aidscaptions*, 3: 49–51.

Reinders, H. S. (2008), *Receiving the Gift of Friendship: Profound Disability, Theological Anthropology and Ethics*, Grand Rapids, MI/Cambridge: Eerdmans.

Reno, R. R. (2010), *Genesis*, Grand Rapids: Brazos Press.

Reuter, C. (1994), *My Life as a Weapon: A Modern History of Suicide Bombing*, trans. H. Ragg-Kirkby, Princeton: Princeton University Press.

Reynolds, T. (2008), *Vulnerable Communion: A Theology of Disability and Hospitality*, Grand Rapids, MI: Brazos Press.

Riesebrodt, M. (1993), *Pious Passion: The Emergence of Modern Fundamentalism in the United States and Iran*, Berkeley: University of California Press.

Rivera, M. (2007), *The Touch of Transcendence: A Postcolonial Theology of God*, London: Westminster John Knox Press.

Road to Recovery (a Plymouth-based special interest group in AA emphasising prayer and Christian commitment). http://www.roadtorecoverygroup.org.uk/ [accessed 8 November 2014].

Robertson. R. (1970), *The Sociological Interpretation of Religion*, Oxford: Blackwell.

Roszak, T. (1970), *The Making of a Counter Culture: Reflections on the Technocratic Society and Its Youthful Opposition*, London: Faber.

Ruether, R. R. (1983), *Sexism and God-talk. Toward a Feminist Theology*, Boston: Beacon Press.

Ruether, R. R. (1987), 'Asceticism and Feminism: Strange Bedmates?', in Linda Hurcombe (ed.), *Sex and God. Some Varieties of Women's Religious Experience*, New York, 229–50, London: Routledge & Kegan Paul.

Ruether, R. R. (1998), *Women and Redemption: A Theological History*, London: SCM Press.

Ruether, R. R. (2002), *Sexism and God-talk*, London: SCM Press.

Russell, L. M., edited by J. S. Clarkson and K. M. Ott (2009), *Just Hospitality. God's Welcome in a World of Difference*, Louisville, KY: Westminster John Knox Press.

Sabar, G. (1997), 'Church and State in Kenya, 1986-1992: The Churches' Involvement in the "Game of Change"', *African Affairs*, 96 (382): 25–52.

Said, E. ([1978] 2003), *Orientalism*, London: Penguin.

Sakamoto, I. and Pitner, R. O. (2005), 'Use of Critical Consciousness in Anti-Oppressive Social Work Practice: Disentangling Power Dynamics as Personal and Structural Levels', *British Journal of Social Work*, 35 (4): 435–52.

Sammet, K. (2006), 'Religiöse Kommunikation und Kommunikation über Religion: Analysen zu Gruppendiskussionen', in P. Steinacker, W. Huber and J. Friedrich (eds), *Kirche in der Vielfalt der Lebensbezüge. Die vierte EKD-Erhebung über Kirchenmitgliedschaft*, 357–99, Gütersloh: Gütersloher Verl.-Haus.

Sammet, K. and Erhard, F. (2012), 'The Observation of the Unobservable: Ideas of afterlife in a sociological perspective', in M. Rotar, C. Rotar and A. Teodorescu (eds), *Dying and Death in 18th-21st Century Europe. Annales Universitatis Apulensis, Series Historica, Special Issue*, Alba Iulia: Universitatea "1 Decembrie 1918".

Schugurensky, D. (2004), 'The Tango of Citizenship Learning and Participatory Democracy', in *Lifelong Citizenship Learning, Participatory Democracy and Social Change*, 326–34, Toronto: Institute for Studies in Education, University of Toronto.

Schweitzer, E. (1961), 'The Church as the Missionary Body of Christ', *New Testament Studies*, 8: 1–11.

Seesholtz, M. (2004), 'Remembering Dr. Timothy Leary', *Journal of Popular Culture*, 38 (1): 106–28.

Seid, R. (1989), *Never Too Thin. Why Women are at War with their Bodies*, New York, London, Toronto, Sydney, Tokyo, Singapore: Prentice Hall Press.

Sharpe, E. J. and Hinnells, J. R. (1973), *Man and His Salvation*, Manchester: Manchester University Press.

Silver, C. F., Coleman, T. J. III, Hood, R. W. Jr., and Holcombe, J. M. (2014), 'The Six Types of Nonbelief: A Qualitative and Quantitative Study of Type and Narrative', *Mental Health, Religion & Culture*, http://dx.doi.org/10.1080/13674676.2014.987743.

Slee, N. (2004), *Women's Faith Development. Patterns and Processes*, Farnham: Ashgate.

Slee, N., ed. (2013), *The Faith Lives of Women and Girls: Qualitative Research Perspectives*, Farnham: Ashgate.

Smith, G. (2007), *Isaiah 1-39*, Nashville: B&H Publishing.

Smith, T. W. (2006), 'The National Spiritual Transformation Study', *Journal for the Scientific Study of Religion*, 45 (2): 283–96.

Sobrino, J. (2008), *No Salvation Outside the Poor: Prophetic-Utopian Essays*, Maryknoll: Orbis Books.

Soskice, J. (1985), *Metaphor and Religious Language*, Oxford: Oxford University Press.

Southgate, C. (2008), *The Groaning of Creation: God, Evolution, and the Problem of Evil*, Louisville: Westminster John Knox Press.

Stacey, J. (1990), *Groundwork of Theology*, rev. edn, London: Epworth Press.

Stanner, W. H. E. (1959–60), 'On Aboriginal Religion 1: The Lineaments of Sacrifice, Mime, Song, Dance, and Stylized Movements', *Oceania*, 30 (1): 108–27.

Stefaniw, B. (2010), 'Becoming Men, Staying Women: Gender ambivalence in Christian apocryphal texts and contexts', *Feminist Theology*, 13 (3): 341–55.

Steuernagel, V. R. (2008), 'To Seek to Transform Unjust Structures of Society', in A. Walls and C. Ross (eds), *Mission in the 21st Century: Exploring the Five Marks of Global Mission*, 62–77, London: Darton, Longman and Todd.

Stevens, J. (1993), *Storming Heaven: LSD and the American Dream*, London: HarperCollins.

Stillwaggon, E. (2006), *AIDS and the Ecology of Poverty*, Oxford: Oxford University Press.

Stinson, K. (2001), *Women and Dieting Culture. Inside a Commercial Weight Loss Group*, New Brunswick, NJ, London: Rutgers University Press.

Stolz, J. (2006), 'Salvation Goods and Religious Markets: Integrating Rational Choice and Weberian Perspectives', *Social Compass*, 53 (1): 13–32.

Streib, H. and Hood, R. (2013), 'Modeling the Religious Field: Religion, Spirituality, Mysticism, and Related World Views', *Implicit Religion*, 16 (2): 137–55.

Streib, H. and Hood, R., eds (in press), *The Semantics and Psychology of Spirituality*, Dordrecht, NL: Springer.

Stringer, M. D. (2008), *Contemporary Western Ethnography and the Definition of Religion*, London; New York: Continuum.

Stuerzenhofecker, K., O'Loughlin, R. and Smith, S. (2010), 'Sustainability in the Theology Curriculum', in Paula Jones, David Selby and Stephen Sterling (eds) *Sustainability Education. Perspectives and Practice across Higher Education*, 219–40, London: Earthscan.

Suchocki, M. H. (2005), 'In Search of Justice: Religious pluralism from a feminist perspective', in J. Hick and P. Knitter (eds), *The Myth of Christian Uniqueness: Towards a Pluralistic Theology of Religions*, 149–61, Eugene OR: Wipf & Stock.

Sugirtharajah, R. S. (2001), *The Bible and the Third World: Precolonial, Colonial and Postcolonial Encounters*, Cambridge: Cambridge University Press.

Sumney, J. (2008), *Colossians: A Commentary*, Louisville: Westminster John Knox Press.

Surin, K. (1990), 'A "Politics of Speech"', in G. D'Costa (ed.), *Christian Uniqueness Reconsidered: The Myth of a Pluralistic Theology of Religions*, 192–212, Maryknoll, New York: Orbis.

Sutcliffe, S. and Bowman, M. (2000), *Beyond New Age: Exploring Alternative Spirituality*, Edinburgh: Edinburgh University Press.

Sutton, M. (2014), *American Apocalypse: A History of Modern Evangelicalism*, Cambridge, MA: Harvard University Press.

Tanner, K. (1993), 'Respect for Other Religions: A Christian Antidote to Colonialist Discourse', *Modern Theology*, 9: 1–18.

Tanner, K. (1997), *Theories of Culture: a New Agenda for Theology*, Minneapolis: Augsburg Fortress.

Tart, C. (1999), 'Introduction: What TASTE is about?' *The Archives of Scientists' Transcendent Experiences*. http://www.issc-taste.org/main/introduction.shtml [accessed 16 August 2013].

Taves, A. (2009), *Religious Experience Reconsidered*, Princeton, NJ: Princeton University Press.

Taves, A. (2013), 'Building Blocks of Sacralities: A New Basis for Comparison across Cultures and Religions', in R. F. Paloutzian and C. L. Park (eds), *Handbook of the Psychology of Religion and Spirituality*, 138–61, New York: Guilford.

Tertullian (1963), 'On the Resurrection of the Flesh', in A. Roberts, J. Donaldson, and A. Cleveland Coxe (eds), *Ante-Nicene Fathers*, vol. 3, 545–96, Grand Rapids, MI: WM. B. Eerdmans Publishing Company.

Throsby, K. and Gimlin, D. (2010), 'Critiquing Thinness and Wanting to be Thin', in R. Ryan-Flood and R. Gill (eds), *Secrecy and Silence in the Research Process. Feminist Reflections*, 105–16, London & New York: Routledge.

Tillich, P. (1958), *Dynamics of Faith*, New York: Harper.

Tinker, G. E. (2008), *American Indian Liberation: A Theology of Sovereignty*, Maryknoll, NY: Orbis Books.

Todd, A. (2013), *Military Chaplaincy in Contention. Chaplains, Churches and the Morality of Conflict*, Farnham: Ashgate.

Towner, W. S. (2001), *Genesis*, Louisville: John Knox Press.

Townsend, M. (2007), 'A Scientific Case Study: The Orb Zone Theory', *Association for the Scientific Study of Anomalous Phenomena*. http://www.assap.ac.uk/newsite/articles/ Orb%20Zone%20Theory.html [accessed 16 August 2013].

Travis, T. (2009), *The Language of the Heart: A Cultural History of the Recovery Movement from Alcoholics Anonymous to Oprah Winfrey*, Chapel Hill: University of North Carolina Press.

Turpin, K. (2008), 'Disrupting the Luxury of Despair: Justice and peace education in contexts of relative privilege', *Teaching Theology and Religion*, 11 (3): 141–52.

Turpin, K. (2014), 'Liberationist Practical Theology', in K. Cahalan and G. Mikoski (eds), *Opening the Field of Practical Theology. An Introduction*, 153–68, Lanham, MD: Rowman & Littlefield.

Van der Leeuw, G. ([1933] 1999), *Religion in Essence and Manifestation*, trans. J. E. Turner, Gloucester, MA: Peter Smith.

Van Gennep, A. ([1908] 1960), *The Rites of Passage*, trans. M. K. Vizedom and G. Caffee, London: Routledge and Kegan Paul.

Van Henten, J. W. (2012), 'Noble Death and Martyrdom in Antiquity', in S. Fuhrmann and R. Grundmann (eds), *Martyriumsvorstellungen in Antike und Mittelalter*, 95–106, Leiden: Brill.

van Otterloo, A. H. (1999), 'Self-spirituality and the Body: New Age Centres in the Netherlands since the 1960s', *Social Compass*, 46 (2): 191–202.

van Otterloo, A. H., Aupers, S. and Houtman, D. (2012), 'Trajectories to the New Age: The spiritual turn of the first generation of Dutch New Age Teachers', *Social Compass*, 59 (2): 239–56.

Varga, I. (2007), 'Georg Simmel: Religion and spirituality', in K. Flanagan and P. C. Jupp (eds), *A Sociology of Spirituality*, 145–60, Aldershot: Ashgate.

Village, A. (2015), *Empirical Theology*, https://www.yorksj.ac.uk/education--theology/faculty-of-etrs/our-departments/research/research---theology--religiou/practical-theoolgy/empirical-theology.aspx [accessed 16 April 2015].

Voas, D. (2012), 'Religious Census 2011 – What happened to the Christians?' *British Religion in Numbers*. http://www.brin.ac.uk/news/2012/religious-census-2011-what-happened-to-the-christians/ [accessed 16 August 2013].

Voas, D. and Bruce, S. (2007), 'The Spiritual Revolution: Another false dawn for the sacred', in K. Flanagan and P. C. Jupp (eds), *A Sociology of Spirituality*, 43–61, Aldershot: Ashgate.

Vogt, K. (2003), 'Becoming Male', in J. M. Soskice and D. Lipton (eds), *Feminism & Theology*, 49–61, Oxford: Oxford University Press.

Von Rad, G. (1970), *Genesis: A Commentary*, trans. John Marks, London: SCM Press.

Waltke, B. (2001), *Genesis: A Commentary*, Grand Rapids: Zondervan.

Walvoord, J. F. (1974), *Armageddon, Oil and the Middle East Crisis*, Grand Rapids: Zondervan.

Wambuii, H. (2006), *The Politics of HIV/AIDS and Implications for Democracy in Kenya*, Michigan: Edwin Mellen Press.

Ward, G. (1999), 'Theology in a Culture of Seduction', in Robert Hanniford and J'annine Jobling (eds), *Theology and the Body: Gender, Text & Ideology*, 47–61, Leominster: Gracewing.

Ward, P., ed. (2012), *Perspectives on Ecclesiology and Ethnography*, Grand Rapids, MI; Cambridge, UK: William B. Eermans Publishing Company.

Watts, J. (1987), *Isaiah 34-66*, Waco: Word Books.

Webb, B. (1997), *The Message of Isaiah*, Downers Grove: InterVarsity Press.

Weber, M. (1966), *The Sociology of Religion*, London: Methuen.

Weber, M. (1978), *Economy and Society. An Outline of Interpretive Sociology*, ed. G. Roth and C. Wittich, Berkeley, Los Angeles, London: University of California Press.

Webster's New Collegiate Dictionary (1980), Springfield, MA: G. & C. Merriam Co, cited in Tart, C. (1999), 'Introduction: what TASTE is about?' *The Archives of Scientists' Transcendent Experiences*. http://www.issc-taste.org/main/introduction.shtml [accessed 16 August 2013].

Wenham, G. (1987), *Genesis 1-15*, Waco: Word Books.

Werblowsky, R. J. Z. and Bleeker, C. J. (1970), *Types of Redemption*, Leiden: Brill.

Wesley, J. (1811), 'The Great Deliverance', in J. Wesley and J. Benson (eds), *The Works of Rev. John Wesley*, vol. 9, 189–203, London: Conference Office.

Wessinger, C., ed. (2011), *The Oxford Handbook of Millennialism*, Oxford: Oxford University Press.

West, G. (2009), 'Liberation Hermeneutics after Liberation in South Africa', in A. J. Botta and P. R. Andinach (eds), *The Bible and the Hermeneutics of Liberation*, 13–38, Atlanta: Society of Biblical Literature.

Westermann, C. (2004), *Genesis*, trans. D. Green, London: T & T Clark.

Whisenant, E. (1988), *88 Reasons Why the Rapture will be in 1988*, Edgar Whisenant Publishing.

White, W. (2014), *Slaying the Dragon: The History of Addiction Treatment and Recovery In America*, 2nd edn, Bloomington, IN: Chestnut Health Systems.

White, R. A. (1990), 'An Experience-Centred Approach to Parapsychology', *Exceptional Human Experience*, 8: 7–36.

White, R. A. and Brown, S. V. (2000), 'Triggers of Potential Exceptional Human Experiences', *Exceptional Human Experiences Network*. http://www.ehe.org/display/ehe-pageab52.html?ID=72 [accessed 16 August 2013].

Whitehead, A. N. (1978), *Process and Reality: An Essay in Cosmology*, corrected edn, ed. D. R. Griffin and D. W. Sherburne, New York: The Free Press.

Whitehouse, H. (2004), *Modes of Religiosity*, Walnut Creek: Altamira Press.

Whitmer, P. O. with VanWyngarden, B. (2007), *Aquarius Revisited: Seven Who Created the Sixties Counterculture that Changed America*, New York: Citadel Press.

Wicker, B. (2006), *Witnesses to Faith? Martyrdom in Christianity and Islam*, Aldershot: Ashgate.

Wilber, K. (1999), 'Constant Consciousness', *Shambala Sun*. http://www.shambhalasun.com/Archives/Columnists/Wilber/WilberJan99.htm [accessed 16 August 2013].

Willey, P. and Willey, E. (1998), 'Will Animals be Redeemed?', in A. Linzey and D. Yamamoto (eds), *Animals on the Agenda*, 181–89, London: SCM Press.

Williams, K. and Harvey, D. (2001), 'Transcendent Experience in Forest Environments', *Journal of Environmental Psychology*, 21 (3): 249–60.

Wilson, B. R. (1996), *Religious Experience: A Sociological Perspective*, Oxford: Religious Experience Research Centre.

Wilson, B. R. (1970), *Religious Sects*, London: World University Press.

Wilson, B. R. (1973), *Magic and the Millennium*, London: Heinemann.

Wilson, B. R. (1999), 'Introduction', in B. R. Wilson and James Cresswell (eds), *New Religious Movements*, 1–11, London: Routledge.

Wilson, R. M. (2005), *Colossians and Philemon: A Critical and Exegetical Commentary*, ICC, London: T & T Clark.

Winerman, L. (2014), 'Words Matter', *Monitor*, 45 (3): 20. http://www.apa.org/monitor/2014/03/words-matter.aspx.

Wohlrab-Sahr, M. and Sammet, K. (2006), 'Weltsichten – Lebensstile – Kirchenbindung: Konzeption und Methoden der vierten EKD-Erhebung über Kirchenmitgliedschaft', in J. Hermelink, I. Lukatis and M. Wohlrab-Sahr (eds), *Kirche in der Vielfalt der Lebensbezüge. Die vierte EKD-Erhebung über Kirchenmitgliedschaft*, vol. 2, 21–32, Gütersloh: Gütersloher Verl.-Haus.

Wohlrab-Sahr, M., Karstein, U. and Schaumburg, C. (2005), '"Ich würd' mir das offen lassen": Agnostische Spiritualität als Annäherung an die "große Transzendenz" eines Lebens nach dem Tode', *Zeitschrift für Religionswissenschaft*, 13: 153–73.

Wojcik, D. (1997), *The End of the World as We Know It: Faith, Fatalism, and Apocalypse in America*, New York: New York University Press.

Wolf, N. (1991), *The Beauty Myth. How Images of Beauty are used Against Women*, New York, London, Toronto, Sydney, Auckland: Anchor Books, Doubleday.

Woodhead, L. and Heelas, P. (2000), *Religion in Modern Times: An Interpretive Anthology*, 431–75, Oxford: Blackwell.

Wouters, E., van Rensburg, H. C. J. and Meulemans, H. (2010), 'The National Strategic Plan of South Africa: What are the prospects of success after the repeated failure of previous AIDS policy?', *Health Policy & Planning*, 25: 171–85.

Wright, N. T. (1986), *Colossians and Philemon*, Grand Rapids: William B. Eerdmans.

Wulff, D. (2000), 'Mystical Experience', in E. Cardeña, S. J. Lynn and S. Krippner (eds), *Varieties of Anomalous Experience*, 397–440, Washington, DC: American Psychological Association.

Yamamoto, D. (1998), 'Aquinas and Animals: Patrolling the boundary?', in A. Linzey and D. Yamamoto (eds), *Animals on the Agenda*, 80–89, London: SCM Prespapers.

INDEX